KIỀU CHINH
An Artist in Exile

KIỀU CHINH
An Artist in Exile
A Memoir
First Edition, 2021
Second Edition, 2022

English Translation:
IAN BÙI

English Editor:
MARY LEE GRANT

Book Interior Design:
TRỊNH Y THƯ, 2021
LÊ HÂN, 2023

Cover Design:
NINA HÒA BÌNH LÊ

Cover Photo:
THOMAS ĐẶNG VŨ

Publisher:
VĂN HỌC PRESS, 2021
NHÂN ẢNH PUBLISHER, 2023

ISBN: 9798391459231

In memory of my Father, Mr. Nguyễn Cửu.
For my children
Mỹ Vân, Hoàng Hùng, Tuấn Cường,
and my dear grandchildren.

KIỀU CHINH
An Artist in Exile

A Memoir

Translated from Vietnamese by
IAN BÙI

Edited by
MARY LEE GRANT

With Introduction by
ALISON LESLIE GOLD

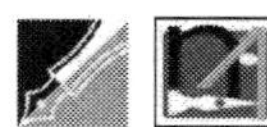

Văn Học Press, California, 2021
Nhân Ảnh Publisher, California, 2023

CONTENTS

INTRODUCTION

by Alison Leslie Gold

Having been brought together by a powerful television executive, I met Kieu Chinh for lunch in Venice California on a creamy California winter day. We did not know much about each other, just that I, a writer, (just coming down from the publication of my new book) was looking for a new subject for my next book (and only a very special subject would do,) and that Kieu Chinh (according to our executive) had quite an extraordinary story to tell.

Not a single eye remained unturned as she and I strolled along the Boardwalk, chatting and getting acquainted. Her magnificent beauty was awesome, quite poignant and Zen, there in that coarse, carnival atmosphere as the soft winter sun poured gently over us. Quickly we connected to each other — as women, as artists, as friends.

A palmist intruded upon our reverie, offering to read our palm. With amusement we agreed, Kieu Chinh offering her upturned palm first to the wizened jet-black eyes of the seer who took it and studied it carefully with narrowing eyelids while we both held our breath.

Finally the palmist spoke.

"She's someone famous," she announced with total certainty, "and she'll have a bright future!" She concluded dropping her hand and reaching for mine.

Later we laughed over this, and we laugh about it to this day...

Kieu Chinh is an unusual woman who had lived what seems like five different lives. She survives as a poignant witness, an experiencer of the turbulence of our most controversial time. I wish her five more lives, and the further deepening that time and a full heart offer to those special few who endure and forge on.

I salute her as a woman with museum-quality beauty.

I salute her as an artist of rare talent.

I salute her as a true and noble friend.

– Alison Leslie Gold

PREFACE

I don't think I would have needed to write a memoir if it wasn't for a dying wish from my father, Daddy Cửu, and from my godfather, writer Nguyễn Ngọc Giao. Both said: "You have to write a memoir."

Similarly, I am indebted to writer Mai Thảo who kept reminding me: "Don't forget what your father said. Write the memoir!"

"But I'm not a writer," I protested. "How can I write?"

Mai Thảo, whom I respected like the oldest brother in the family, turned serious and said: "You don't need to be an author. Just write like you normally tell a story. A kind of *language parlant* [speaking language]. I can edit it for you if needed."

"OK. Sure..." I would say, just to get off the topic. Nevertheless, I did start jotting down on pieces of paper things that were happening around me, just so I wouldn't forget them. But then I got sucked into the humdrum of daily life and the memoir became a low priority. Besides, I still had Mai Thảo to help me "*if needed,*" so there was no hurry.

Every now and then he would needle me, "How far have you gotten?"

"Umm... well... Just a few things here and there."

"You must do it regularly," he said with a stern professor's look. "Keep the pace steady. Don't let it sit too long!"

Unfortunately, I did let it sit too long. Way too long. Mai Thảo is gone. He's been gone twenty years.

The pieces of paper that went into this memoir came from many different places at many different times — an airport lounge, a hotel room, early morning in my backyard, a sleepless night in bed... Through the years they started to pile up. But my busy schedule and all the traveling relegated them into a corner of the office. It wasn't until 2020 that they finally saw the light of day, all because of a virus.

COVID-19 shut down airports, shops, restaurants, schools... We all went into lockdown mode. To kill the time — and to find some distraction from the daily bad news, I took out my pile of paper and started reading, hoping that I would finally be able to fulfill the promise I made to myself.

But as I waded in, I discovered that the story wandered all over the place. Perhaps I was too emotionally involved when certain events took place that I just poured my heart out onto paper (literally, since I don't use a computer) without thinking much about structures or forms.

But by and by, a story began to take shape in digital form through tremendous help from family and friends. I can't list everyone's name here because it would take up too much space, but you know who you are. From the bottom of my heart, I say "Thank you!"

It would be remiss to not mention two dear friends, Nhã Ca and Trần Dạ Từ, and their two daughters — Hoà Bình and Sông Văn. They have been by my side throughout the entire process.

And I especially want to thank poet Trịnh Y Thư, who edited the original version in Vietnamese and was responsible for the layout of both versions. Without him this memoir could not have been realized.

I am not an author. I don't write novels. These were just pieces of paper that collectively tell the story of one woman's sojourn and the people she met along the way, many of whom are no longer alive. I hope you'll read this memoir with empathy and an open mind.

I wish everyone love and peace. Please accept the sincerest appreciation from an *Artist in Exile.*

– Kiều Chinh

PART I

Hà-Nội, 1937-1954

Prologue

"It's time," says James Kimsey before a sea of cameras, "to lay to rest the bitterness that has been gnawing at us all these years."

Twenty years after the war ended, the U.S. and Vietnam reestablished diplomatic relations. Around the same time, the first of 51 elementary schools sponsored by our non-profit Vietnam Children's Funds (VCF) was completed. As a co-founder of VCF, I was to travel with my co-chair, journalist Terry Anderson, and our principal sponsor James V. Kimsey, founder and CEO of America Online, to Việt-Nam to cut the ribbon on April 24, 1995.

The event would take place in Đông-Hà, Quảng-Trị, near the 17th parallel that once divided my home country and where in 1967 the Battle of Khe-Sanh took place.

On April 17, members of VCF departed for Việt-Nam from various locations in the U.S. I was the only Viet-American in the group, leaving from Los Angeles. From Washington, D.C., James Kimsey flew to LAX to join me. Terry Anderson departed directly from New York and we all would rendezvous in Việt-Nam.

In the VIP lounge of Cathay Airlines, David Jackson, news anchor for Fox Television, began my interview by recalling that it seemed every major turn in my life had occurred in an airport: forty years ago I migrated to the South from a Hà-Nội airport; twenty years later I boarded an airplane to the U.S. to begin a new life in exile; now, after another twenty years, I was flying back to my home city and country.

As a veteran who fought in Vietnam, James Kimsey was able to succinctly express his bottled up emotions upon returning to the old battlefields. But I knew that I was incapable of making such a sharp and clear resolve. Việt-Nam is where my parents, I, and even my children, were born. Imprints of the three wars that our wretched land had to bear, to me, were scars carved so deep in my flesh and bones that I would never be able to forget. It may be possible for James to "*lay to rest the bitterness that has been gnawing at us*," but for me it's inconceivable.

"Cheer up!" David said as he handed me a copy of the *Los Angeles Times* dated April 17, with a story about me with my photo on the front page. "Tonight, I will be watching *Kieu Chinh Returning Home* on the news segment of Fox Television while you're in the air. Bon voyage!"

The paper accompanied me onto the plane. We flew through the night. Most passengers were asleep, and all the noises had died down save the humming of the engines. Looking at the nebulous darkness rushing by outside the window, I felt like I was flying back in time to a previous incarnation. The past flowed in and out of my mind like a stream of consciousness, flooding my senses.

I just had to close my eyes and I could see it all again.

Kim-Mã Estate

The road is at a slight incline, with tamarind trees on both sides leading toward Bovine Mountain (Núi Bò) which looks like, as its name suggests, a gigantic cow resting in the field under the big blue sky. At a distance, a horseman leisurely weaves among the shadows of the trees along a hillside ridge. The horse is white; so is the man's shirt. He is Dad. I am five years old, full of wonder and joy, riding around Bovine Mountain nestled in Dad's arms.

Phi-Mã seems just as joyful as the little girl as he gallops along the dirt path up the hill. Every now and then, a hamlet appears below. Smoke gently rises from rooftops and hangs effortlessly in the air. As they make their way down the hill, a small school with red-tiled roofs comes into view; there are children playing. As soon as he sees the thick groves of fruit trees, Phi-Mã slows his pace. He knows he's getting close to home. This is the last curve of the dirt path around the mountainside. Phi-Mã slowly turns into our private road, then stops. The man hands the reins to his old butler Ba Kỷ, who leads Phi-Mã to the barn where another horse, Phi-Phi, is waiting. While waiting for her father to stop by the garage to check on Tư, the chauffeur, who's buffing the Citroën, the little girl hangs around the barn to help old Ba Kỷ feed the horses. As she and her Dad cross the backyard to go into the house, Toto runs out to greet them with his tail wagging excitedly. She picks up Toto then goes inside to meet her mother, her older brother and older sister.

It was a peaceful spring scene in the wonderful, almost fairytale childhood which I shared with my siblings.

Kim-Mã Estate was a traditional house with five main rooms situated in the middle of a vast orchard facing Bovine Mountain. In front, there was a long wall connected to a row of mossy brick columns. At one end was the front gate, with a tiled awning in Oriental style, that opened into the main courtyard leading to the main house. At the farthest end was the dirt road that led to the barn, used to house horses and vehicles.

In one corner, next to the main gate, was a round pillar that supported a miniature temple. Inside the temple there was a stone urn full of spent joss sticks, skeletal remains of the incense that we burned on holy days and death days.

From the front gate, as you walked past the bricked courtyard you would come to a long veranda with a balcony. This was the veranda that appeared in many of the childhood photos that I still possess. Near the left corner were Dad and oldest brother

Lân. Lân was three years old, wearing a black velvet jacket, a black fedora hat and sandals with white socks, perched on the balcony. Dad was standing next to him in a dapper gray suit, holding and looking dotingly at his firstborn.

On the right corner was Mom in her traditional *áo dài [ow-yaï],* also in black velvet and the traditional head scarf, posing with me and my older sister. Tĩnh was five, with a chubby face and short "carré bombé" haircut, standing only up to my mother's hand. Next to her was a three-year-old Chinh, holding an obviously impatient Toto in her arms. At the front doors, by the bonsai ochna plant was Ông Nội, my paternal grandfather, in his traditional fine silk dress and headdress. On his chest hung the official government name tag displaying his rank.

In my childhood memories, my grandfather was a tall, slender man with a silky beard as beautiful as a wizard's.

For generations, the Nguyễn family on my father's side were landowners at Mọc Cự-Lộc village in Hà-Đông province, a historic land just outside Hà-Nội on the bank of the Tô-Lịch river.

My grandfather Nguyễn Phan was an official in the government. He inherited all of his family's holdings. A scholar belonging to the Chinese-based Nho educational system, he was an advocate for development and for the opening up of the country to Western ideas. In Mọc Village, his hometown, my grandfather built many traditional Vietnamese structures such as the triple gate and the hexagon temple. But he also constructed the more modern Kim-Mã Estate and Đồng-Xuân Hotel — some of our family's major properties in Hà-Nội.

Our Nguyễn clan at Mọc Cự-Lộc was known not only for its wealth. Since my great-grandfather's time, the family also was known for its paucity of male heirs. My grandfather was the only son out of six children. And of his three children, my father was the only son — the youngest.

In traditional Vietnamese society, there's even a saying about how male and female children are treated differently: "One son counts as a birth, ten girls count as none." That is to say, only the birth of a son merits recording. Girls are considered "outside the family." Only sons are respected because they're the ones who carry on the family traditions. For example, when my father, Cửu, was a child, even though he was the youngest of three children, everybody on both sides of the family called him Big Brother Cửu.

My father was born on July 1, 1910. At that time, Vietnam already had been a French colony for 36 years. Chinese influence was receding, the Latin alphabet was replacing Han characters, and French culture was overtaking the ancient Nho traditions.

In an old Nguyễn family photo taken in 1913, everyone wore solemn Vietnamese dresses while Big Brother Cửu, at three years of age, was all decked out in a Western outfit with a formal jacket and high boots. Behind him is his young father in the perfectly traditional silk dress and headdress. When he became older, my father studied French instead and graduated from Bưởi High School, the premier academy in Hà-Nội at the time. There clearly was a formidable East-West cultural gap between my father and his father, yet their father-and-son bond was kept intact.

" Daddy Cửu", as he was called by many, was tall and elegant; his voice had a warm tone, his hair was full and fluffy, his eyes were large and brooding. Most special of all were his hands, with their long, lean fingers. To me, Daddy Cửu was a refined and handsome man. He liked to wear comfortably large white shirts with simple black slacks. Nothing fancy, yet always neat and smart looking.

In 1932, the Nguyễn of Mọc Cự-Lộc became married into the Nguyễn clan of Gia-Lâm. My mother, Nguyễn thị An, was born in 1911. She was one year younger than my father. I only knew "Mother An" as a gentle and kind-hearted woman with very long hair, down past her knees.

Unlike my paternal side, who were landowners tied to their farms and properties, my maternal grandfather, Ông Ngoại, was a high-level government official working for the Indochina railway. The family's genealogy records noted that for many years he supervised the building of the Yunnan – Đà-Lạt rail lines. My maternal grandparents had six children — four sons and two daughters, each born in a different locale as the family had to travel wherever my grandfather's work took him.

My mother was the third child; she and her next older brother Nguyễn văn Nghị were born in Yunnan when the rail line was begun in China. The two of them were nearest to each other in age and thus had a very close relationship growing up together. But after my mother got married, Uncle Nghị was sent to France to study and later became a world-renowned physician known as Dr. Van Nghị, famous for bringing Asian medicine, such as acupuncture, to the West. The two never saw each other again.

My mother also had three younger siblings. The next one was Uncle Nguyễn văn Thành, a doctor, born in Nha-Trang, and Aunt Cam born in Bảo-Lộc. Uncle Thành was very close to my father while Aunt Cam was always by my mother's side.

Idyllic Days

One of my father's major properties was the Kim-Mã Ranch and Estate. That was where most of my childhood memories sprouted and grew.

The landscape and scenery of Kim-Mã Estate, in my innocent eyes and tender memory, was an endlessly green space. Every nook, every cranny of the place gave me a different feeling, a distinct scent. It felt as though the place was both alien and familiar, and absolutely captivating.

In front of the gate were two big jacarandas, their overarching branches brightly colored in the flowering season. Our ancient-looking main house sat hidden among rows of ancient-looking trees. The front yard was shaded by golden apple and pomegranate trees, with ylang flowers spicing the pathway with their distinct fragrance.

In the back yard were planted fruit trees such as bananas, persimmons, grapefruits... There was a horse barn, a rainwater tank, even a small pond to raise fish and grow water spinach. The garage was where my father's black Citroën was kept; my mother had her own private rickshaw.

The main house was expansive and full of traditional furniture. The carved altar cabinet, the square table-bed made from sindora wood and its accompanying cupboard, the long wooden couch set, tall ceramic vases of all kinds, and many antique statues and paintings that belonged to my grandfather. Both he and my father were avid antique collectors.

Even now, as I age, the images of Kim-Mã Estate are still fresh in my memory. Every time I look at the old black-and-white family photos, I always feel a rush of nostalgia transporting me back to those idyllic days of childhood.

Kim-Mã Estate was also where many of my father's best friends used to gather. Dad had many friends whom he truly loved. There were those he went to school with like Đỗ Trí-Lễ the educator, Nguyễn Mạnh-Hà, Hà Văn Vượng. Then there were famous poets and writers like Vũ Hoàng-Chương, Đinh Hùng, Ngọc Giao (my godfather), Lê Văn Trương, Hoàng Cầm... literary giants at the time. Thus our living room became a sort of late 19th- early 20th-century "Parisien salon litérature." At these gatherings they would discuss poetry, music, politics... My father could play the violin; he also wrote poems.

My mother always made the most special dishes for Dad's friends. She had the highest regard for them, and they all respected her in return. The atmosphere at these gatherings was always cheerful, full of laughter and warmth. My grandfather always attended; sometimes he would recite a poem or join in a poetry duet.

My father loved antiques. Mr. "Antique" Dzương was a close friend of Dad's. His home full of antiques on Hàng Trống street was well-known throughout Hà-Nội. It sat overlooking Hoàn-Kiếm lake; I used to accompany Dad on his many visits there. In the garage, next to Dad's Citroën was Mom's rickshaw. Dad loved his car, so he always drove himself. Tư was my mother's rickshaw puller. Uncle Hùng was my father's car aficionado friend; he was called Hùng the Racer because he once won a race from Hải-Phòng to Hà-Nội. Uncle Hùng dressed and carried himself quite distinctly from Dad's other friends. He always wore a leather jacket, a driving cap, high leather boots and a pair of big sunglasses. Dad liked to tell the story of the time I nearly got crushed under uncle Hùng's motorcycle. On that day, he drove his motorbike over and parked it in our front yard. He and Dad stood nearby smoking and talking while I, only three years old, climbed on the motorbike and caused it to tip over. Luckily both men were able to catch it in time and save me.

Although he had a car, Dad still loved horseback riding. He also had a close friend who was a horse lover like him; his name was Phúc. Uncle Phúc was owner of the orange grove Bố-Hạ, the most famous orange variety in all of the North. From when I was little until the time I was a young woman, I went with Dad many times to uncle Phúc's ranch, riding horses in his orange grove.

The Four Seasons of Hà-Nội

Spring in Hà-Nội left deep imprints. Not least was the fine misty dust otherwise called spring rain. I loved those practically invisible aerosols. They touched your face and your clothes but left no trace, neither wet nor cold. They were like clear and colorless confetti.

But our Hà-Nội springs also were filled with the myriad tasks that kept my mother, her helpers and us children, too, occupied in the weeks and days leading up to the Lunar New Year celebration we call Tết.

Every New Year's day my mother prepared a sumptuous feast to welcome back the spirits of our ancestors from both sides of the family, to show our gratitude and respect. Days before, the family altar would have been meticulously cleaned. Our butler, Ba Kỷ, was always given the honorific but important job of polishing the brass incense burner and candlesticks.

In another part of the house, the kitchen and the back patio, things were less solemn and much more boisterous. Everyone was busy with something. Pickling leeks; peeling onions; salting cabbages; tenderizing meat; making sausage; cleaning banana or phrynium leaves to wrap sweet rice cakes. My siblings and I, needless to say, were just as excited whenever Mother allowed us to participate in her well-oiled chain of production which occurred only once a year.

Beyond those tasks and before the arrival of spring, marked by the all-important New Year's Eve and New Year's Day, mother also had to make new clothes for us. We would wear them on New Year's Day as we went to greet Grandpa to wish him health — and to receive our little red envelopes.

New Year's Eve was great fun also. While waiting for Mother to finish making the ancestral offerings, Dad played cards with Grandpa, Ba Kỷ, and brother Lân. Meanwhile my sister Tĩnh and I would follow Mother outside to place incense at the mini-temple, without neglecting to put some at each of the old trees in the front yard. It was as though the trees were imbued with spirits and played a part in protecting and blessing us throughout the year.

Next came the most important part — lighting incense at the main altar and bowing to the ancestors, the spirits, and everything under the heavens. Then we would go outside and recite the midnight prayers — sending them to the four corners of the earth and the ten gates of Buddha as we welcomed the new year.

After all that was done, everyone went to the front yard to light firecrackers. It was a noisy and rambunctious affair. According to my mother, at the moment the old meets the new, sounds of firecrackers drive away all the bad luck and disappointments of the past year as we usher in a better and more prosperous new year.

Even now, I still seem to smell that distinctive odor of firecrackers and see their red paper skins splattered all over the front yard, or fluttering on tree limbs like little flowers. In the morning, as I walked out to the garden, I still could see their shredded remains strewn everywhere as though a wind had come through last night to generously sprinkle peach petals all over our yard. They gave me a feeling of joy and a strange yearning for something that hadn't quite come into focus.

I can't remember how long those firecracker skins were left in our front yard before they were cleaned up. I only remember that Mother forbade anyone to sweep anything on New Year's Day. It was strictly forbidden because, as my mother explained, it is our traditional belief that sweeping out the trash on New Year's Day meant sweeping away all the good luck of the new year.

If Hà-Nội springs were known for the mists that looked like clear colorless confetti and for the joys of Tết, then its summers were marked by the droning of cicadas among the jacaranda trees. Their songs rose and fell like musical notes floating in the clear blue Hà-Nội skies.

But if I had to choose my favorite Hà-Nội season out of the four, then after spring, autumn would definitely be it.

Hà-Nội in autumn had light breezes that felt like a silky scarf of the most pleasing colors on the elegant dresses worn by its ladies. Autumn leaves covered the yards at Kim-Mã Estate like a golden rug. I loved walking on the dead leaves just to hear them rustle beneath my feet. Those settings, those colors, like the weather, draped over Hà-Nội like a new jacket, a sharp contrast to the airy summer shirt she was wearing just a few months earlier.

But besides its lovely weather, Hà-Nội autumns also gave us a wonderful green snack made from rice flakes called "*cốm*" [kohm]. My mom said that long before the start of autumn, the communes or villages that made *cốm* already got started for the "*cốm* season" by prepping those lovely green flakes with their distinctive scent so that they would eventually reach every corner of this city known for its traditions and elegance.

Dad said that right outside of Hà-Nội there were many towns that made good *cốm*, like Mễ-Trì Hạ, Mễ-Trì Thượng. But best of all was a village called Vòng, with its famous brand of "*Cốm Vòng*."

I once asked Dad why *Cốm Vòng* was so famous. He said he didn't know. Perhaps because it was the oldest, even though its *cốm* was made from the same kind of young and milky grains of sweet rice, and its processes were pretty much the same as well. *Cốm* connoisseurs who could discern the taste and fragrance of good *cốm* would tell you that autumn is the best season to fully enjoy it. That's the time when the morning dew, followed by the cool autumn breeze, hastened the aging of the lotus leaves but still left them pliable enough for use as linings, like a piece of green silk that was subtly scented with which you wrapped this delicate gift before presenting it to relatives and friends.

During *cốm* season, we children loved hearing the "ding-dong, ding-dong" of the doorbells, rung by the vendor woman who knew our mother well. Groups of *cốm* sellers going into town early in the morning liked to stop outside our estate to take a break. And this particular woman would ring the doorbell so that our mother could come out and choose the best batch.

I loved watching these *cốm* sellers. They wore only plastic sandals, yet they moved briskly. They dressed in traditional long black skirts, dark brown brassieres and black head covers resembling the shape of a crow's beak — "mỏ quạ." The tips of their poles curled upward to serve as hooks to hang baskets full of *cốm*, lotus leaves, and strings made from bamboo used for tying. Starting at the crack of dawn, they always moved in groups with a certain rhythm and grace that looked like something out of an old painting.

And while my sister and I hung around Mother waiting for her to get ready, my brother Lân already rushed to open the gate. I followed my Mother to the front and watched her pick out those divine packages of lotus-scented *cốm*.

Afterwards, Mother and Aunt Cam split the *Cốm Vòng* and persimmons into equal parts, lined them up in rows, then placed them onto wooden trays. Brother Lân, all dressed up nicely, would ride with mother on the rickshaw to each of our aunts and uncles to give everyone a package. She also made a special steam dish of *cốm* with rock sugar for Ông Nội — our paternal grandfather. My father, on the other hand, liked his *cốm* fresh and raw, but sometimes he'd also dip bananas in it. I liked *cốm* also, especially when Mother used it to make sweet congee desserts.

And she never forgot to take some to our maternal grandparents in Gia-Lâm, either.

Mother often took us to see her father. And of course, each would be given a small pack of *cốm* to snack on to make the journey seem shorter.

How can I put into words all the happy memories of my childhood. The image of my mother with her long black hair that reached past her knees. She used to wash it with a special concoction made with sun-dried locust fruits [gleditsia flora] in a copper bucket. After each washing, she'd swing in a hammock to let it dry. Sometimes she let me brush her hair or dry it with a small hand fan. The subtle scent of locust from her hair would fill my nostrils. How could I ever forget?

But that bucolic and fairytale life was violently upended when war came. I was born in 1937. That was also the year the Japanese invaded China and then, a few years later, Vietnam. It was during those tumultuous years that I first saw a corpse.

Father liked to ride his horse, Phi-Mã, in the morning. Being his favorite, I was usually brought along for the ride, nicely nestled in his arms. I'll never forget that day. Phi-Mã was in full stride up the slope on Bovine Mountain when he suddenly neighed loudly and halted, stomping his hoofs in a most unusual manner. Almost at the same time, my father and I caught sight of it. A dead Japanese man was hanging limply on a tree limb by the roadside. Knowing I was in shock, my father held me tightly and pulled on the bridle with his other hand to turn Phi-Mã around. We immediately went back to the house.

The corpse was a terrible omen.

I remember that the year was 1943. Father had the trees in our backyard felled and cleared to build a bunker. Those were the days when I saw bombers flying overhead. Sirens would go off constantly. Everyone would hustle like mad to jump into the bunker. One time, after the entire household had gotten in, they noticed I was missing. My father rushed back into the house. I was running around looking for my dog Toto. He probably was too scared by the siren and was hiding somewhere. When I was a child, that sound also frightened me; it filled my mind with dread and thoughts of destruction and death.

World War II had broken out and the Japanese army invaded Vietnam. Allied planes started bombing.

The air raid sirens sounded day and night, incessantly, putting us all on constant edge. Every time I heard the ear-piercing sound, my body would shrink as though disaster was about to fall on our heads.

By the middle of 1943, the Japanese had thrown the French out of Vietnam. Not long before that, Allied planes bombed Hà-Nội non-stop. During that period, my mother was pregnant with my youngest brother. When she was in the last month of her pregnancy, Mother went into the hospital to get ready for the birth. As fate would have it, the section that she was in was hit by a bomb. My mother and my youngest brother - named Nguyễn Quỳnh, who had just been born but not yet had his birth certificate registered, were killed!

From that calamitous moment on I never saw my mother again, nor my brother, killed so prematurely. It was the first tragedy that visited our family.

I can still remember my father carrying me in his arms as he walked behind two coffins: a white horse-drawn carriage for my brother, a black horse-drawn one for my mother. I could hear my father's sobbing voice: "Oh my love! Oh my son!" as the two coffins were lowered into the earth.

To avoid the bombings, right after the funerals my father decided to move us all back to his parents' hometown.

Along the way I saw with my own eyes bodies littering the roads. It was the Great Famine of 1945.

Mọc Village

After the Hà-Nội bombing that killed my mother and newborn brother, Dad decided that our family should take refuge in Mọc Village, his hometown. It was here that we three children and our old butler, Ba Kỷ, lived some very peaceful days with my grandfather in an old-style three-room house.

There was a semi-circular pond in front with lotus flowers. Out back was a fish pond, next to it was a spacious yard. My brother, sister and I spent many days playing there. We watched sharecroppers spread the grain out to dry, crush the rice, dry the hay — the small mountains of hay which we loved to run around and around. I liked to climb on top of the rice mortar, but I was too tiny to stomp on that giant thing to operate it. Lunchtime was great fun. We shared simple meals with the sharecroppers and their children — packed rice, sesame salt, tiny shrimp, dried fish, boiled vegetables...

I loved the red dirt roads with tall bamboo lining both sides, reaching toward the sky. The winds were filled with the smell of the rice paddies, the sounds of the grain being crushed and the milling of the rice, pigs oinking, cocks crowing... and the laughter of children.

We played all day in these bucolic settings with the other village children. Daddy Cửu stayed in the city to work, but on weekends he came home to see us and Grandpa. I always looked forward to being with Father again. Those were such happy times. Ba Kỷ would cook Dad's favorite dishes — crab soup with water spinach, taro with white eggplant, crispy fried perch dipped in ginger fish sauce, fried, and tofu with soy paste.

At night, I would sit next to Father and listen to him recite his latest poems to Grandpa. Ông Nội would nod and comment on his son's poetry. Whenever Dad was home, I got to sleep with him, cuddled in his arms.

In Grandpa's three-room house, I did not like the middle room where the three-story altar stood with colorful flags and our ancestors' name plaques. In front of it was a three-piece cupboard and a dark wooden daybed. Every afternoon a man we called "Mr. Piper" would come to serve opium for Grandpa. He wore a black traditional dress and shiny, black sandals. He would take the smoking paraphernalia out from the cupboard and arrange them on the daybed. He would then unroll a thin mattress and place it to the right of where Ông Nội was lying. He'd lie on the other side of the opium tray and serve Ông Nội on this side. As Grandpa smoked, I would sit or lie at his feet. I enjoyed watching how Mr. Piper lit the kerosene lamp, loaded the pipe, then heated it up, making a sizzling sound and emitting a marvelous smell. Grandpa would take one long drag then sip a small cup of black tea poured from a pot insulated in a rattan basket.

I would look around the room, at the shiny wooden columns and the underside of the red tiles on the roof. Every now and then I would see a lizard which made me turn away quickly. I was scared of lizards. Actually, there were many things in that house that scared me, but nothing worse than the empty coffin to the right of the altar. Ông Nội said it was reserved for him. There used to be another one on the left also, but it would already have been used to bury Grandma. One time when we were playing hide and seek, my sister Tĩnh and I looked everywhere but couldn't find our brother Lân. As we passed by the coffin he suddenly popped the lid and sat up, scaring both of us to death. I screamed and cried; I did not play with him for several days.

Time passed, Ông Nội began to get weaker. One day, Dad came home before the weekend and stayed with us without going back to the city. He said he wanted to be with Ông Nội. Then the day came when Grandpa breathed his last, in Dad's arms.

It was raining hard that night, with thunder and lightning. I woke up in the middle of the night and didn't see my father in bed. I followed the light from the kerosene lamp and came to the middle room. There on the daybed, inside the mosquito net, Dad was lying next to Grandpa. I was so frightened, thinking my father was dead too. Dad heard my crying, got out of the net and held me close. He carried me into the next room where we normally slept, but I kept crying. I asked why he was sleeping next to Grandpa. He explained: "Because there's a storm. If there's lightning and a black cat jumps over the body then... the dead would wake up! I had to stay next to Grandpa to watch over him."

Ông Nội's funeral was very large. Almost everyone in Mọc Village came to pay their respects. The procession stopped when the coffin got to the village gate. You could hear the crying amidst the monks' prayers interspersed with the sounds of bells and wooden tocsins. This was the gate that my grandfather built and donated to the village.

After Ông Nội's burial, my father gathered up everything and took the three of us along with old Ba Kỷ back to the city.

My peaceful childhood from that moment on shifted in a different direction. Even though I had lost my mother at a young age, I was more than compensated by my father's overflowing love. But step by step, the march of cruel fate was approaching, except I was too young to know it. I could only vaguely sense that something terrible was awaiting us!

By the time we got back to Kim-Mã Estate after our long stay at my grandfather's house, the place had been burned to the ground, reduced to a pile of rubble. My childhood home was nothing more than piles of bricks. Most of the old trees had been cut in half or obliterated by bombs, some had not even finished burning. I could see images of my childhood being guillotined by war. All those loving memories, despite being no more than ashes now, clung desperately to the earth in a last ditch effort to claim they still existed!

Ever since then I have been haunted by sirens and fires, to the point of having nightmares. It was clear that Kim-Mã could not preserve any remnants of my fairy tale childhood. And my mother and newborn brother became more like a figment of my imagination.

Little House in Ngọc-Hà

After selling the hotel near Đồng-Xuân market, my father arranged to buy a small house in Ngọc-Hà district near the Arboretum. It was a very small house without any front or back yard, situated right behind the house of Dad's friend, professor Đỗ Trí-Lễ.

Mr. Lễ had built a big bunker in his backyard. He knocked out a large hole in the wall between our two houses so that we could run into his bunker whenever there were air raid sirens. This was the time when the Việt-Minh were fighting the French. We were not living particularly well because of the famine.

Every morning, before we went to school, Mr. Ba Kỷ would give each of us a boiled potato. Lunch typically was thick congee with rock candy. In the afternoon we'd have rice mixed with corn and maybe a little bit of vegetables. Some days we might have dried fish.

On the way to school one morning, just as I got to the main street and was about to take a bite of my boiled potato, a boy about my age snatched it from my hand. I stood there gaping, watching him stuffing it into his mouth as he ran away.

Another morning, at that same corner, I witnessed a thin, emaciated man snatch a rice cake from the stall of an old woman. As he ran away, the old woman called after him:

"Go ahead. Eat it, sonny. It's a brick!"

Apparently the sweet rice cake she had on display was just a brick wrapped in phrynium leaves!

Every day on our way to school, we saw dead people on the side of the streets. Ox-drawn carts traveled around to collect the bodies.

It was the Great Famine of 1945 which took away over two million lives.

On one Sunday morning, as Mr. Ba Kỷ was making breakfast for us, gunshots rang out, even before we could sit down to eat. We all dropped everything and ran to the bunker at Mr. Lễ's house. The sound of gunfire came closer and closer. Finally, we heard the sound of French boots stomping inside the house. Everybody held their breath and listened. I was so scared. Dad held me tighter in his arms.

Next, we heard the French shouting right outside of our hiding place. Dad told me to hang on tight to his back as he raised his arms. He told my brother Lân to hold my sister's hand as we slowly walked out of the bunker with Mr. Ba Kỷ, whose hands were also held over his head.

Seeing that my father was carrying a child with two other children in tow, the French soldiers held their fire. But they tied up the three men. Realizing that both my father and Mr. Lễ spoke French, they told us that the Việt-Minh were in the area and that everyone had to be moved out.

They tied my Dad, Mr. Lễ and Ba Kỷ to the back of a Jeep and drove slowly toward the Arboretum. My brother Lân grabbed me and my sister by the hand and ran after them. As I looked back, I saw flames. French soldiers were setting the Ngọc-Hà neighborhood on fire.

When we got to an area inside the Arboretum where French soldiers were stationed, I saw many tanks and big trucks. They allowed us to sit under a tree near where the Jeep was parked. Dad and Mr. Lễ were talking to a French officer, and everyone had been untied. By lunchtime, I was getting hungry. There was a shirtless soldier sitting on a tank eating. I kept looking up at him. He threw down a pack of biscuits in my direction. As I crawled out to get it, the soldier fell down on the ground next to me. A Việt-Minh sniper had shot him. Dad quickly crawled out to pull me back to the tree.

We waited there until late afternoon when the officer came back and said they were moving out of the Arboretum. He told us we also had to leave because the area wasn't safe. Mr. Lễ said he knew Father Grass at a Dominican Church nearby, so the officer had one of his men drive us there. At the church, we met the family of Mr. Nguyễn Mạnh-Hà who also had come there seeking refuge; his wife was French and they had two children. We all occupied one long room. People were lying all over the floor.

On our second day there, the church ran out of food. Father Grass told us that most of the owners of the nice villas around the area had fled and their homes were empty. He said even though it was dangerous for adults to go outside, it was safer for kids. He gave us children each a burlap sack and told us to go foraging for whatever food we could find. So the three of us and Mr. Ha's two children put the sacks on our backs and began going house to house "stealing" food.

We broke into one large empty villa. As the other kids went into the kitchen, out of curiosity I went up to the second floor to look around. After he finished stuffing his bag, my brother noticed I was missing. He went upstairs and found me standing speechless in front of a dead woman lying totally naked on the floor. He grabbed my hand and quickly got us out of there. After that incident my father did not allow us to go looking for food anymore.

One night it rained really hard. As we were sleeping, we heard loud knocks on the door. Father Grass rushed in, all wet; he quickly closed the door and blocked it with a desk. In a frightened voice, he told us that the Việt-Minh had entered the priests' quarters on the other side of the church and killed a young French priest. He said it was no longer safe for us to stay.

So once again, we had to pack up and find another place to shelter.

The House on Lê Trực Street

After many months full of madness and tragedies — having his home destroyed, his wife and son killed, his possessions gone — my father found a safe home for us. Uncle Cát, a wealthy friend who owned many properties, loaned my father a house on number 10 Lê Trực street.

It was a two-story villa built in the French colonial style, with a wrought iron gate and surrounded by a wall. A tall White Champaca tree guarded the front of the graceful villa; a lush grapevine adorned the gate. In the middle of the backyard, an old starfruit tree stood sentinel next to a rainwater tank. The rear garden overflowed with banana, guava and other fruit trees. Many different kinds of flowers bloomed along the wall. There was even a fish pond filled with water-fern, on its opposite side was a small pagoda. In the evening you could hear the pleasing sounds of Buddhist chants, bells and wood blocks in the dusky air, like a lullaby. They calmed one's mind, beckoning us to ponder the fleeting nature of earthly life: insignificant and impermanent.

At the end of Lê Trực street lay the Septo sports field. Every day, many young people bicycled past our house on their way there to exercise. I, too, went there often with my brother Lân to jump rope or run laps around the field.

The house wasn't very far from the Albert Sarraut School, which my brother Lân attended. And even closer, if memory serves, were the One-Pillar Pagoda and the Toad Garden.

Dad took me with him everywhere during those days. One time, we visited uncle Phúc's orange grove at Bố-Hạ. Dad and I rode horses with him around his ranch. He and Dad taught me to ride. Actually, it was mostly me sitting on a small donkey as Dad pulled it slowly behind his horse. I still remember to this day the ecstatic feeling of being on horseback in Dad's arms again after such a long time away.

I also remember the time we went to visit the famed writer Lê Văn Trương in his tiny second floor studio. I think the only physical asset this famous author owned was a small coffee table in the middle of the room. There were no chairs. Guests had no choice but to sit ... on the floor. The room, the furniture, even the four walls conspired to say that this puny little space, occupied by one of the giants of Vietnamese literature, had no colors other than black. Even the curtains were black; the whole scene was quite radical and bizarre.

I asked myself how could this man, living in this environment, bring into his novels such heroic characters idolized and beloved by so many readers? Is it because only behind these impenetrably dark curtains could the artist's soul escape to some fantastic locales far, far away?

On weekends, sometimes Dad would bring me with him to visit Mr. Hà Văn Vượng. His house, if memory serves, was near the Opera House on a leafy boulevard lined with beautiful French-style villas. Unlike uncle Trương's humble studio, uncle Vượng's house was palatial with a vast garden. There was a gigantic bird cage to house his peacocks. They were brightly feathered birds, with beer bottle green and deep red colors on their tails. I doubt any artist could mix such precise hues and shades to replicate what the hands of mother nature had produced.

Uncle Vượng had a special room with an easel and lots of canvases. I don't know if it was because his English wife was moving back to London with their children that led him to painting as a way to find peace and solace. But speaking of uncle Vượng, I can't neglect to mention his wife.

She was my first English teacher. A sweet and patient woman, she took time to explain to me the subtle differences in meaning between different words, and how to pronounce them correctly (that is, with the proper British accent) using a textbook with a French title: "Anglais sans Peine" — "English Without Pain."

I felt very proud to have received a special kind of love from Mrs Vượng. Because I didn't have a mother, I was especially grateful for the affection and tenderness from this kind and noble woman.

And thus I wasn't so surprised when uncle Vượng needled Father once: "Save your Chinh for my son Anh, will you?" His son Hà Văn Anh was studying in London at the time. I think Dad just smiled without saying anything.

Besides uncle Trương and uncle Vượng, there was another close friend of Father's that I have to mention — uncle Dzương, also known as "Antiques Dzương" of Drum Street. He and my father shared a love for photography.

To satiate their passion, they often went for days on shooting trips to faraway places that I'd never heard of . Sometimes Dad and uncle Dzương would let us kids tag along, to teach us a little bit about geography. perhaps.

Among the black-and-white photos from that period still in my possession were those of me and my sister taken at the zoo, Nghi-Tàm Arboretum, Toad Garden, Thầy Pagoda or the Hundred-Room Temple. But the most memorable ones, for me, were those taken on our trip to Đồ-Sơn Beach. I can still remember the early dawns when there was absolutely nobody around. The beach was empty and clean of footprints. My shadow reflected on the pristine sand as though from a mirror sprinkled with morning dew. On those mornings, I wore an exercise outfit and had many photos taken by Father. It felt like a once in a lifetime trip. In the evening, Father also took pictures of me in my long flowing dress and conical hat, standing on the beach looking toward the horizon. On the back of one of those photos my Father wrote down a couplet by the great poet Nguyễn Du:

My gaze reaches the sea
as evening fades, lonely a sail.

But memories with Dad were not limited to summer days. When winter came, Dad gave me even more things to remember him by. They were those chilly evenings that he took me to the movies.

Locking arms with him on those cold winter nights and Sharing his overcoat on our way to the Majestic, Philharmonic or Cầu Gỗ (Woodbridge) theaters were just magical. The owner of the Philharmonic, a Frenchman, was Dad's friend, There were two seats reserved in the loge for us; it's where we always sat.

To me, those were halcyon days spent heaven with a most wonderful man whom I was fortunate enough to call Dad.

Thanks to Dad, I fell in love with the movies from a young age. He always took time to thoroughly explain the meaning of every movie we saw. I liked films like *Le Cid* and *Limelight* by Charlie Chaplin.

I can remember many others, like *Les Plus Belles Années de Notre Vie* (*The Best Years of Our Lives*) which teared me up when I saw scenes of destruction brought on by war and of families separated. On our way home Dad would always pull me close to him to keep me warm. And as we walked, he would discuss the film, pointing out the more interesting or important aspects. When I reminisced years later, I realized that he was using the movies to educate me, to expand my perspective on life and the arts.

But back then, the part I liked the most was that he never failed to stop by "Le Grand Magasin" shopping center on Tràng-

Tiền to buy some French roasted chestnuts for me, and Cotab cigarettes for him. Sometimes, when he was in a particularly good mood, Dad would bring home a bottle of red wine and a pack of my favorite dark chocolate.

An avid reader, he might also pick up a book or two and some magazines like *Ciné Revue* and *Ciné Monde*. They were ostensibly for him, but I was welcome to read them as well, of course.

And when he'd finished his "duties" to his child and to himself, he'd call a cyclo pedicab to take us home. On the way back he always let me sit on his lap and held me tight to keep me warm. I always wished that the ride home would last much longer.

As I think back about it now, I feel so sad for my father. He lost his wife when he was quite young — and because there was no TV back then, there was pretty much nothing for him to do in the evening other than play his violin then take a book with him to bed.

Those were days when my father was trying to resettle and stabilize his life. He accepted a job as assistant to uncle Vượng who was the Minister of Finance at the time.

Brother Lân was going to school at Albert Sarraut and taking accordion lessons with the musician Nguyễn Hiền. He loved sports, particularly weight lifting, rope jumping and rowing. He also was an excellent table tennis player, even winning a tournament once. We had a ping pong table at the house — actually two. His friends used to come and practice; they were on the school team and were all very good. The two best players were "Tall" Hiệp and "Dark" Trương; not too shabby were "Skinny" Khuê and Năng Tế.

Besides going to a regular school, my sister Tĩnh also attended a homemaking class. Because we didn't have a mother,

Dad made sure both of his girls studied cooking and other domestic arts. I also learned knitting. I attended a Catholic school — St Paul's, and studied piano with Mr. Duyệt. I had a close and very pretty friend in piano class; her name was Bích Vân. We both thought each was the other's "best friend forever" and that nothing would ever be able to separate us.

During my time at St.Paul's with the Sisters, I was known as a devout student. I recited Christian prayers each morning and night. I attended church every Sunday. One time I asked Father for permission to be baptized. He said:

"I don't forbid you from believing in Jesus. All religions teach us to do good. But I advise you not to get baptized because our family history is steeped in Buddhism and in ancestor worship. You are a girl. Later on, when you get married, you will have to follow your husband's family traditions. You don't know yet whether that family will be Buddhist or Christian."

The four of us had a peaceful life together during the time at 10 Lê Trực. As for me, I consider those days to be my "childhood heaven," always in the arms of my father's love. Perhaps I was the only one who knew how much I loved him. My mother passed away when he was in his early thirties. My father was handsome, refined, well-tempered and talented.

Ever since we moved into the house on Lê Trực, my father's friends became fewer. Only the closest ones would come around, like uncle Ngọc Giao, uncle Dzương, uncle An on Peach Street and uncle Phúc from the Bố-Hạ orange grove.

At night my father stayed home and read. Sometimes he even read dictionaries; his friends liked to joke that he was a walking dictionary. How could I not love my father?

I don't know if it was because he was lonely, but my father began to smoke more than usual. He would drink at least one or two glasses of wine at dinner. He often sat pensively before his wine glass. Every now and then he'd write a poem. He even had a book of poetry titled "Hidden Gems."

One day, a pretty lady started to come visit our father. She always had some treats for us. Dad said she was a well-known poet in the literary world. I didn't know what my brother and sister thought about our father's new friend. Myself, I simply thought that it was good that he'd made another friend in his literary circle, just like all his other male friends.

One afternoon I found my father pacing around the living room with a cigarette in his hand, looking very tense as if he was trying to solve a difficult problem. I was too afraid to ask him what it was, so I just watched with a certain disquiet and nervousness.

At last, he called the three of us into the living room. Once we were seated, he calmly announced that he was going to marry the literary lady friend whom we were quite fond of.

His announcement hit me hard. He said the words slowly and with difficulty, especially when he suggested that he wanted to remarry.

The first thought that entered my mind at that moment was that it meant his love for me would be diminished as he began sharing it with his new wife.

Even though I liked her fine, perhaps I was too young to understand the loneliness of a man who had lost his companion at such a young age. My reaction was abrupt and strong. I stood up and ran out of the house, toward the pagoda on the other side of the fish pond.

There I hid under a tree for a long time, skipping dinner. I held my face and cried and cried. As evening fell, Dad became concerned and went looking for me. He finally found me curled up under a tree behind the pagoda, shivering. He took me into his arms to warm me up and promised that he'd never, ever marry anyone.

"Our family will be just as before," he said. "Just the four of us." And he kept that promise. My father stayed single until the day he died!

As I think back about all that now, I'm filled with remorse. I was acting in a most foolhardy and thoughtless manner! My behavior was childish and based on a selfish love. I wish now that in his later years, when his three children were all grown and gone, my father had a companion by his side in his last moments on earth, someone to close his eyes for him as he moved on to a different plane.

I'm so sorry, Dad! I'm so sorry!

Leaving

Dad seemed worried and concerned. His friends rarely came over anymore. And when they did, there wasn't that fun atmosphere like before. They talked in low voices with a solemn tone. Brother Lân's friends, too. Whenever they came, it wasn't to play ping pong but always to discuss something. Something grave and serious.

One night, his friend Tế came over, but my brother wasn't home. Tế called me out to the grapevine and told me that he'd decided to enlist in the army. He would enter the Thủ-Đức Reserve Officer School near Sài-Gòn, so he'd be gone for awhile. I looked up at him without saying anything. He took my hands and kissed me. It was my first kiss.

A few days later, my brother and I and a few friends of his went to see off their friends who were leaving for Ngọc-Hà training camp. There were so many. Besides Tế, there was Nguyễn Trọng-Bảo, Trần Đức-Sơn...

In the days that followed, I received many letters from Tế from Thủ-Đức, full of feeling and passion. My adolescent, first love blossomed during this time of war, in a Hà-Nội that was no longer peaceful. The situation was tense and changing rapidly from day to day.

Right after my sister's wedding, Tĩnh moved with her husband's family to France. I was devastated. After so many years of living together, growing up together, eating, even sleeping together, now she was gone. I had no idea when we'd see each other again. In our last meal together before she boarded the ship, with all four of us, Tĩnh cried and cried. Dad drank more than usual. I drank with him too. It was the first time I got drunk.

The year was 1954. The Geneva Conference had just concluded with an agreement that divided the country into two zones at the 17th parallel. Communist in the North, Nationalist in the South.

I was too young to understand all the politics behind it. I just knew that one day, after Dad met with his friend Hà Văn Vượng, he called us in and told us that we had to go South. And we must pack quickly.

The next morning, Dad and brother Lân brought everything in the house outside to conduct an estate sale. The front yard where my brother and his friends used to play table tennis was now filled with furniture; even the family altar was there. Valuable antiques were put on the ping-pong table. Everything was up for sale — everything. The house was completely emptied.

When we opened up the iron gates, people poured in. It was a big crowd, noisy like a small market. I looked on in horror as strangers picked up our personal belongings and made remarks about them, haggled over the price, then walked off with things that we had grown up with. My brother refused, however, to relinquish his bicycle.

Now that my sister was gone and most of our stuff was sold, the house became totally empty. Only Dad, brother Lân and I remained with a few essential personal items. Dad got each of us a small back sack containing emergency items like medication, dried food, and a little bit of money. That night, we all slept together inside our mosquito net on the floor.

In the middle of the night, I was wakened by my brother. He made a sign for me to be quiet and took me outside. At the gate, his ping-pong friend "Tall" Hiệp was sitting on a bike, waiting and holding my brother's bike in his hand.

Lân hugged me, then said: "Chinh, I must go with Hiệp to the front. I won't migrate. You go with Dad, and take care of him for me."

I started to panic: "No! You can't go! You have to ask for Dad's permission!"

"He won't let me," my brother replied. "We must leave now."

Hiệp looked at me, stuttering: "Chinh, I have to go... Please take good..." Then he quickly said, "I love you, Chinh."

I pretended like I didn't hear him. My brother let go of me and climbed on his bicycle. I grabbed the handlebar really hard:

"No, you cannot go!"

He tried to remove my hand, "Chinh, please..."

I shook him off and rushed inside, calling: "Daddy! Daddy! Brother Lân..."

By the time my father ran outside, there wasn't a soul on Lê Trực street. Dad started yelling: "Lân! Lân! Where are you, son...!"

His voice dissolved into the emptiness. There was no sight of the two young men and their bicycles. They'd disappeared into the night.

In the darkness of the house, my father sat against the wall. His cigarette flickered now and then. He was chain smoking. I came over and lay down next to him, not saying a word. He took my hand, pulled out from his pocket a gold bracelet and put it on me:

"Keep this, in case of need."

I held his hands tightly, overcome with emotions.

"Try to sleep a bit," he said. "We'll leave early tomorrow."

But I couldn't sleep. And neither could he.

The next day, Dad and I went to the airport in Hà-Nội — I can't remember now if it was Bạch-Mai or Gia-Lâm airport. I don't really know how to describe the chaotic scene at the airport. Dad held my hand tightly as we fought our way through the crowd and found a place where we could stand and wait.

Around noon, large DC-3 military planes began to arrive and take off. Each time one plane landed, people started to run toward it. One wave after another, rushing the planes. It was getting quite hot, and my father placed his hand over my head to shield me from the sun as much as he could.

All of a sudden, my father saw in the sea of people his friend Nguyễn Đại-Độ, also the father of Tế. Unlike us, they had the whole family with them; about a dozen or so, with grandkids and house maids and all. So we went over to stand next to them. Dad talked to uncle Độ as we waited. It wasn't until after sunset, when the last plane landed that we could get on. As the rear hatch opened downward, people started to climb in. It was tumultuous, chaotic, disorganized and loud. Dad closely followed uncle Độ's family. Once they'd gotten on, he suddenly picked me up and threw me in after them. In the midst of engine noise and the cacophony of people shouting, my Father yelled:

"Chinh, you go on first. I'm staying to look for your brother. I will join you later."

"No! No! Daddy, no!!" I screamed and tried to jump out. All I saw was him standing there like a lifeless person, watching. I raised my hand high so he could see me and screamed:

"Daddy!!!"

I tried to get out, but the crowd pushed me down to the metal floor. I struggled to stand up and looked toward the rear of the airplane as the rear hatch pulled up.

That was the last time I saw my father and heard his voice. I sat curled up in a fetal position and cried until the plane landed.

PICTURES
PART I
Hà Nội, 1937-1954

My paternal grandfather in front of Kim-Mã Estate.

A rare photo of my father's family. My grandfather stands in the middle with his hands on my father's shoulders, who wears a Western style outfit with leather boots.

My maternal grandfather, Nguyễn Văn Luận.

An old photo, taken in 1918, of my mother's family.
My mother is on the far left.

Daddy Cửu at a young age.

My mother Nguyễn Thị An at young age

A tall, lean Daddy Cửu (left) and mother (right), Nguyễn thị An, in black velvet "áo dài" and gold necklace.

My father (far right) with his buddies in Hà-Nội.

My father riding his horse on the way to Bovine Mountain.

My mother (left) and her sister, Cam, in the family rickshaw.

My father and my brother Lân at Kim-Mã Estate.

My mother, my sister Tĩnh, and me holding our dog, Toto. It's the only photo I have with my mother.

My father, my grandfather, my brother Lân, and my mother.

My mother's last photo; she was pregnant with my youngest brother at the time.

Kiều Chinh (left), my sister Tĩnh, and my brother Lân in the backyard of the house on Lê Trực Street, Hà-Nội.

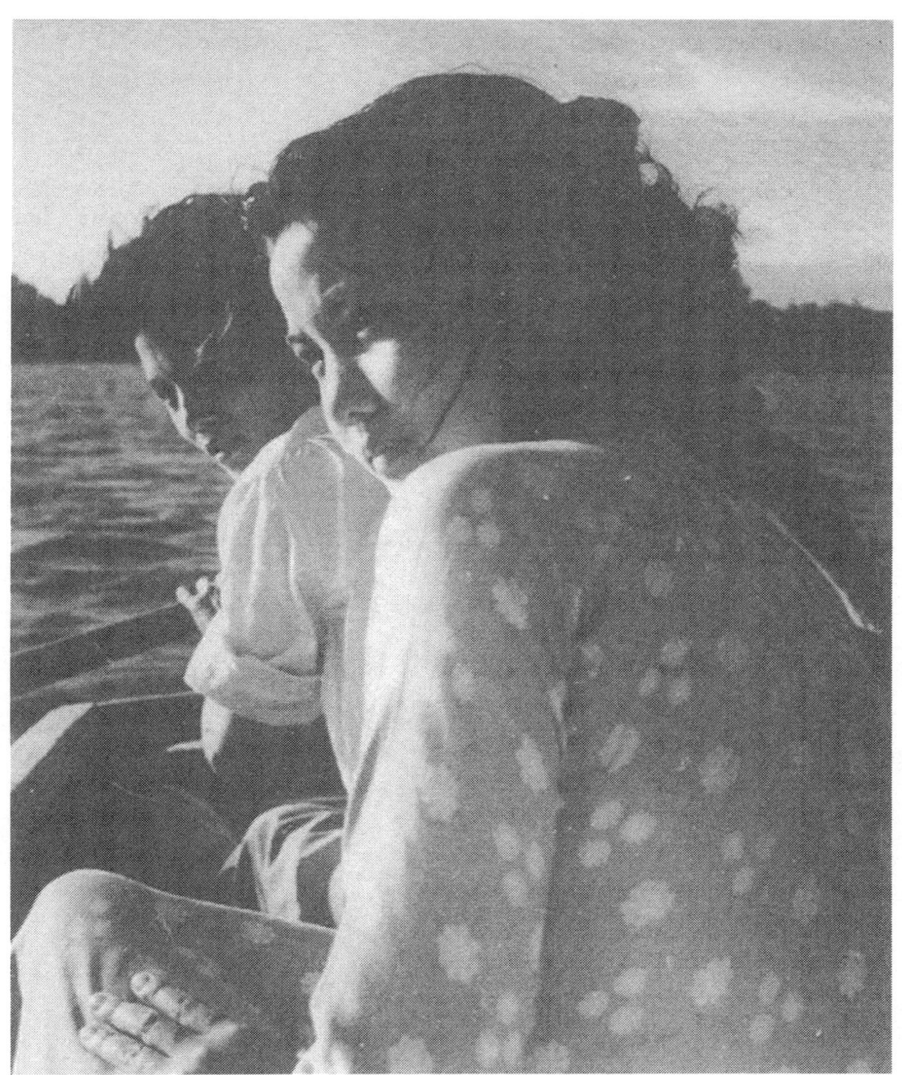

Brother Lân and me rowing on West Lake (Hồ Tây), Hà-Nội.

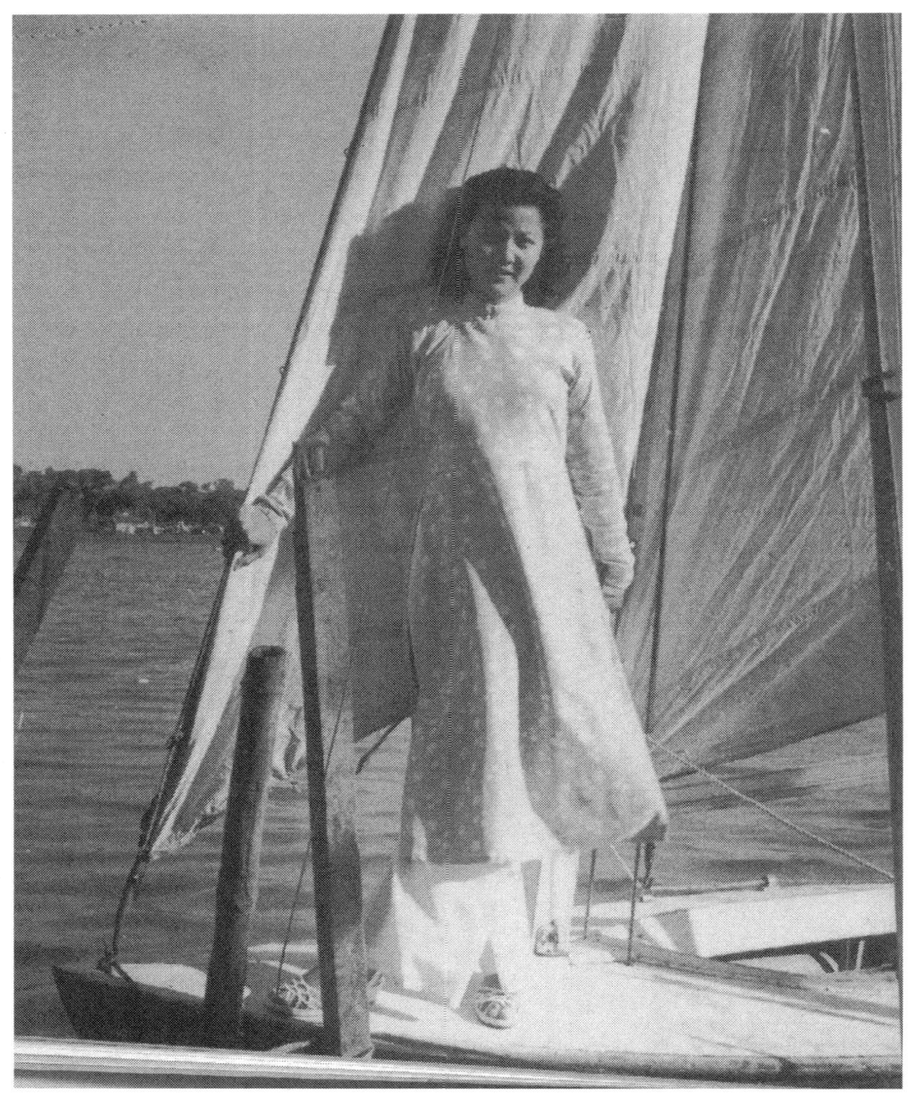

West Lake (Hồ Tây), Hà-Nội.

Kiều Chinh (left), and Tĩnh, riding bicycles at the Toad Garden in Hà-Nội.

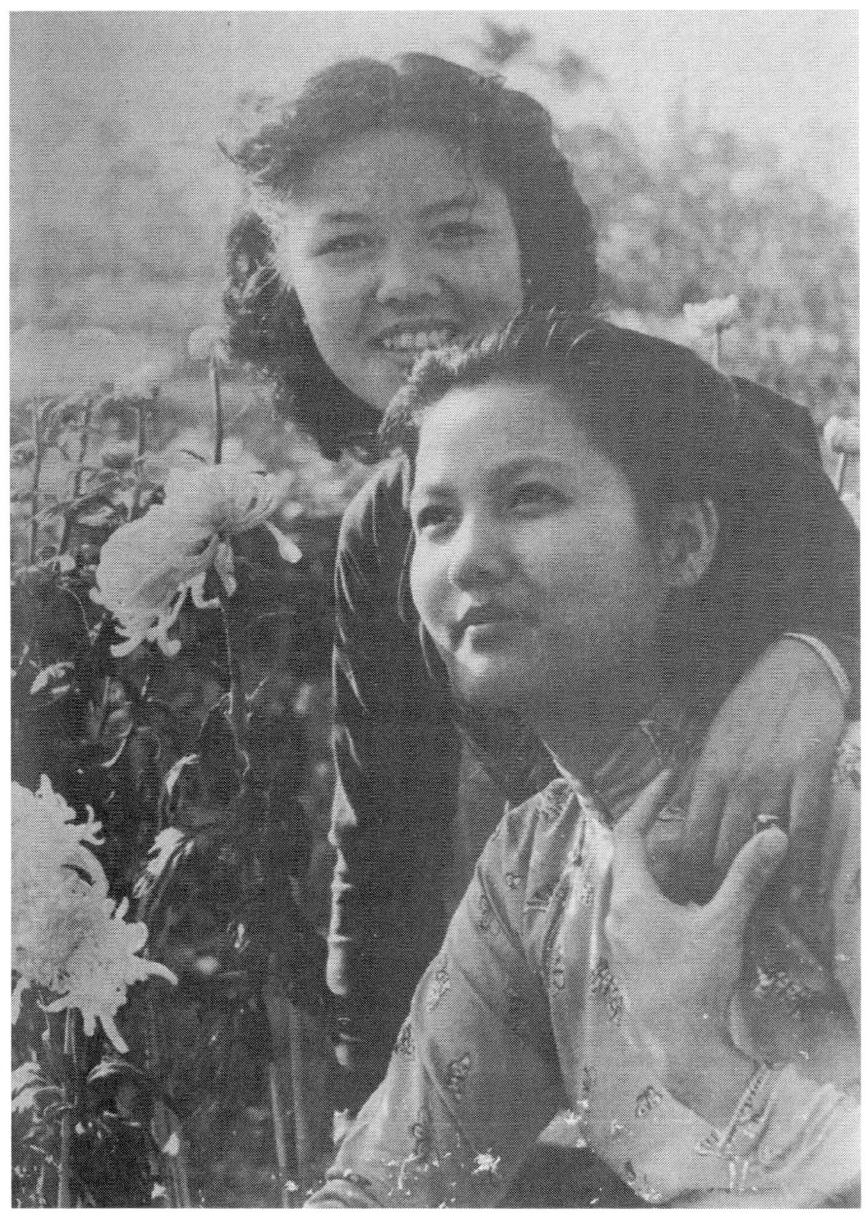

My sister Tĩnh and me at Nghi-Tàm Flower Garden, Hà-Nội.

At Nghi-Tàm Flower Garden, Hà-Nội.

In the haystack

With two puppies at the Arboretum, Hà-Nội.

Kiều Chinh's class at St. Paul's Catholic school in 1948.
(in the second row from left, Kiều Chinh in black uniform is the seventh person after nun Suzanne)

With Bích Vân (left) my best friend at young age.

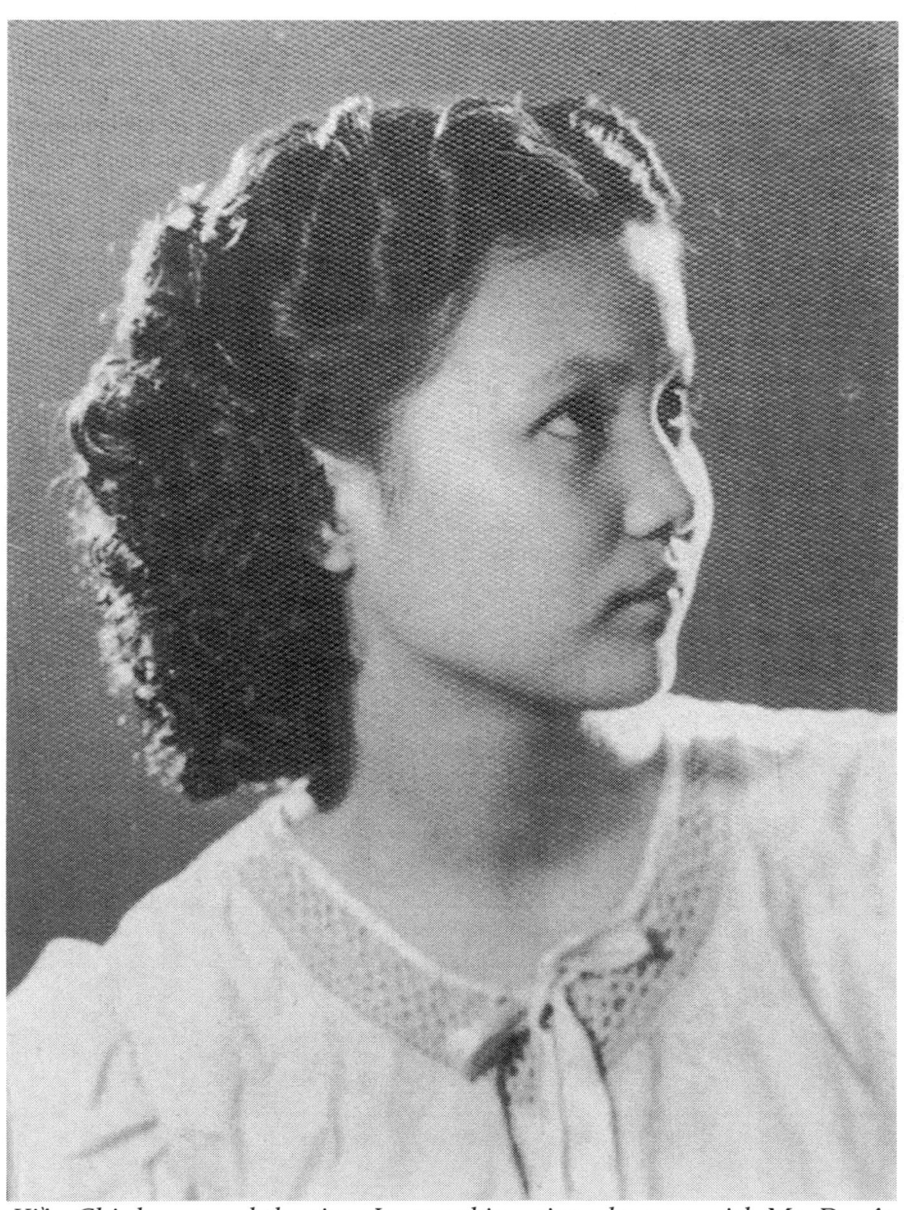

Kiều Chinh, around the time I was taking piano lessons with Mr. Duyệt (circa 1949-1950).

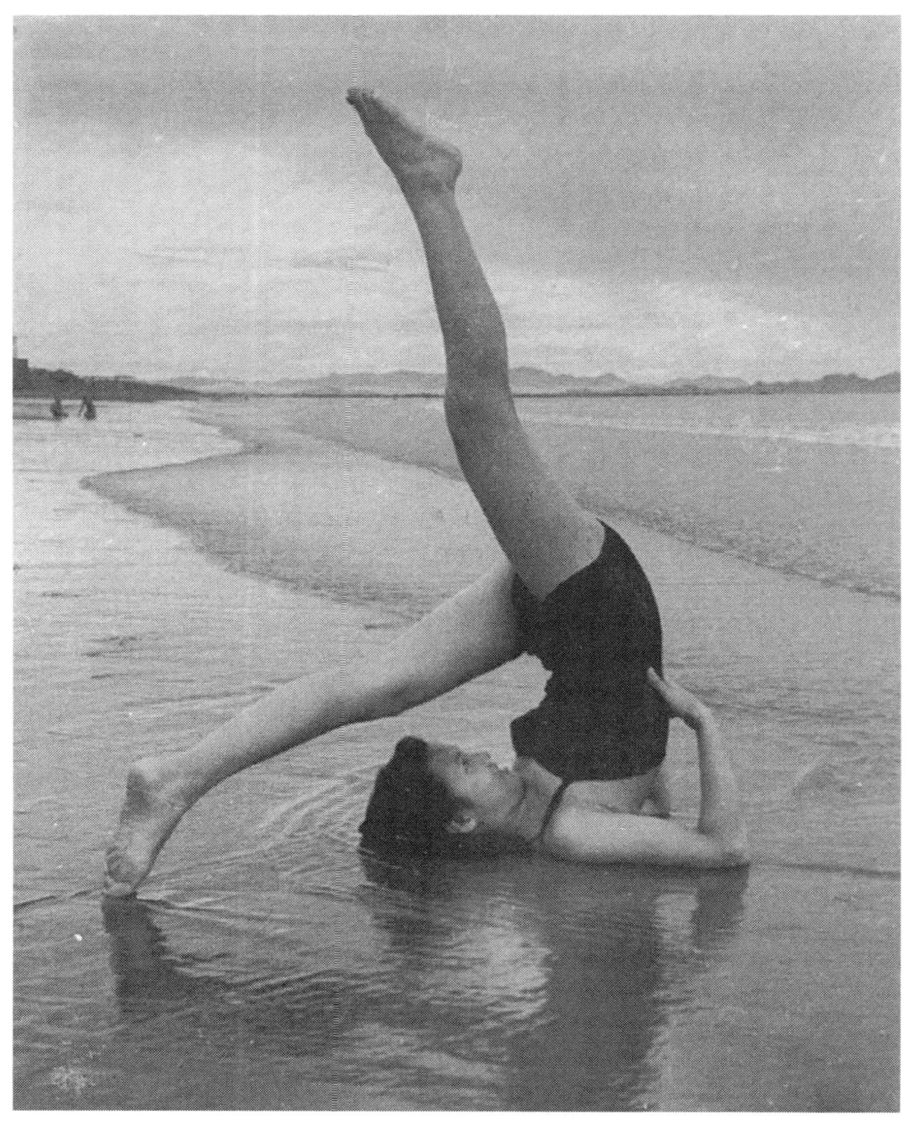

On Đồ-Sơn beach at dawn. Photo by my father.

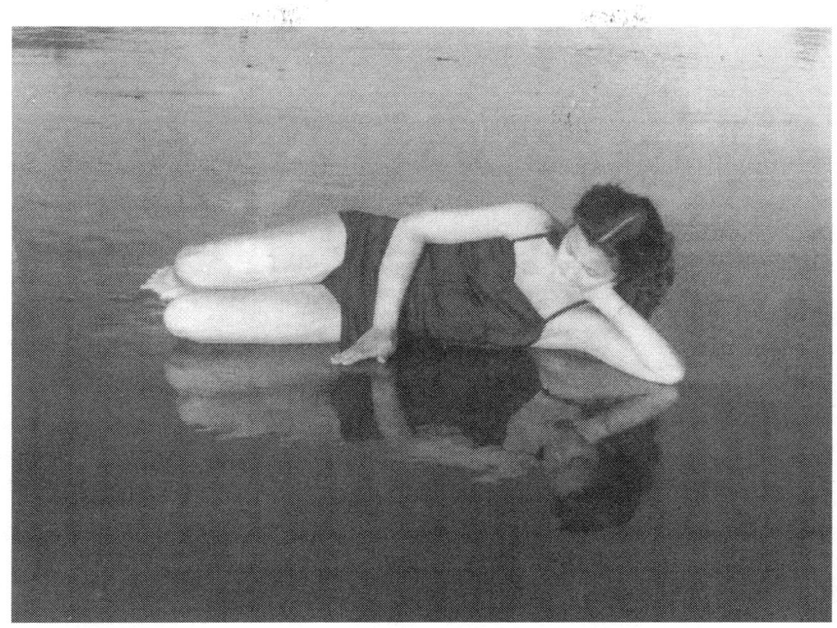

My reflection on Đồ-Sơn beach. Photo by my father.

In áo dài and conical hat on Đồ-Sơn beach. Photo by my father.

Last picture with my father, our last Tết (Lunar New Year) together.

PART II

Sài-Gòn, 1954-1975

All By Myself

It was the first night of August, 1954. The DC-3 rumbled and shook as it touched down in Tân-Sơn-Nhứt. It was raining hard outside. Was it a sign that Sài-Gòn chose to meet and greet this suddenly "orphaned" girl with a tempestuous downpour?

The rain followed me to the bus that took us to the camp whose name I couldn't remember. I just called it "Refugee Camp." They let us out at Petrus Ký Boulevard, in front of Petrus Ký High School.

While I was still trying to get my bearings among a sea of strangers, I heard someone call my name whose voice I immediately recognized. It was my childhood best friend Bích-Vân from Hà-Nội. I was like a drowning person who was thrown a lifeline.

We hugged each other; tears welled up in our eyes.

That night we talked nonstop on the dirt floor of the camp. Bích-Vân asked many questions about my family, especially about my brother Lân and our neighborhood. She made me feel simultaneously happy and full of self-pity. Seems like self-pity is a dark cloud that never leaves me alone; it has hung over my head and has followed me around ever since I left my brother and father.

In the darkness of the camp, I had to make sure my friend couldn't see the silent tears rolling down my cheeks.

After such a long and terrible day, I finally fell asleep near daybreak. In my nightmarish dreams I heard myself scream "No,

Daddy! No!" when my father pushed me onto the airplane and shouted "Chinh, you go on first. I must stay to find your brother. I will join you later."

When I awoke, beads of sweat were rolling down from my head even though it was chilly outside. I immediately wanted to tell Bích-Vân about my nightmares, but was surprised to find her gone. Where she slept there was note: "Chinh, stay here. Don't look for me. I've decided to return to Hà-Nội. Be strong. Good luck."

I sat there stunned. I couldn't register anything that was happening around me. The image of Bích-Vân and so many questions swirled around in my head. What made her decide to go back to the North after talking to me, when only a few days earlier she had secretly left her family to go South all by herself?

And another question was, why didn't she tell me so I could join her?

(It wasn't until years later that I found out that Bích-Vân also became a film actress in the North just like I was one in the South.)

As the sun came up, I joined the crowd of people lining up to register and get some food. Uncle Độ came and said he'd already registered my name under his family. As we waited in line he revealed that my father had asked him to take care of me for him until he and brother Lân could make their way to the South.

Uncle Độ's family, now with me included, swelled up to 17 persons. A nephew of his came to pick us up and brought us to a residence on Red Cross Boulevard (Hồng-Thập-Tự). A few days later the entire family moved to a small apartment on Nguyễn Tri-Phương street which his nephew had kindly let us borrow. The place was tiny. It was more like a long tube, with an even tinier "attic".

With 17 people packed in, the place felt like it could combust at any given moment. There were the two parents and two grandchildren. Their father — Nguyễn Giáp-Tý, the oldest son, was an officer working on the Six-Party Ceasefire Committee based in Đà-Lạt (which was why he'd hired a maid name Sâm to take care of his two boys.) And then there were two daughters, Mùi and Dậu with their children.

At the time Tế (who gave me my first kiss) was training at the Thủ-Đức Reserve Officers School as part of its 4th graduating class. The only son at home was the youngest one, Nguyễn Chí-Hiếu, who was a classmate of mine for a short time when I was in Hà-Nội. (Hiếu later entered the Đà-Lạt Military Academy — the Westpoint of South Vietnam, and became a decorated officer serving in the Airborne branch of the ARVN[1]).

I was assigned to the "attic" with Sâm, the maid. There was a small ladder that we had to fold sideway and then hook into the wall after each use to make room for walking around. The attic barely had enough room for two small mats, one for me, one for Sâm.

There was a window that opened to the back alley where I took out the trash each day. It was also how I was able to look up to the sky every night to send my wishes and dreams to the stars, or sometimes watch the foreboding yet spectacular southern storms threaten overhead.

The window was in fact an outlet that allowed me to truly be myself at night. The faraway stars would beam down through that tiny opening their little sparks of consolation and comfort, offering glimmers of hope that I'd soon be reunited with my father.

It was but a cheap sedge mat plus a small window that someone probably had knocked out just for some air, but to me

---

[1] The acclaimed wartime author Phan Nhật-Nam, in an article titled "Remembering our senior Red Beret brother, Colonel Nguyễn Chí-Hiếu" spoke highly of him as a hero of the ARVN. He participated in most of the bloodiest battles of our 20-year war. His conduct and leadership abilities were recognized and lauded by Americans who fought alongside him. He died on December 5, 2007, in Southern California.

these were a microcosm of my whole world. The happiest moment in the day for me was when I'd finished all my tasks and were able to lie down on that mat. So many times it patiently listened to my stories and heard me share my humble wish that I'd see Dad again one day. It was also on that little mat that I spent many private moments with the postcards that my father sent from Hà-Nội. They were the simple types with preprinted form greetings that one just had to circle the line one wished to say. Nothing too personal. But through them my father was able to keep my spirit up. He never failed to end each with a short but encouraging message such as "Your loving father," "Your dearest Dad," "Be courageous," etc.

That mat was also the only guest invited to see me light a candle to mark my 17th birthday. The first birthday without my father or brother present. It was just me and my shadow that night, watching the candle slowly melt away. My 17th birthday came and went quietly on that September night in 1954, like many other hardships I would have to endure.

As stipulated by the Geneva Accords, there was a 300-day period of free movement between the North and South, and Hải-Phòng was the free port where Northerners could be evacuated. I counted every minute of every hour of those 300 days, desperately waiting to hear the good news that Dad had found brother Lân and they were on their way South. We would be reunited and living together again — rich or poor, I didn't care.

Every day at six o'clock I listened to Radio France-Asie for news on the evacuations. As each day passed my hopes became fainter and fainter. Finally, the 300 days were up. Hải-Phòng port was closed. The evacuation ended. My heart sank. All my hopes were completely extinguished, like the last leaves that fell from the tree before winter arrived.

When the final broadcast from Radio France-Asie finished with its familiar tune "Hirondelle" (The Swallow) for the very last time, it was a death knell to me. I understood. That was it. A dead end. There was no more road, no more light at the end of the tunnel.

Ever since the communist Bamboo Curtain came down, I stopped holding out any hope of ever seeing my father again. I fell into a state of despair and apathy. I walked around like a zombie, a robot that performed housework — washing, cleaning, cooking for Mr. and Mrs. Độ. There was only one person my age in the family, Hiếu, from whom I received a lot of subtle emotional support. Every now and then I'd get a letter from Tế sent from Thủ-Đức. There was also Lịch, the sister of Tế's friend Nguyễn Trọng-Bảo, who visited often and helped me through that difficult period of utter depression.

Marriage

It was a spring day in 1955 in Sài-Gòn. I was sweeping the front yard when a Jeep braked in front of our house. A man in a camouflage uniform jumped out, walked up to me with a backpack in hand:

"Chinh!"

"Oh, Tế!"

We both were so happy to see each other. Tế had changed so much. None of that boyish, college student look, he was now a handsome looking soldier in a time of war, so impressive in his paratrooper uniform with the red beret stylishly tilted just so.

With his usual warm voice, he placed his hand on my shoulder and led me inside: "How have you been?"

Tế had just graduated from Thủ-Đức Reserve Officer School. His homecoming and his buoyant personality enlivened the atmosphere. I also was happy to receive much of his attention and affection.

A few months later, Tế announced that he'd been selected to go to the U.S. for training at Fort Benning in Georgia. It would last one year. All the paperwork had been completed, it was just a matter of waiting for the departure date. This news caused great concern for Mr. and Mrs. Độ. They feared one year in America was just too long.

One afternoon, while I was washing clothes in the back, Sâm, the maid, excitedly came looking for me. As soon as she saw me she started speaking in a most animated voice as if this was the juiciest slice of gossip:

"Miss Chinh, I heard our lady was afraid uncle Tế might marry an American woman while he's in America!"

Not getting any response from me by this "hot off the press" news, Sâm was taken aback a little bit. But she quickly reloaded and tried again, this time with even more emphasis:

"It's true, Miss Chinh. I heard that uncle Tế will be leaving for America in a few weeks. He'll stay there for a whole long year before they let him home. That's why Mr. and Mrs. Độ want him married quick, else it'll be too late."

She stopped and looked me, searching for a reaction before letting out what she surely thought was an unmistakable hint to help me get it:

"I also heard... that they... really, really like YOU, Miss Chinh."

A few days later Sâm came to me again, this time in the kitchen, and whispered:

"Mr. and Mrs. Độ want to see you, in the living room..."

There wasn't anyone home at the time. Mr. and Mrs. Độ were sitting on the bed, in front of a teapot. Mrs. Độ spoke first, in a serious tone that wasn't at all like when she reminded me what to buy at the market. As a matter of habit, I sat down on the floor. But this time she pointed me to go sit on the bed near Mr. Độ. He looked at her, then turned to me and said very slowly:

"There's an important matter that we must let you know. The reason we've been holding off so long is because we've been waiting to hear from your Daddy Cửu. I tried to reach him through many methods and many ways, and today I finally got his response. Here's the letter from your father which I've just received. It is addressed to you. I'd like for you to read it here and let me know your answer."

My hands started shaking. Oh my God! News from Dad! I prayed that it would be about when we could see each other again. My heart pounding, I began to read:

My dear daughter Chinh,

Mr. and Mrs. Độ are kind enough to want you to marry Tế. I have agreed. I know you're still young and haven't gotten your education, neither are you mature enough to start a family. But the situation cannot be changed. I cannot see you, cannot do anything to help you while the North and South are separated like this. I put my trust in uncle Độ. From now on they are your parents. You must obey them and fulfill your duties as a daughter-in-law. You must take care of them as you would your own parents.

You know how much I love and care for you. Remember my words, Chinh. I cannot write more. I love you so much.

Your Daddy Cửu.

My father's short message not only extinguished any faint hope I might have had of ever seeing him again, but his resoluteness threw my life on to a totally different path, a new life. And I was barely 17 years old.

I knew Mr. and Mrs. Độ would be studying my facial expressions as I read the letter, so I tried my best to not show any emotions. But because they had asked to hear my answer right away, as soon as I folded up the small piece of paper, I spoke meekly:

"Yes, sir. Yes, ma'am."

And that was how my girlhood came to an end, and how my womanhood and motherhood began. It was just as abrupt, sudden and shocking as the day I was separated from my father at a Hà-Nội airport.

That night, after finishing all the chores, I went up to my sedge mat. I reread Dad's letter over and over again. I tried to imagine where he was and his state of mind when he wrote this important message. But I couldn't see anything other than a rough, unusual handwriting, as though he had to write it the shortest amount of time possible. I also noticed that the piece of paper was quite yellow and of low quality.

(It wasn't until 30 years later that I learned that my father's terse letter was the last thing he wrote to me. And it wasn't from the house on number 10 Lê Trực but from prison.)

For my part, I can still remember clearly how I held his letter close to my chest that night, put it against my lips and whispered that familiar phrase: "Oh, Daddy..."

Like all the nights before, only the stars were there to answer me, with their usual glimmering. My tears silently flowed, "Oh, Daddy..."

Once Mr. and Mrs. Độ, whom I now called Dad and Mom, had chosen a fortuitous day, the wedding took place in a format that could not have been simpler. There was not the traditional procession by the groom's family to the bride's home to ask for permission to receive her — because the bride was already living with the groom's parents! It was just a small ceremony of tying the red string before a makeshift family altar. Sâm was ordered to move downstairs to sleep on a cot so that the newlyweds could have the "attic" to themselves. The two single mats were replaced by a double mat. And that was it.

The wedding date was set for July 3, while the groom was to leave for the U.S. in the first week of September. In a way, my wedding reception was also a farewell party to see my husband off to a distant land that existed only in my imagination. As for guests, my new parents ordered exactly two tables at a restaurant in Chợ Lớn. Only a few close friends from Hà-Nội were invited. One was a friend of my oldest brother-in-law's, Kỳ Quang Liêm, a paratrooper who also was my husband's training officer at Thủ-Đức. And a brother and sister pair: Nguyễn Trọng-Bảo and his older sister Lịch. Sister Lịch later became a great source of stability for me when I went through a tough period of loneliness and despair. Brother Bảo became a

Brigadier General and in 1972 he was killed in a bloody battle in the highlands.

I'd always thought weddings were big deals. As it turned out everything went by quietly and just as quickly returned to normal. Like my father had written, "*the circumstances can't be changed.*" Or, like he had told me once long before: "Of my three children, you're the most romantic, most intelligent, but also most idealistic. That's why you'll be the one most easily disappointed. My advice for you is to close one eye when you look at life. This world and the people in it aren't what you wish them to be. Only by clearly understanding this will you be able to avoid the pains of disappointment..."

Before Tế left for the U.S. he often took me to the movies on weekends, something I enjoyed tremendously. There was one film that I'll never forget, *From Here to Eternity* with Montgomery Clift, Burt Lancaster and Frank Sinatra. It was shown at the brand new Eden theater. After the movie we walked hand in hand through the mall. Everybody thought we were the most perfect couple — a handsome officer with his pretty young Northern bride.

But those outings also reminded me so much of the time I went to the movies with Dad in Hà-Nội.

After Tế was gone for three months, I discovered that I was pregnant. The baby was growing quite fast, but I didn't have any maternity clothes. Sâm gave me a pair of her old pants so that I could tailor them into something that fit. I suddenly realized that I had no money, not just for myself but also to take care of the baby! I had never been concerned about Tế's salary as a second lieutenant. I figured he should give it to his parents to help with family expenses. I just felt sorry for him for having to be so far away so soon after the wedding.

Even though I didn't say anything to sister Lịch, she nonetheless noticed and knew that I was having financial issues. One day she came up to me as though she was the oldest sister in the family and said: "You can't go on living like this. You have to stand up and be strong. Get a job so you can support yourself and take care of your child. Love yourself first..." Then after a short pause she continued:

"There's an agency called MACV; they're hiring. You can speak English, and I'm sure they'll hire you on the spot. Get that job now before your tummy gets too big."

MACV was, of course, the United States "Military Assistance Command, Vietnam" headquartered on Trần Hưng-Đạo Boulevard.

And she was right. I went to apply and was hired right away. But there was a problem persuading my parents-in-law. As soon as I told my mother-in-law, her answer was both negative and swift:

"Look at our family. Are we so desperate that our daughter-in-law has to go to work?" After pausing for a few seconds, she continued:

"And who will take care of cooking and cleaning if you're gone all day?"

I softly answered: "Once I start working I will be able to hire a helper. She will take over what I've been doing, and probably will do a much better job, too."

She said nothing. I had no idea what she was thinking. So I went to brother Bảo and sister Lịch for advice. I figured being older and well respected by my in-laws, they'd be able to help. When I approached sister Lịch about it, she immediately agreed to intervene. Lịch came and talked to my mother-in-law, explaining how a family in this day and age would need two incomes in order to take good care of the children, etc. Fortunately, her arguments won over my father-in-law. He told his wife:

"Just let Chinh give it a try for a few months. If it doesn't work out she can always quit. What is there to be scared of?"

And so I zealously went to work, just as sister Lịch advised me to. I understood that my needs were no longer just a pair of pants big enough for my expanding belly. Too many things were waiting for me up ahead.

I used my first month's pay, without being told by anyone, to help with the family expenses and to pay Chấm, our newly hired helper who took over my old tasks. I also bought a box of Chinese tea, two brass candlesticks and a bronze Buddha statue as gifts for my parents-in-law. The small statue changed how my mother-in-law saw me, as if I was the only one who knew what she'd been wanting, since the little makeshift altar in the house didn't have such a statue.

Even though we were living apart, I wrote Tế regularly to keep him abreast of what was going on. In the beginning, he also wrote back and would send me small presents like a night gown or pajamas. They were the letters of a young couple, full of love and yearning. When I announced that I was pregnant, or that I had a job, he was very happy. But as time went on, the frequency of his letters to me started to lag behind that of the letters I sent him. I didn't want to speculate; I just prayed that he wasn't sick or facing some difficulties.

One day, when I was in my seventh month of pregnancy and the baby had become quite active, I received a letter from the Department of Defense. They wanted me to come in for a talk. There I met an older officer who handed me an official request by Second Lt Nguyễn Năng-Tế to stay in the U.S. for an extra year, and for the permission to marry an American woman!

I was petrified while holding Tế's unbelievable letter in my hand. Everything became one big blur. I couldn't hear anything except maybe sounds of sledge hammers banging against rocks or ocean waves crashing on the sand.

Looking at my swollen belly, the old gentleman asked me in a sympathetic voice: "You are legally married to Second Lt. Tế, right?" I nodded: "Yes, sir." "Then don't worry," he said. "Go home and take care of the baby. Military rules don't allow anyone to have two wives, or bigamy."

Two months after that day, Sâm accompanied me to the hospital. We rode in a motorized cyclo. The date was April 19, 1956. It was raining very hard. After three long hours of excruciating pain, I gave birth to a daughter. Her cries were drowned out by the thundering rain as my tears flowed non-stop, joining the downpour outside.

I wanted to name her Bích-Vân (jade cloud) after my best friend who left Sài-Gòn to go back to Hà-Nội. But her grandfather suggested that since she was born while her father was in America, we should call her Mỹ-Vân instead. Mỹ is America in Vietnamese.

After six months working for MACV I got a raise. With the extra money I was able to hire an extra helper so that Chấm could take care of the baby full-time. Mỹ-Vân could flip over by the time Tế was finishing up his one year of training.

On the day he and his fellow officers returned to Vietnam, I asked for time off and took Mỹ-Vân to the airport to meet her Dad. The terminal was filled with joyful voices of wives reuniting with their husbands, children with their fathers. I, too, held Mỹ-Vân in my arms in excitement and anticipation.

The last person to get off was our family friend Nguyễn Trọng-Bảo. There was no Tế. I began to panic, not believing my eyes. Once he saw me standing there with the baby, lost amongst a crowd of happy families, Bảo came over and gently said: "Tế asked to stay. He didn't tell you?"

I shook my head and held my three-month-old child even tighter. My poor baby. Even if she were three years old she still wouldn't understand why her mom was squeezing her so hard. She wouldn't be able to comprehend that her mother was trying to lean on her, a helpless baby, as she searched for some ways to cope with the shock of having to carry on in the days ahead.

A few months passed. One day I was over at sister Lịch's house for a death day celebration. It was the first time I saw Tế's familiar handwriting again, in a letter he wrote to brother Bảo. Bảo said:

"It's a private letter to me, but sister Lịch said I should let you see it. It even has some photos. Tế talks about his days in the U.S., and mentions your name in one line..."

I saw the line: "... I feel so sorry for Chinh, but I can't leave Marjorie." It was a color photo of Tế holding an American-looking baby.

So that was it! In my mind things couldn't have been any clearer. My marriage had ended just as it began — abruptly, and quickly.

Back at the house, I briefly told my parents-in-law what happened and asked for permission to take my baby and leave. I don't know if they were as shocked as I was when they heard this unimaginable story, but Mỹ-Vân's grandmother said:

"No families are run that way. Your father [in law] and I are still here. You and your child are the ties that bind. How can he not return? We will not accept anyone else to take on our name as daughter-in-law. So stop entertaining those negative thoughts."

Late that night, after I'd put the baby to sleep, I returned to my little diary and quickly jotted down the things I wanted to tell Dad. This time it was just a short call for help. I wrote to him and to the gods: "Dear Daddy, please tell me what I should do."

I don't know if my plea actually reached some spiritual being somewhere, but a friend of my sister-in-law Mùi told me one day after she heard about my predicament:

"Sheesh! It's not that hard, you know. There's an underground network that transports people to the North to join the People's army. The bus will take you to Phnom Penh first, from there it's a straight shot to Hà-Nội. The only thing is, it'll cost you three gold teals."

"To Hà-Nội!" The words were like a shot of rejuvenation drug to my ear. I would go back to our old house with Dad. Mỹ-Vân will have a maternal grandfather. I couldn't believe how I hadn't thought of this simple solution before.

I clung to this woman like the last life-saving buoy that God had mercifully sent down from above for me and my baby. "Thank you so much," I said. "Could you help me arrange it please?"

I made a quick calculation in my head. My path to rebirth was not illusory; in fact, it was within reach. I still had the golden bracelet that my father gave which I'd carefully stashed inside my luggage. And with next month's pay coming up, I should be able to pay for the "border crossings" back to Hà-Nội. I furtively began plotting for the trip with the excitement of a child about to relive her fun-filled days.

On the first of the following month, with my pay firmly in hand, I went home and excitedly climbed up the attic. Before I could realize what had happened, a horrific and messy scene came into view. The window's bars had been broken. My luggage, with my bracelet, my diary, Dad's letters, my night-gown that Tế sent from America, my cash savings. All gone!

Gone with my luggage was not just everything I owned, however little that was, but much worse was my dream of going home, of escaping a marriage that I never truly had a chance to enjoy.

The sudden sense of hopelessness drove me insane. I fell to the floor and started screaming like mad, causing great concern downstairs. The first person who ran up to see what was going on was Hiếu. But it was already too late. There was nothing left. Not a single trace.

Another year passed, Tế had to return after his one-year extension expired. Due to my failed "border crossings", our marriage resumed and lasted for another 25 years. Mỹ-Vân had two younger brothers — Hoàng-Hùng and Tuấn-Cường.

I stayed with my in-laws until my mother-in-law passed away in 1972 after years of ill health. In her later years she came to understand and love me more. Every time she went either to the pagoda or to her many "medium" sessions, I was always the one who carried the trance paraphernalia for her. Many of her friends even thought I was her real daughter. I was secretly proud that I had a "Mother," not just a mother-in-law.

Movie Career Launch

Many people know that my first film was *Bells of Thiên-Mụ (Hồi Chuông Thiên-Mụ)*, made by Tân-Việt film company, directed by Lê Dân and produced by Bùi Diễm, who later became ambassador to the U.S. But as a matter of fact, the first time I received the command "Action!" from a director was much earlier.

Even though my in-laws were Buddhist, I often went to Mass at Notre Dame Cathedral like I used to when I attended St Paul's School in Hà-Nội. One weekend afternoon, when Tế was still in the U.S., I went to Mass and afterward strolled down Tự-Do (Freedom) Boulevard toward Café Givral. Suddenly an American crossed the street, tapped me on the shoulder and asked if I could speak English. I looked at him, said nothing and kept on walking. Perhaps realizing that it was impolite to touch me on the shoulder, he apologized profusely and explained that American director Joseph Manquiewics and his film crew had been watching me from the Continental Hotel across the street. They thought I had the right look for the main character in a film that they were planning to make in Vietnam. He asked again if I spoke English, then invited me over to meet the film crew.

I took the script for *The Quiet American,* based on the novel by the English author Graham Greene, and brought it home. After reading it that night, I thought I might want to give a try. I vaguely felt that I needed to find something to do that I could be passionate about in order to fill the emptiness in my soul. I started to imagine myself in a movie. What a chance encounter this was; it could very well be the light at the end of the tunnel.

But when I asked for permission from my in-laws, they were very negative, especially my mother-in-law — she couldn't understand why I would want to be a film actress. After learning that the main character, Phương, was a Vietnamese woman living with an Englishman who later fell in love with an

American, both of them vehemently opposed the idea. Films were still a new art form in Vietnam at the time, especially to the older generations whose traditional view of singers and actresses was that they didn't belong in proper society.

And so the next day I returned the script to director Joseph Manquiewics. My refusal took everyone by surprise. I apologized to Mr. Manquiewics and explained to him the reason was because my in-laws did not approve. Everybody looked shocked; something like this would never happen in Hollywood. But even so, they still invited me to a reception which took place sometime later. It was there that I got the chance to meet some of the Vietnamese in the world of filmmaking, like Bùi Diễm and the famous actor Lê Quỳnh.

And even though I had declined, Director Manquiewics still asked me to appear briefly in a cameo role with no dialogue. My character was a Vietnamese girl walking near a Chinese temple in Chợ Lớn who was stopped by the main character (played by the English actor Michael Redgrave) because he mistook her for someone else. After realizing it was a mistake, he apologized to her and went on his way. That was it! But it was in this timeless classic that I heard the command "Action!" for the first time — and from the world-renowned Joseph Manquiewics, no less!

Not long after missing out on *The Quiet American,* I was asked by producer Bùi Diễm to star in *Bells of Thiên-Mụ*. This time, I answered him right away that there was a good chance my in-laws wouldn't allow it. However, Bùi Diễm understood Vietnamese culture. He and actor Lê Quỳnh (a friend of Tế and whose mother went to the same pagoda as my mother-in-law) came to our house and asked them to let me play the role of a Buddhist nun. As a pious Buddhist, she was very happy to hear that I would play a nun, while my father-in-law liked the idea from the beginning.

And thus predestination once again led me, the girl who had to be separated from her father in Hà-Nội to go South, down yet another twisting path of history.

The beginning of my film career was indeed as a Buddhist nun amidst the bells and scenery of Thiên-Mụ Pagoda in 1957.

So there I was — born in the North, raised in the South, and entering the movie world in Central Vietnam.

During the entire shoot, I was still nursing my own sorrows. Playing a young nun in simple earth-brown clothing and listening every day to the sounds of temple bells in the beautiful setting of Thiên-Mụ Pagoda by the Perfume River, really helped me clear my mind and left me with many beautiful memories.

After finishing with the film, I returned to my normal routine of being a mother and daughter-in-law as though nothing had changed. My in-laws, and Tế's family in general, seemed comfortable seeing me as an actress. As for me, those days spent on the set far away from the family was just a short dream. And after the dream was over I had to wake up to reality again.

The project took place around the time Tế came back from America. It was a little awkward for us at first, but it didn't take long before we got pulled along by the stream of life and the flow of fate once again. As a soldier, Tế had to move from place to place. Châu Đốc near the Cambodian border for awhile, then the central coastal city of Qui Nhơn.

I lived with my in-laws. Sometimes I'd travel to visit my husband wherever he happened to be stationed. My mother-in-law increased the amount of joss sticks and the frequency of her prayers as her sons were deployed (by this time Hiếu also had become an officer in the Paratrooper Division). Like her, I was constantly fearful about what tomorrow might bring; I just tried to live my best each day so that I have nothing to regret later.

Two years after *Bells of Thiên-Mụ*, in 1959, I was invited by director Thái Thúc-Nha to star in *Forest Rain* (Mưa Rừng) alongside actor Hoàng Vĩnh-Lộc and stage actress Kim-Cương.

While speaking of Thái Thúc-Nha and his company, Alpha Films, please allow me to make a quick detour to talk about this extraordinary person in South Vietnam's 20-year cinematic history.

Alpha Films was the largest and only private production company in South Vietnam at the time. It had its own studio, equipment, and professionally trained staff. Its CEO was not only knowledgeable in filmmaking, he also was fluent in both French and English. That's probably why foreign journalists and filmmakers liked to visit Alpha Films whenever they were in country.

After *Forest Rain,* I was asked to participate in a few other films like *Clouds of Ages* (*Ngàn Năm Mây Bay*) and *Parting of the Heart* (*Ngã Rẽ Tâm Tình*). But the most significant projects were co-productions between Alpha Films and foreign companies. I played the lead role in *A Yank in Vietnam*, initially called *Year of the Goat*, starring alongside the actor-director Marshall Thompson.

In one of the receptions that Alpha Films hosted on its company rooftop, guests included personnel from the U.S. Embassy and Sài-Gòn's elite. It was there that I met the author Mai-Thảo, founder of one of Việt-Nam's most prestigious literary journals. He later penned a glowing review of me in one of the leading movie magazines in Việt-Nam.

After becoming refugees in the U.S., we met each other again as part of a group of exiled artists that included people like singer-songwriter Phạm Đình-Chương, playwright Vũ Khắc-Khoan and composer Lê Trọng-Nguyễn. Mai-Thảo became like an older brother to me, and we were close friends until he died in 1998. In his only book of poetry which he published shortly before his death, there's even a poem that he wrote about me.

After the success of *A Yank in Vietnam* I was invited to work with several other foreign film companies. In 1964, I had the chance to play the lead female role alongside Burt Reynolds in *Operation CIA.*

After that film, Filipino director Rolf Bayer, known for his film *Cry Freedom,* asked me to play the lead opposite Leopoldo Salsedo, the top Filipino actor at the time who was known colloquially as "King" Salsedo.

Filming took place in the western province of Tây Ninh near the Cambodian border. At night we had to sleep in bunkers to avoid Việt-Cộng rockets. Actor Nguyễn Long later wrote a detailed piece about the making of this difficult film. (See Appendix).

At the movie premier in Manila I was greeted as a most honored guest. They even rolled out a red carpet at the airport for me. We were escorted to our hotel by the Filipino Department of Defense. Leopoldo and I were paraded through downtown, protected by military Jeeps equipped with big machine guns. Fans lined the streets, military planes flew overhead to drop welcoming leaflets. Paramount Pictures organized a press conference and cocktail party at the Manila Hotel for us. It was quite a scene.

Also, on this occasion, I was invited to cut the ribbon to inaugurate New Frontier Cinema, the largest movie theater in Quezon City at the time. But even more special was that in Manila I was reunited with an old friend from Hà-Nội, Hà văn Anh, son of Dad's close friend Hà văn Vượng who at one point asked my father to "save Chinh" for his son.

Travels

The first time I ever went abroad was actually 1963, to attend the Asian Film Festival in Tokyo. I was accompanied by Mr. and Mrs. Thái Thúc-Nha, and Ms. Kim Huê, the owner of Alpha Films, who later became like a sister to me. We visited several film studios in Tokyo. One of them, Toho, was the creator of Godzilla.We were greeted by Japan's top actors including Akira Takarada, who starred in the Godzilla movies, and Masumi Okada. Masumi, a versatile actor born in France and known as Fanfan, became my good friend and came to see me when he visited Sài Gòn once.

At the reception in Kyoto I also had the chance to meet Japan's number one actor — Toshiro Mifune, known for films such as the *Seven Samurai.* Our delegation was taken on a terrific sightseeing tour of this ancient city.

In the years that followed, I returned to Tokyo many times when the film company I was in charge of, Giao-Chỉ Films, was making *The Faceless Lover (Người Tình Không Chân Dung),* directed by Hoàng Vĩnh-Lộc. The negatives were processed at Toho Studio because at that time we didn't have the ability to process 35mm color film in Việt-Nam. This turned out to be a blessing in disguise as the original was preserved in Tokyo after the Fall of Sài-Gòn. Years later, I was able to fly to Japan and bring the negatives to the U.S.

The following year, 1964, I was invited to the 11th Asian Film Festival in Taiwan. There I met American actor William Holden, who had starred in some of Hollywood's most popular films, like *Sabrina* and *Bridge Over the River Kwai*. It was a most memorable encounter because he actually saved my life.

For the last day of the Festival, the organizers had prepared two excursions for participants to choose from. One was to visit a museum in Taichung on the west side of the island known for its rich collection of antiques and precious stones. The other was Quimoy Island near China's coast, with its unique village whose inhabitants lived completely underground.

I had signed up to go to Taichung with Thái Thúc-Nha and his wife because she loved jade and precious stones. The night before we left, William Holden called and asked me which trip I was taking. When he heard I was going to Taichung, he said that we could see that museum anytime and suggested that I should go to Quimoy with him instead, because this was a very rare chance. I said I had already signed up, but if he could help rearrange it, then we'd be happy to go with him. He did just that. And so the next morning, Bill came to pick the three of us up at the hotel.

Quimoy was truly a unique experience. It's a small city completely underground — schools, markets, hospitals... Nothing was above ground. Residents had to live like this to avoid rocket attacks from the mainland. That evening, before we left, each of us was given a balloon on which we could write a message and release it into the sky.

I wrote: "Daddy, I hope you're safe. I love and miss you." Bill wrote: "Freedom to All!"

Back in the city that night, we attended the closing ceremony and party at the presidential palace, attended by President Chiang Kai-Shek. Inside the vast hall, tables were lined up in a U shape. They were arranged alphabetically by country names. On a dais was the president's table, with Mr. and Mrs. Chiang Kai-Shek and their honored guests.

The president opened the party with a short welcoming speech. As the band was warming up, he said: "My wife and I are too old and cannot waltz. But I would like to request that our distinguished guest from Hollywood, Mr. William Holden, ask any lady in this room to a dance to kick off the evening for us."

All eyes fell on Bill, waiting. He stood up at the first table on the left, "America," and crossed over the dance floor to the last table on the right, "Vietnam." With a polite bow, he extended his hand and asked me to dance. The band struck up a waltz and off we strutted.

The music reverberated throughout the hall. Bill wore a smoky black suit; I was in a white *áo dài*. We were the only people on the dance floor. Everybody was watching us. Suddenly the music stopped.

The president came to the microphone to apologize and said he had some important news to share. The plane carrying 69 people on the trip back from Taichung had exploded in mid-air.

There were no survivors!

Among the victims were many famous actors and filmmakers from Hong Kong, Taiwan and the other countries. We were all stunned. Some people gasped; others burst out crying. Everybody knew we'd have to wait until the next day before the authorities could find the bodies.

The following day, it was widely reported on TV and in newspapers that among the dead were Mr. and Mrs. Thái Thúc-Nha and the actress Kiều Chinh — apparently our names had not been scrubbed from the flight manifest!

But that was how William Holden saved our lives. I met Bill many more times in Hong Kong after that near death escape.

One time he brought me to the hill where he shot *Love Is a Many-Splendored Thing* with Jennifer Jones. It was fabulous! He had plans to visit Sài Gòn at the invitation of Thái Thúc-Nha, but never could make the trip because of too many projects.

We became friends. Bill gave me his business card and told me that if I ever visited the U.S., I was welcome to stay with his family in Palm Springs, California. Bill died on November 12, 1981. I'll never forget what a gentleman this giant in the film world truly was.

Back to Hong Kong, in 1965, I was invited by entertainment mogul Mr. Run Run Shaw, owner of Shaw Brothers, to visit their studios. I was introduced to many of their directors and actors. Shaw Brothers was an indescribably big movie studio in Hong Kong. It took up an entire hill and had multiple films rolling simultaneously all the time. There I met many great Chinese actresses such as Ly Chin, Li Li-Hua, Ivy Ling Po, and Linda Lin Dai as well as directors Griffin Yueh, King Churn and producer Raymond Chow.

I believe Raymond was working with Shaw Brothers at the time because in all my subsequent trips to Hong Kong it was always he who picked me up at the airport in his Rolls Royce! Raymond Chow later became an important player, having his own film studio called Golden Harvest and produced the famous kung-fu flicks starring Bruce Lee.

After 1975, I did meet Raymond again in the U.S. He was partnering with an American studio to make the movie *Company C*. He called and invited me to the studio for lunch.

One time, director Robert Wise (*Sound of Music*) went to Sài Gòn with the American film director Jules Dassin (who had moved to France after he was blacklisted during the McCarthy Era) to explore the possibility of making a new movie in Việt-

Nam. Thái Thúc-Nha asked me to join the welcoming party and meet with them. At first, the two directors wanted me to play the lead role in a movie they planned to shoot in Sài-Gòn. But after a long period of waiting, the project fell through because the government of South Vietnam refused to issue a permit, citing "political issues" with the script.

Robert Wise then proposed that I starred a different movie called *The Sand Pebbles* which would be filmed in Taipei. He told me I'd be in the lead female role opposite Steve McQueen.

After many more months of waiting, I finally received a telegram from Robert Wise inviting me to Hong Kong to talk.

An elaborate party took place at the Hotel Peninsula where I met not just Robert Wise, but also Steve McQueen, as well as many important guests from Hong Kong and the film crew. After the party, Robert Wise asked if he could walk me back to the President Hotel in Kowloon where I was staying.

During our walk, I could tell that he was feeling bothered and uncomfortable. I knew there must have been some bad news. Finally, Robert Wise explained the reason he had to bring me to Hong Kong was because there was something he couldn't tell me by phone or letter. It had to do with a major problem they ran into with *The Sand Pebbles*.

The backdrop of the story was Taiwan so he wanted to shoot it there. But after months of delay the Taiwanese government decided not to approve the project. Once again, the team had to make changes to the script; they finally got approval to shoot in Hong Kong but with a new financial backer. Unfortunately, the new financier insisted that the leading female must be a Hong Kong actress.

As he finished, I could tell he felt like a giant boulder had been lifted off his shoulders. But his last words to me were: "I feel terrible. I want to give you something worthier than an apology."

After I'd become an artist in exile in the U.S., I called Robert Wise one day when I happened to be in Hollywood. He invited me to the studio in Burbank for lunch. He was working on *The*

Hindenburg at the time. During our lunch in the studio cafeteria, Robert Wise gave me something beyond my wildest expectations.

He called the manager over and instructed the man to type up a letter for him to sign, introducing me to director Francis Ford Coppola, a close friend of his. Robert Wise knew that Coppola was about to make a film having something to do with Vietnam.

I was even more surprised when Francis Ford Coppola actually called and asked me to come see him. He told me he was planning to make a movie called *Apocalypse Now*. It would be filmed in the Philippines, and all the main characters would be male. There was only one female role, a very small and fleeting role. My character would be the wife of the main character, played by Marlon Brando. But more importantly, Coppola wanted me to be on the set throughout the filming to act as an advisor, making sure all the details about Việt-Nam were accurate — costumes, scenery, dialogue etc.

I was elated; I couldn't have been happier. For someone who was just trying to get into Hollywood like me to have the chance to work with a big name like Francis Ford Coppola was simply unthinkable. And to be the wife of Marlon Brando, too!

But as the departure date approached, the studio informed me that they couldn't get me an entry visa into the Philippines. At the time, I didn't have a passport — only a green card, because I wasn't a U.S. citizen yet. If I left the country, I ran the risk of losing my permanent resident status and would have had to start the immigration process all over again when I returned — that is, if I was even allowed to re-enter the U.S. at all!

Besides, the Filipino government wouldn't have issued a work permit for me anyway!

Fate had cruelly denied me the chance to work with the most celebrated director and actor in Hollywood. I thought an opportunity like this would never come again. I felt so deflated and dejected.

Saying that doesn't mean I don't acknowledge all the good luck I've had from the day I serendipitously walked into the movie world. Indeed, film acting had taken me by the hand and led me all over Asia since 1963. Prior to 1975, I was invited to just about every Asian Film Festival. I even got to travel to Europe for the first time, to attend the Berlin Film Festival.

It was a very memorable trip. I went with famous Vietnamese actor Lê Quỳnh. We visited many places — Frankfurt, the Bonn Wine Festival, and even took a boat trip on the Rhine. I was interviewed by German TV along with iconic American actor Jimmy Stewart, known for films such as *It's a Wonderful Life* and *Mr. Smith Goes to Washington.* He was someone I really admired. In the interview, Jimmy Stewart revealed that he had a son who served in Vietnam.

On this trip, I also met French actor Jean Marrais, whose life story inspired Francois Truffaut's masterpiece *The Last Metro,* about Nazi-occupied Paris. He invited me to cross the Berlin Wall with him in a car provided by the French Embassy. How could I pass up the opportunity? To me, the Berlin Wall was like the 17th parallel separating North and South Vietnam.

Jean Marrais and I sat in the back of an official embassy vehicle flying the French flag, driven by embassy personnel. The crossing evoked so many emotions. We were not allowed to step outside at any time. Looking out, I could see that East Germany was radically different from West Germany — the streets, the shops, the clothes people wore. In short, it was dark and depressing. A very sad city.

It made me miss my Dad and my brother even more.

And Hà-Nội, too.

Ambassador

Since very early in my career, I was looked after by many big names in the movie industry — William Holden, Robert Wise, Francis Ford Coppola, Jean Marrais... There was another person that I would be remiss not to mention: actor-director Rolf Bayer.

Rolf was the representative in Asia for several major Hollywood studios. I met him at Alpha Films. When he went back to Sài-Gòn for the second time, he quickly became a friend not just to me but also to my husband's family. The reason he returned to Sài-Gòn was to ask me to play the lead role in a second film he was making with 20th Century Fox & Arbee Productions. It was called *The Evil Within*. I would play an Indian princess alongside famous Indian actor Dev Anand.

The film's success brought me an unexpected benefit. I was invited back to India to attend the New Delhi Film Festival, where local papers lauded me as the "Goodwill Ambassador from Vietnam." As a result, the government of South Vietnam issued me a special diplomatic passport called "Goodwill Ambassador of the Arts from the Republic of Vietnam."

The Faceless Lover

Around this same time, I was elected Chairwoman of the Vietnam Film Association. In 1970, I founded Giao-Chỉ Films with the help of many good friends, especially the well-respected director Hoàng Vĩnh-Lộc who directed Giao-Chỉ's very first film: *The Faceless Lover (Người Tình Không Chân Dung).*

The Faceless Lover was a very special film in my career. It left me with many indelible moments as well as painful memories. It was special not just because the story was about the horrible war we were embroiled in at the time, but also because of the many incredible friendships forged during its making that I will cherish all my life.

The film was shot entirely on location, even on battlefields where fighting had previously taken place. The hardest part of all was when we filmed at a military hospital in Nha-Trang. I got to witness the horrors of war up close on the faces of the wounded soldiers. Most had lost one or more limbs. Some were blinded in one eye or both. There were so many of them, some had to share beds — lying at opposite ends. Seeing how bored and depressed the men were, I bought dozens of transistor radios to give to the soldiers in the hospital wing where we set up.

But what I felt most keenly, and which has stayed with me to this day, was an unspeakable pain in the eyes of the women. Young wives. Old mothers. They sat in stoic silence, resigned to the meaninglessness of war. Their agony came not just from the physical wounds on the bodies of their men but perhaps from a cut somewhere deep inside their souls. It's difficult to describe and impossible to forget. I call it the real and permanent wounds of war.

The film was an unequivocal success. It was called the best Vietnamese film to date even by the toughest Sài-Gòn critics. *The Faceless Lover* was the first Viet language film to open at REX, the biggest movie theater in town, and earned for Giao Chỉ Films 45 million VND at the box office.

After its successful run in Việt-Nam, the film was screened at the Asian Film Festival in 1973 and brought home two major prizes: Best War Movie and Best Actress. It also was the last movie made in Việt-Nam in which I acted.

After I left Việt-Nam in 1975, director Hoàng Vĩnh-Lộc stayed behind. Vũ Xuân-Thông, a Special Forces lieutenant colonel who played the lead role, was thrown into a re-education camp. Thông wrote to me while in prison, and I was able to write him back. Over a decade later, after he was released, Thông was brought to America through the help of U.S. Special Forces. I waited for hours at Los Angeles Airport to greet my old friend and hold him in my arms once more.

Minh Trường-Sơn (the other male lead) was able to escape by boat after a few years living under communist rule. In 1981 I got news that Minh and his family had successfully made it to San Jose, California. I immediately flew up to see them. It was an emotional reunion seeing Minh and his wife Ngoc again with their four children: Khanh, Chinh, Cường and Giao. His children all call me "Mommy Chinh."

Through Minh I learned that after 1975, Hoàng Vĩnh-Lộc suffered tremendous economic hardship and died under very difficult circumstances. He was a big man, over six feet tall, but the family couldn't afford anything but a cheap coffin for the celebrated director. Minh had to use force to fit his friend's legs in. When they tried to lower him into the ground, rainwater from the night before kept pushing the coffin back up. He and actor Huy Cường had to stand on both ends of the coffin to push it down long enough for the others to fill up the grave with dirt.

Many people may not know this, but Hoàng Vĩnh-Lộc was also a songwriter and lyricist under the pen-name Dạ Chung. The lyrics for the title song, "The Faceless Lover", were written by him and put to music by Hoàng Trọng. They were all very precious people to me.

I want to thank these lifelong friendships.

I want to thank *The Faceless Lover*.

I want to thank *"The soldier who left his helmet among these tall wild grasses*[2]*."*

Hoàng Vĩnh-Lộc and I had plans to make two more films based on two of my favorite books: the classical "*Male and Female*" *(Trống Mái)* by Khái Hưng (1896-1947); and the controversial modern love story "*In the Arms of Youth*" (*Vòng Tay Học Trò)* by the contemporary female novelist Nguyễn thị Hoàng.

Unfortunately, our dream would never materialize as history had its own cruel plans for Việt-Nam.

2 Lyrics from the title song, *The Faceless Lover*.

Sisters Again

On my first trip to Europe to attend the Berlin Film Festival in 1968, I decided to stop in France on my way back to see my sister Tĩnh and Uncle Nghị, my mother's older brother. It should be noted that during the war it was exceedingly difficult to get an exit visa out of South Vietnam.

To me this was a big deal. A very big deal. I had not seen anyone from my immediate family since 1954. I had not seen my sister since she got married. And I had never met Uncle Nghị.

I let my sister know of my plan and my itinerary ahead of time. We both waited with nervous anticipation. From Marseille, she and Uncle Nghị went to Paris to pick me up at Charles de Gaulle Airport. The moment was too emotional to describe. Fourteen long years since the day she left Hà-Nội for France, it was the first time I could see her and hold her in my arms. Tears of happiness poured down our faces as our joys mingled.

We kept holding each other's hands as though we were afraid if we let go it would take another 14 years or longer before we could see each other again. Her three children also came: Pascal, David and pretty Lysa.

Uncle Nghị was the only relative on my mother's side living abroad. I don't know if he realized it, but for me, seeing him for the first time was like seeing my own mother again after so many years riding the roller coaster called war. When he held my hands, I felt like the warmth from my mother's hands was coursing through my veins. Childhood memories came rushing back.

I sat next to sister Tĩnh and her children on the train ride back to Marseille. We passed through many towns, cities and seemingly endless fields of flowers that stretched to the horizon. The rhythmic, metallic sound of the wheels against the rails droned like a long but peaceful song about heaven on earth. Every now and then it made me think bout Dad and brother Lân, wondering where they were, what they might be going through, whether they were dead or alive. Then I would sigh, trying to suppress the lump rising in my throat.

Although the train ride was long, I was at last standing in front of my sister's pretty little house on Didier Boulevard. She and her husband lived a simple life.

Our first family meal together after so many years apart, in my opinion, could not have been more wonderful. One day before, Tĩnh had taken the time to make some of the dishes that she believed, according to her best recollection, were her baby sister's favorite food. There were crabmeat egg rolls, crab noodle soup and salted shrimp. She insisted on making everything herself so that she and I could relive the happy times we spent together. And what could have made us happier than to be able to look into each other's eyes and drink our fill of the sight of one another. Then we'd raise our wine glasses for a toast. Then another. And another. I can't recall if we were drunk from the wine, or if we simply couldn't stop pouring into each other's glass all the emotions that had been bottled up inside as we reminisced about Dad and brother Lân. And about a Hà-Nội of fourteen years ago, on the night the four of us were together for the last time, when we also were very drunk. It was, of course, my sister's wedding day.

That night, I slept with Tĩnh. Her husband Đăng elected to sleep in another room with the children. We had the whole night to talk, to tell each other everything about our lives in the past fourteen years, like only sisters could.

The next morning, I woke up to the sound of knocking on the door. Tĩnh had already been up. She came in with a tray of breakfast of coffee, fresh orange juice, bread... She brought it to the bedside and said:

"You slept very well, so I let you sleep. Brother Đăng has already gone to work and the kids have gone to school. It's just the two of us. Today I will take you to see Uncle Nghị, then we'll sightsee Marseille. Show me what you want to wear and I'll iron it. There's a fresh towel in the bathroom for you.

She took care of me like a mother would her child, not omitting even the tiniest detail. At times I wanted to cry.

In contrast to my sister's pretty but humble home, Uncle Nghị's house was an imposing two-story villa right on Rue de Coq. His wife was French. They had four children: Patrick, Christine, Johan and Luc. Mixed blood, they were distinctively good looking.

While my sister and Uncle Nghị's wife prepared lunch, my uncle took me upstairs to show me the house. We went into in his office to talk. I finally was able to see how wealthy my uncle was. Besides all the expensive furniture and other possessions, he had a library full of rare books and many books written by him — Docteur Van Nghi. They were books on acupuncture. Not only was he a regular medical doctor, Uncle Nghị also was a renowned acupuncturist. On the wall hung many pictures of him attending various conferences, as he was president of the Acupuncture Association of Europe. There also were news articles cut out from *Paris Match* and pictures of him posing with the President of France.

There was a long wooden table in the middle of the room with only two antique armchairs — one at each end. He sat in one and I in the other. In that position, he began telling me, the niece who lost her mother at a young age, about himself and about his sister. Meeting his sister's offspring so unexpectedly through the sheer serendipity of history visibly moved my uncle.

He told me that my presence in his office, which for many years had been kept silent, had aroused all sorts of sentiments. Images from a long lost past suddenly reappeared. He said he could still picture my mother as a young, innocent girl. He described his parents' home and all his siblings. After asking me to tell him about my situation in Việt-Nam, he wistfully said:

"I miss Việt-Nam." His voice dropped a notch when he uttered the word. I knew right away that what he meant by "Việt-Nam" was really Hà-Nội and his younger days, with both the paternal and maternal sides of our family. And my generation also. But however we looked at it, Hà-Nội could only exist in our minds now.

On our way home, my sister took me up to the statue of Mary at Notre Dame de La Garde high on a hill. From that vista one could look down and see Marseille laid out like a beautiful painting. I sat down on a bench and took in the tranquility of the scene which, as its natural beauty readily confessed, could not have been any more calm and peaceful. Just at that moment church bells could be heard pealing in the air as if from a distant dreamscape. I squeezed my sister's hand as though to tell her to pay attention to the sound which seemed to carry with it a familiar fragrance that was quickly dissolving into space.

It was at that very moment that I decided to ask my sister about our father and brother. I knew that she received news about them from time to time because you still could send letters between France and North Vietnam.

This time it wasn't my hand squeezing hers but the reverse. Her first words were "I'm sorry." She said she had to apologize because she had been intentionally hiding the bad news about them from me. She explained that she did it out her love for me. She didn't want me to suffer knowing the truth about the punishing years our father and brother endured as they were sent from one prison to the next.

My heart sank. The air was still. There was no sound. Before me there was no Tĩnh, no Marseille. Even I didn't exist. I could only picture my father and my brother flailing away like some sort of walking dead that I couldn't quite imagine nor give a name to. I sat there motionless until evening fell. The church bells rang again. But this time I could not discern any fragrance other than that of a dark fog that was spreading itself in broken segments over the forests and the rocks.

Tĩnh hugged me and softly said: "Let's go home, Chinh."

I stood up and followed her.

The following day Tĩnh showed me her photo albums. I asked her to give me some pictures of our family when we were still happily together. She also let me read several short letters that Dad and brother Lân sent. In every letter they always asked: "How is Chinh these days?"

In one letter, my brother said he just got married. His wife was Lan, the older sister of my best friend Bích-Vân. Eventually they had two daughters: Loan and Liên.

Before going back to Sài-Gòn, I went with my sister to buy a Rolex watch and a bicycle for Dad and brother Lân. According to my brother, those things were the easiest to sell. The money could feed a family for months. Not only that, my brother said the bicycle wasn't just personal transportation but also a "wagon" which you could use to transport things for hire!

In those days Hà-Nội had no cars. And no petrol, either.

We spent our last day together increasing our collection of memories by wandering along the wharf of Vieux Port Marseille, watching fishing boats return and men bringing up cases and cases of fresh fish, while old men sat in groups drinking and smoking cigars. We picked a table near the road to people watch. The port sat just across the street. The sun was slowly setting, painting the whole scene in a lovely blond hue. I suddenly had a crazy wish that Dad and brother Lân were here with us to raise a glass of wine and enjoy a bowl of Marseille's famous bouillabaisse, in perfect harmony and peace.

The day I left was difficult. We couldn't let each other go. Who knew when we'd see each other again? My sister cried.

Once back in Sài-Gòn, every now and then I'd write a letter to Dad and brother Lân and send to my sister so she could forward it to them for me. And even though the things she was telling me about the horrific conditions they were facing filled me with anguish and sadness every time I thought about them, at least I was able to write Dad and send him a little bit of money via my sister.

But little did I know that those letters were causing a problem. One day, I was called in for questioning by the Security police. All three of the brothers in my husband's family were officers in the ARVN. Not only that, the oldest one,

Nguyễn Giáp-Tý, and my husband Nguyễn Năng-Tế were serving on the Ceasefire Monitoring Committee. I also accompanied my husband to dinners at various embassies, thus all my communications to my family in the North had been closely monitored. The Security police officer advised me to cease all communication, otherwise they would have to start investigating not only me but my husband as well.

Family

Family In Time Of War

Patriarch Độ had three sons and three daughters. Miss Mão (Tế's next older sister) had a husband, Dr. Dương Như-Hoà, who lived in France but came back to Vietnam and became the first Director of the Nuclear Research Center in Đà-Lạt. Mr Độ's oldest son was Nguyễn Giáp-Tý, a former sergeant in the Imperial Guard unit that protected Emperor Bảo-Đại in Đà-Lạt; he later became a member of the International Ceasefire Monitoring Committee. Nguyễn Năng-Tế was a Second Lieutenant in the Paratroopers Unit, 1st Battalion. The youngest son, Nguyễn Chí-Hiếu, went to the Đà-Lạt Military Academy and later rose to become a Colonel in the Airborne 5th Battalion. Hiếu participated in many famous battles like An-Lộc, Mậu-Thân.

Tế came home after spending two years in the U.S. I gave birth to our first son, Hoàng-Hùng, right before Christmas 1958. Tế also joined the Ceasefire Committee and was sent to Quy-Nhơn in Central Vietnam. I stayed with my parents-in-law. Tế would come home whenever he had leave.

In July, 1961, while I was nearly full-term pregnant with our third child, I went to Quy-Nhơn to visit Tế. On the train ride back to Sài-Gòn my water broke. Tuấn-Cường was born prematurely on July 20.

Growing up in a country that was constantly at war, I was

fully aware of the fact that nobody knew what tomorrow could bring. When I picked up the newspaper each day, I always skipped the front page news and went directly to the obituaries, trying to see (or not see) if there was anybody I knew. And that day did come: "Second Lieutenant Nguyễn Khắc-Nhật has been killed in battle."

Nhật was the eldest son of the eldest son in my husband's family, the one responsible for carrying on the family traditions. He was a tall, handsome young man, well loved by everyone.

When his father was in charge of the Nuclear Center in Đà-Lạt, Nhật stayed with us to go to school in Sài-Gòn. After graduating from high school he went into the military academy and became a young officer. He was killed on the first day of battle. The news hit my brother- and sister-in-law hard. Indeed, a heavy pall was cast over the entire family.

The year was 1968. The Tet Offensive had broken out all over the South. Sài-Gòn and Huế were hit the hardest, especially Huế. Bloody battles raged, destroying most of the ancient Imperial City. Thousands of civilians were savagely murdered by communist forces; many were buried alive.

In Sài-Gòn, the area around the Phú-Thọ Racetrack near our house was where the offensive began. That night, deafening gunfire started to ring out to greet the new year. I started to imagine a terrible tragedy. Could my brother be on the other side? What if he was one of the men attacking us? If they entered our house, would he and my husband be shooting at each other? I could only close my eyes and prayed:

"Most merciful Jesus, please do mot let that happen to my family or any family, North or South. Our country and our people are suffering too much already!"

At daybreak, as the gunfire ceased, we ran over to Minh's house, which was on the other side of the racetrack. Minh was a school friend of mine. She and her husband had four children. The two older ones went to school at Fraternité (Bác-Ái), same as my children, so her husband Đạt would come by every day to pick up my children and give them a ride.

A ghastly scene greeted us when we arrived. Her house was

completely destroyed. Minh sat like a zombie amidst the carnage holding her youngest child. Next to her were the bloodied bodies of Đạt and two of their children. She recounted, sobbing:

"Last night we heard gunfire real close to the house and thundering footsteps. We grabbed two children each and hid underneath the two beds next to each other. They shot through the door... They shot all over our house... They shot... my husband... and both of the children under the bed on the left..."

We took Minh and the two surviving children to come stay with us for awhile. At night, even when there was no more gunfire, my heart broke every time I was awakened by Minh's nightmarish screams.

A few years ago, I had the chance to see Minh again in Australia, where she's living with her youngest child. Her oldest daughter, Minh-Phương, who was a classmate of my oldest daughter Mỹ-Vân, is currently living in Texas with her husband.

The Passing of My "Mother"

Mrs. Nguyễn Đại-Độ, my mother-in-law, died in 1973 after years of ill health. She was nearly blind by the end. All her children came back to see her, even the oldest daughter Mão from Canada. Before she died, my mother-in-law called out:

"Chinh, where is Chinh?"

I grabbed her hand: "Yes, mother. I'm right here."

With the dying breath of someone who knew they were about to leave this earthly plane, she whispered:

"I have six children, plus their husbands and wives; that makes twelve, but you're the only one who's been with me the whole time we've been in the South. You have given your all to this family... I want everyone to know that."

As her voice grew weaker, I couldn't hold back the tears.

Her funeral was well attended and perfectly executed in the

Buddhist tradition. In sadness I said goodbye to a person whom I had respected and faithfully served for nineteen years just as I would have done for my biological mother.

From that day on, even now in America, on the altar in my house there are always portraits of all four of my parents.

The only sad part is that my father-in-law, Mr Nguyễn Đại-Độ, was not able to emigrate in 1975. After his passing, his children were scattered to the four corners of the earth by the winds of history, some even ended up in re-education camps.

I want to thank you, Father and Mother.

Children Go Abroad

My mother-in-law's passing in 1973 was followed by the death of 2nd Lt. Nguyễn Khắc-Nhật, the eldest son of her eldest son, Nguyễn Giáp-Tý, the carrier of the family tradition and name.

Her maternal grandsons were both in the army as well. It seemed like all the men in the family were serving in the military, like just about every other family at the time.

When sister Mão came back with her husband for her mother's funeral, she said to me: "I want to thank you for taking care of mother during her illness for those of us who couldn't be there. I would recommend that you send your children to Canada to study, to allay some of the family's concerns. They will be with us and will have their cousins to play with. You won't need to worry."

My father-in-law also encouraged it: "The three of them are still young. You should let them study abroad so that their education doesn't get disrupted and we can have some peace of mind. Besides, since you can travel out of the country every now and then to make movies, you can always arrange to visit them." So I accepted his advice and agreed to let my children go live with sister Mão and her husband Hoà. In those days I was doing many foreign films so I could afford to send the children to a private school in Toronto, Canada.

But at the same time it was a difficult decision for me, as a mother, to let my children live so far away. The day they left I was overcome with worries and cried a lot. Nguyễn Xuân-Thu, vice-president of Vietnam Airlines, assured me: "Don't worry, Chinh. I will escort them from Sài-Gòn to Hong Kong on Air Vietnam. Once there I'll make sure they get on the correct Cathay Pacific flight to Toronto."

"You'll see them this summer," said Tế. "Don't worry. Sister Mão and brother Hoà will pick them up at the airport. They'll have their cousins as friends."

At the time Mỹ-Vân was 16 years old, Hùng was 14 and Cường barely 12. That night after they had left I was all by myself in the house. I took out some of their clothes and smelled their scents. And cried. I felt so bad sending my youngest Cường away at such a tender age.

The following year I was able to arrange a trip to Toronto to see my children. On my flight back to Singapore to shoot *Full House,* during the stopover in London the film company arranged an unexpected interview for me in the airport. It was such a pleasant surprise. That interview led to a full-blown press conference for me after I touched down in Singapore and before we started to shoot.

"*Full House*" and the War

Full House was a movie about the youth culture in Singapore, focusing on lifestyles, fashion, partying and so on. We started filming near the end of February, 1975. Merely two weeks later, on March 10 in fact, communist forces overran Ban Mê Thuột in the Western highlands. The final offensive had begun. One by one other provinces were abandoned. Pleiku. Kontum. Central Việt-Nam...

Every day I did my work diligently and professionally. But at night my mind was a mess. I followed closely the deteriorating situation; I read news and analyses from international media sources. It was depressing to hear all of them agree that the collapse of South Vietnam was imminent. Only a miracle could save my country, and none was forthcoming.

Every night I was glued to the TV. Thousands upon thousands of panicking refugees were fleeing south from the Central coast. So much suffering, so many deaths. When the order to evacuate Pleiku was issued, soldiers and civilians alike poured down the highway toward Tuy-Hoà on the East coast. As they tried to cross Ba river, communist forces mercilessly mowed them down. The river became clogged with corpses. It was horrific.

Meanwhile, I kept receiving telegrams from Sài-Gòn and Toronto: "Go to children in Toronto. Don't come back to Sài-Gòn."

But my husband and in-laws were still in Sài-Gòn. How could I just quietly fly to Toronto by myself? My children were safe. It was the lives of my husband, my father-in-law, Sâm and everyone else in the family that were in danger.

On the last day of filming, I participated in the ribbon cutting for a brand new movie theater in Singapore. After attending a perfunctory party that night, I immediately booked a flight back to Sài-Gòn. It was April 16, 1975. The plane was completely empty. I was the only person going into Sài-Gòn when everybody else was trying to get out. One attendant told me this was an emergency flight to pick up diplomatic personnel and expats.

When I got to Tân-Sơn-Nhứt airport, immigration told me I had to convert all foreign currencies into Vietnamese Dong, basically what I got paid for three films — two in Thailand and one in Singapore. I walked into the house with a big sack of cash and was excoriated by my husband and father-in-law not only for coming back but also for not saving the dollars.

Not even day by day but hour by hour we watched as one city fell after the next. Huế. Đà-Nẵng. Quy-Nhơn. Nha-Trang. Cam-Ranh. Phan-Thiết... Then came Bình-Tuy, Long-Khánh... Sài-Gòn went into convulsions; it was total madness. Columns of refugees poured into the city from the north and west while Sài-

Gòn residents themselves tried to leave. People were running in every direction. Cars, trucks, bicycles, motorcycles, military vehicles... all means of transportation available were out on the streets, all hastily heading somewhere.

Rumors reigned supreme. A ceasefire agreement was in the works. A multi-party government recognized by both sides and by the international community was being formed. Central Vietnam would be a buffer zone. The French were bringing Emperor Bảo Đại back. And on and on.

I thought about my father and brother. If any of these rumors were true then there was a chance I would see them again. Yet at the same time, my children in Toronto were telling me to get out of Sài-Gòn as quickly as possible. I understood. They had much better news sources in Canada.

Even my husband and father-in-law said I should leave while my diplomatic passport was still valid. For days I was torn — undecided between leaving and staying. But then the image of the 16-year-old girl traumatically losing her father in 1954 returned. The picture of me in a Hà-Nội airport 21 years earlier came back like a flash. It lit up a path and pointed the way; it clarified my responsibilities. Even if I'd have had to pay a steep price for leaving my husband and his family behind, I had to be with my children. There was absolutely no way I would let what happened to me happen to them once history turned the page and Sài-Gòn had a new master.

At the urging of the family and with tremendous help from Nguyễn Xuân-Thu, vice-president of Vietnam Airlines, I was able to catch a flight. In the middle of the night, way past curfew, Thu drove me to the airport in an official Air Vietnam vehicle flying a VIP flag. On the way, he disclosed there would be a flight to the Philippines early next morning; it would be Air Vietnam's very last flight. He had already made arrangements for AV employees to take care of me upon arrival.

Tân-Sơn-Nhứt airport was packed with panicked people and their luggage. Most were Vietnamese wives and their children either going with their foreign husbands or saying goodbye to them. The cacophony was deafening.

Dawn came. As my departure time neared, the airport fell under a barrage of rocket attacks. The scene became even more chaotic than it already was. Thu dragged me back inside Air Vietnam's VIP lounge. For a whole day no airplane was allowed to take off. I anxiously waited another night in that asphyxiating atmosphere. Thu said he had to go take care of some business. A little while later he came back with some good news: "I got it. There's one Pan Am flight taking American civilian and military personnel about to depart. You must go now. Don't bring anything." I hurriedly swung my handbag around my neck and followed him.

Thu grabbed my hand as we ran across the runway. He pushed me onto the plane; it was fully packed. He jumped up and helped me to a seat reserved for the flight attendant, near the toilet. He held my hand and said: "Bye, Chinh." I watched as he ran out right before the door closed, forgetting to even ask him what my destination was. But no matter, I was on the last Pan Am flight out of Sài-Gòn

Nguyễn Xuân-Thu, thank you!

It was only a week earlier that I flew into Sài-Gòn with a big wad of cash. Now I was leaving with nothing but my handbag, a small phone book, my passport and a few dollar bills.

I didn't know if history was repeating itself or not. Twenty-one years after I left Hà-Nội, once again I was by myself and leaving everything behind. But this time I was leaving my country to start a completely new life — that of *an artist in exile*, far away from her homeland.

Last Days

South Vietnam didn't officially cease to exist until April 30, 1975. That was the day communist tanks rolled down Thống-Nhất (Unification) Boulevard and crashed through the gates of Independence Palace, after Gen. Dương văn Minh (Big Minh)

ordered all military units to stand down awaiting the transition of power.

Before that moment came, however, rumors were flying around about last-minute solutions that would have prevented capitulation. Two of them were particularly appealing, causing many Southerners to hold out hope:

– Set aside a portion of Central Vietnam as a demilitarized buffer zone while all sides negotiated a political solution, with a nationwide poll to decide whether Vietnamese in the South wanted to join the communist North or to remain neutral;

– The South would be a completely neutral zone for a period of two years while its citizens worked out a new form of government.

These were some of the reasons that made more than a few people not want to leave. In the end, hundreds of thousands of military and civilian personnel who served in the Republic of Vietnam were sent to re-education prisons. Millions more tried to escape by boat. The International Red Cross and the United Nations High Commission for Refugees estimated that the number of escapees who perished at sea was about half a million.

The real number, of course, will never be known. But what is known is that a new term — "Boat People" entered the English lexicon to describe those Vietnamese trying to flee the country by boat, regardless of whether or not they reached the shores of freedom.

But those things were political aspects and ramifications of the conflict which I'm sure were covertly negotiated and arranged months before by the superpowers involved in our 20-year war. For ordinary people like us, things were fairly calm as far as our wartime society was concerned. There were no major upheavals in any of the big cities, especially in Sài-Gòn. Tết (Lunar New Year) in February 1975 was celebrated just as joyfully as ever. We wished each other a prosperous new year. We performed age old traditions. We hoped and prayed for peace.

In the period right after our hosting of the Asian Film Festival in 1973, Vietnam's nascent movie industry took off to new heights. New movies were made in rapid succession. New talents emerged both in acting and directing. It was an exciting period of growth for those of us in the movie business. Theaters throughout the South happily welcomed our industry's coming of age.

It was also the busiest period of my professional career. I had just completed two films made in Thailand in which I played the lead. I had signed a contract to star in *Full House* in Singapore. By February, 1975, I was up to my neck with projects which director Hoàng Vĩnh-Lộc and I had in the pipeline. Besides all that, I also had plans to visit my children in Toronto.

On New Year's Day of the Year of the Cat, February 11, 1975, as soon as I finished our traditional celebration with the family, I headed straight to Alpha Films for a party with the Vietnam Film Association. At that party, Thái Thúc-Nha, CEO of Alpha Films, reminded me:

"Madame Chairman, please remember to invite some international stars to our second Vietnam Cinema Day in August."

Obviously, I couldn't do anything for "Vietnam Cinema Day II." By August of that year South Vietnam was no more.

From Singapore to Toronto

As soon as we landed in Singapore, which I'd left exactly one week before, I was immediately taken by immigration police to ... jail! According to them, my diplomatic passport was issued by a government that no longer existed. President Nguyễn văn Thiệu had already resigned.

That night I sat in a cell among all types of people, worried about what would happen to me next. The following morning, on our way to the bathroom, I saw a guard reading a copy of *Female* which had a large photo of me on the front cover. (The magazine did an interview and cover story on me after we finished filming *Full House*.) I excitedly pointed to the magazine and told the guard that the woman on the cover was me, and asked him to let me make a phone call. He gave me an incredulous stare from head to toe, then went back to his reading without saying a word.

In the bathroom with the other prisoners, I suddenly understood. The woman I saw in the mirror, with her disheveled hair and a haggard look, was not at all like the glamorous movie star on the cover of Singapore's famous magazine. Without any make-up available, I did my best to straighten out my hair and fix up my dress.

On our way back to the cell, I begged the man once more, asking him to open up the magazine to the center-fold. So he did. And there, in the middle of the magazine, was a two-page spread filled with a large picture of Kiều Chinh in her resplendent Vietnamese áo dài. It was unmistakable.

The guard nodded and allowed me to make a phone call to the Vietnamese Embassy in Singapore. Thanks to the tremendous efforts by the *Full House* crew and by Ambassador Trương Bửu-Điện, I was released under the condition that I must leave Singapore within 48 hours.

I spent a whole day running around, looking for a place to go. Not a single foreign embassy in Singapore issued an entry visa for me, citing the reason that South Vietnam was about to be history at any moment. They suggested the best thing for me to do was to buy a plane ticket that would fly me from airport to airport, from East to West, until Sài-Gòn officially fell. At that point I would be able to apply for asylum wherever the plane landed.

And so I did. For four days and three nights I traveled from place to place, homeless among the clouds. Singapore. Hong Kong. Korea. Tokyo. Paris. New York... In between these stops were long hours of anxiety at the airports. I drank water from fountains and bathroom faucets. I ate leftover bread from flight meals. In my handbag were just a few crumpled dollar bills worth maybe $50. When in Tokyo I called my sister Tĩnh, letting her know the time my next flight was to arrive at Charles de Gaulle. While I was in the air en route to France, she was on a train from Marseille to Paris.

At long last we were able to see each other, albeit through a glass wall. Tĩnh signaled for me to come to a phone booth nearby. Through the phone she nearly screamed into my ear: "Sài-Gòn is about to fall. Stay here and wait. Don't go anywhere. Don't be scared. Uncle Nghị and I can take care of everything. We'll bring your children over."

I looked at her and shook my head. We placed our hands against each other on the glass wall, crying. I did not heed her advice to stay in Paris and wait. I turned my back and got on the next flight.

From New York I called my children.

At exactly 6 p.m. on April 30, 1975, the plane landed in Toronto. As I hugged my children, my heart was shattered when told that Sài-Gòn had fallen.

I became the first Vietnamese refugee in Toronto, Canada.

PICTURES
PART II
Sài Gòn, 1954-1975

First photo taken in South Vietnam; with Nguyễn Chí-Hiếu on Rue Catinat, Sài-Gòn.

Chinh and Tế after wedding.

Kiều Chinh and Tế with 3 children

With my three children, from left: Mỹ-Vân, Cường, Hùng.

The family with my father-in-law, Mr. Nguyễn Đại-Độ, on the balcony of the house at Lữ-Gia residential complex in Sài-Gòn.

Family photo on balcony of Lữ-Gia house in Sài-Gòn.

At Tân Sơn Nhất airport, Saigon, to say goodbye to children going abroad to study.

Movie career in the period at Sài Gòn

*First movie role as a Buddhist nun, Như-Ngọc,
in "Bells of Thiên-Mụ" directed by Lê Dân.*

Kiều Chinh and Lê Quỳnh in "Bells of Thiên-Mụ."

Kiều Chinh in "Mưa Rừng", shot in Dalat and directed by Thái Thúc Nha.

Saigon era, with "áo dài" and conical hat.

Poster for "A Yank in Vietnam" filmed in Việt-Nam with actor/director Marshall Thompson.

With Burt Reynolds in "Operation CIA" filmed in Thailand. 1964

Poster for the film "Destination Vietnam".

The Philippine Ministry of Defense welcomes the actors of the film "Destination Vietnam": Leopoldo Salsedo and Kiều Chinh in an open-top Jeep parade through the streets of of Manila.

Paramount held a press conference and gala dinner at the Manila Hilton Hotel, Philippines, in 1968 for the film "Destination Vietnam". (Kieu Chinh is in the in the middle of the photo)

Kiều Chinh with original "áo dài"

Modeling the modern "boat-collar" áo dài for the first fashion show in Sài-Gòn, at the grand opening of the Small Manufacturer Center in the early sixties. Mme. Ngô Đình Nhu cut the ribbon and started the trend of wearing this collarless style which was later dubbed the "Lady Nhu áo dài."

With Japan's top movie star, Toshiro Mifune, 1964

Kiều Chinh arrived at Taiwan airport to attend Asian Film Festival, 1965

Kiều Chinh with President Chiang Kai-check at the Asian Film Festival in Taiwan, 1965.

Kiều Chinh and the American actor William Holden at the Taiwan Asian Film Festival. (Thanks to the Thái Thúc Nha family and their daughter Elizabeth Giáng Tiên for these rare photos).

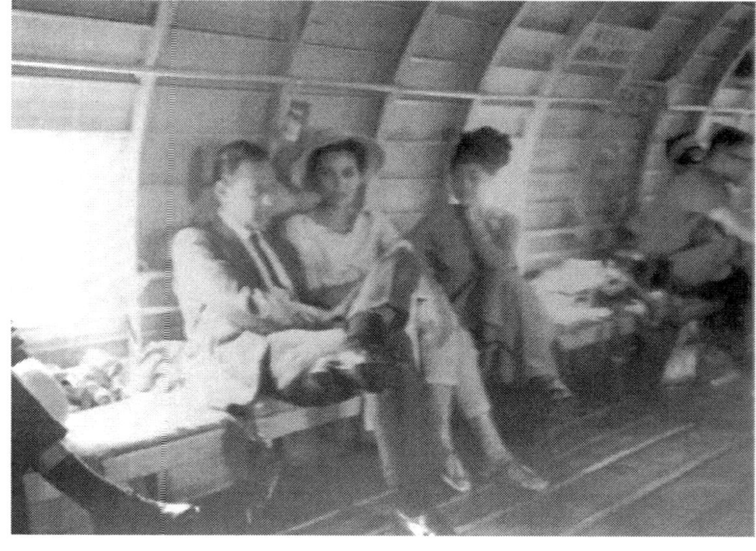

William Holden, Kiều Chinh and Kim Huê (Mrs. Thái Thúc-Nha), on the life-saving flight to Quimoy.

William Holden (right) and Kiều Chinh at the Asian Film Festival.

The 11th Asian Film Festival in Taiwan. From left: Mme Mỹ-Vân, actress Thẩm Thuý-Hằng, Mrs. Thái Thúc-Nha, Kiều Chinh, Mr. Thái Thúc-Nha.

Evening for Shaws

邵氏同人聯歡晚會

聯歡會上，邵逸夫介紹越南影后喬貞與導演岳楓、金銓、李菁等認識。

Host Run Run Shaw introduces the beautiful Vietnamese actress Kieu Chinh to directors Griffin Yueh, King Chuan and 1965 Asian film queen Li Ching.

右起：鄒文懷、凌波、喬貞合影。中越兩位影后敘在一起，這是難得的盛會。

Production Manager Raymond Chow, ... and Vietnamese actress Kieu Chinh.

Hong Kong newspaper with photo of Kiều Chinh being introduced by Mr. Run Run Shaw to movie stars at the Shaw Brothers Studios.

Kiều Chinh and Lê Quỳnh (center) at Berlin Film Festival. On the far right is French actor Jean Marrais.

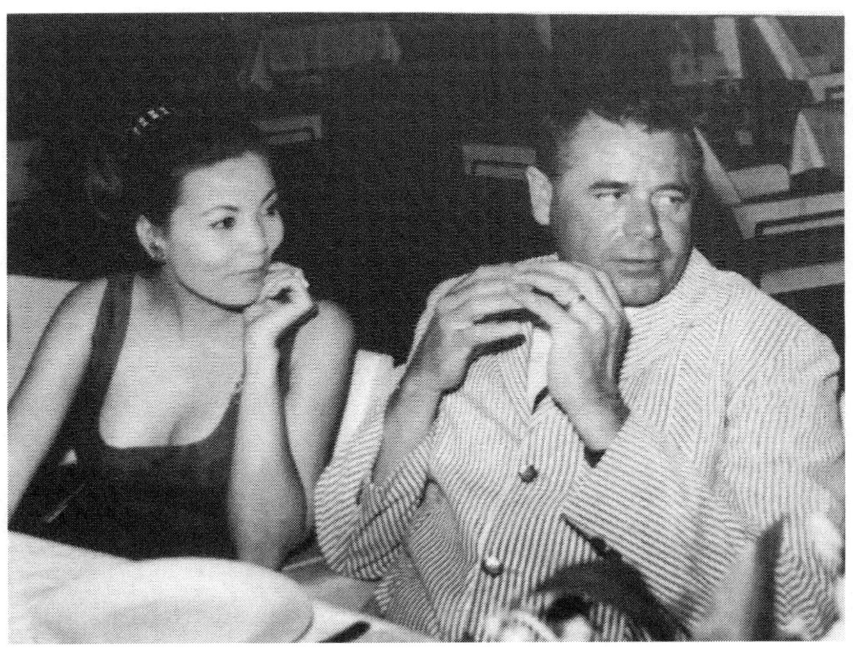

With American actor Glenn Ford, visiting Saigon.

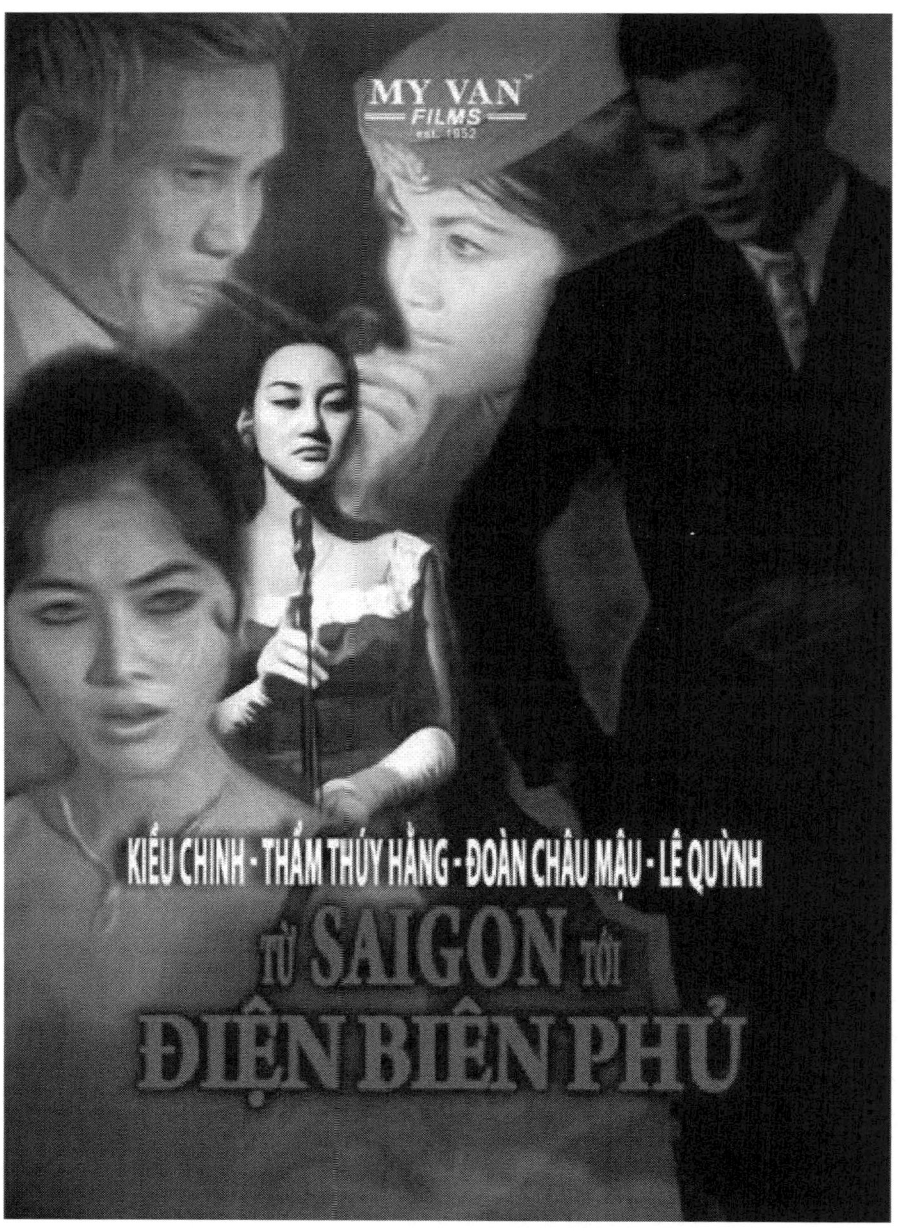

Poster for the movie "From Saigon to Điện Biên Phủ".
Top left corner is the actor Đoàn Châu Mậu. Kiều Chinh is next to him.
Thẩm Thúy Hằng is at the lower left corner.

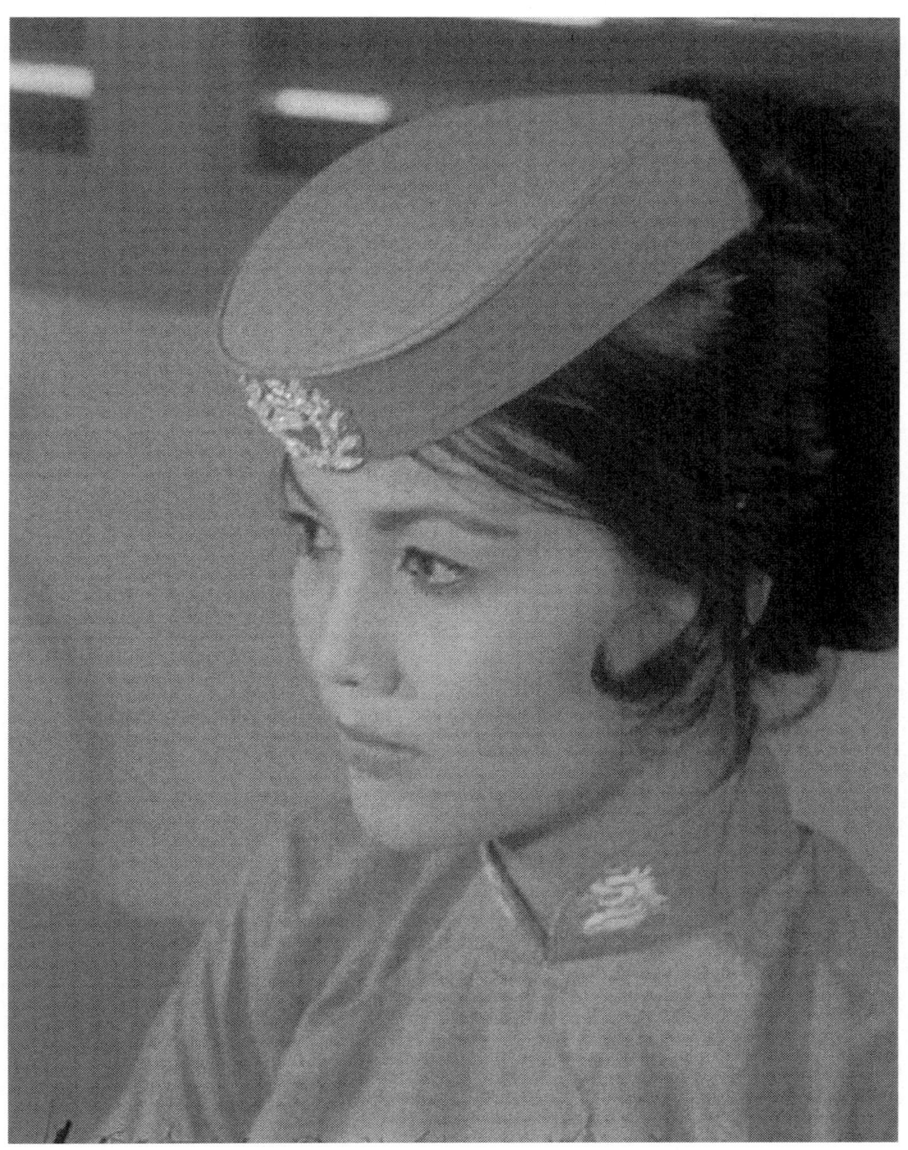

Wearing airline stewardess uniform in "From Sài-Gòn to Điện Biên Phủ."

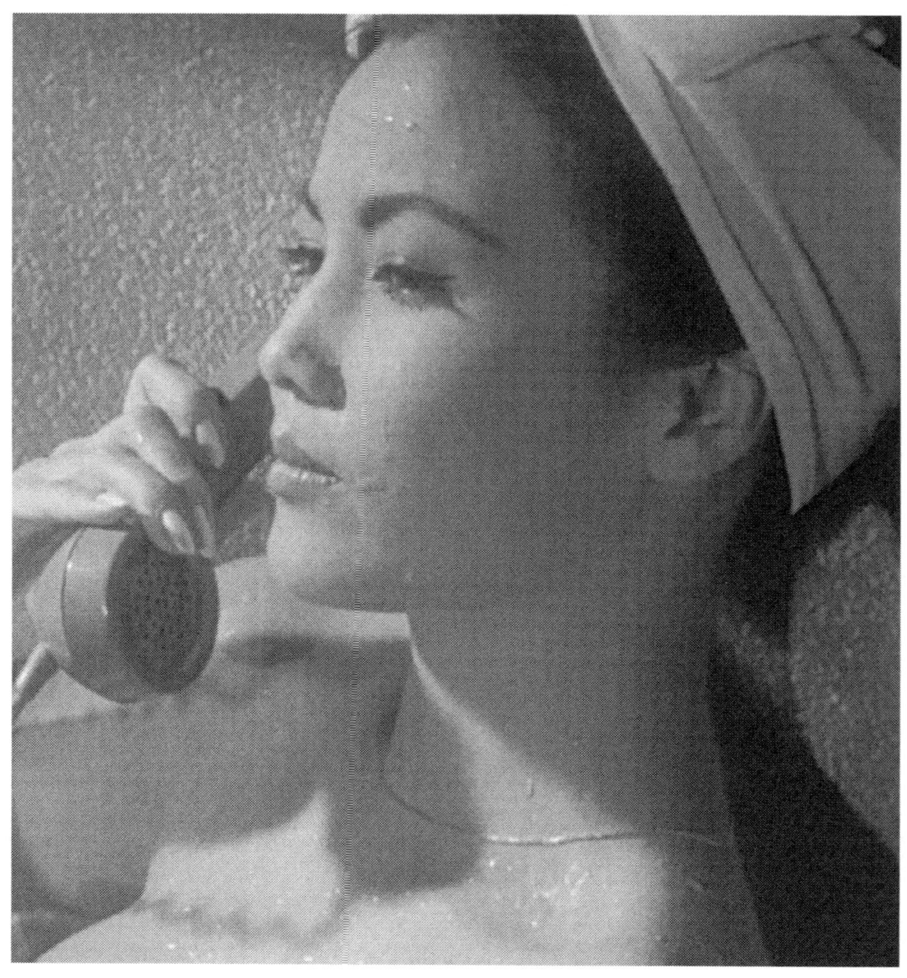

A scene in "From Sài-Gòn to Điện Biên Phủ"

A scene riding a cyclo in "From Sài-Gòn to Điện Biên Phủ"

Poster for the film "Chiếc Bóng Bên Đường" (A Shadow by the Roadside), 1973. From left to right: Thành Được, Kiều Chinh, Kim Cương.

Poster for the film "The Evil Within"

With Indian actor Dev Avnand in "The Evil Within".

From left to right: director Rolf Bayer, actor Dev Anand and Kiều Chinh on the set in India of "The Evil Within"

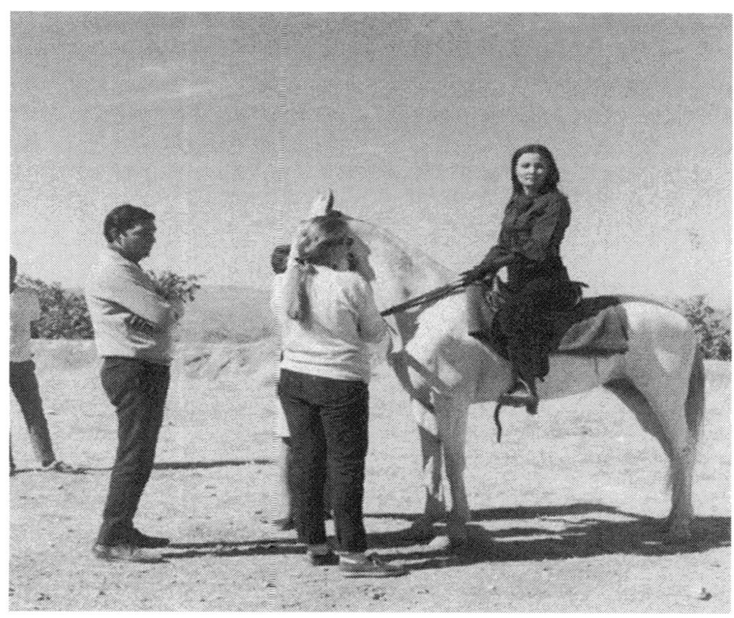

On horseback on the set of "The Evil Within", waiting for "Action!" command from the director.

Kiều Chinh as an Indian princess in the movie "The Evil Within", 1970

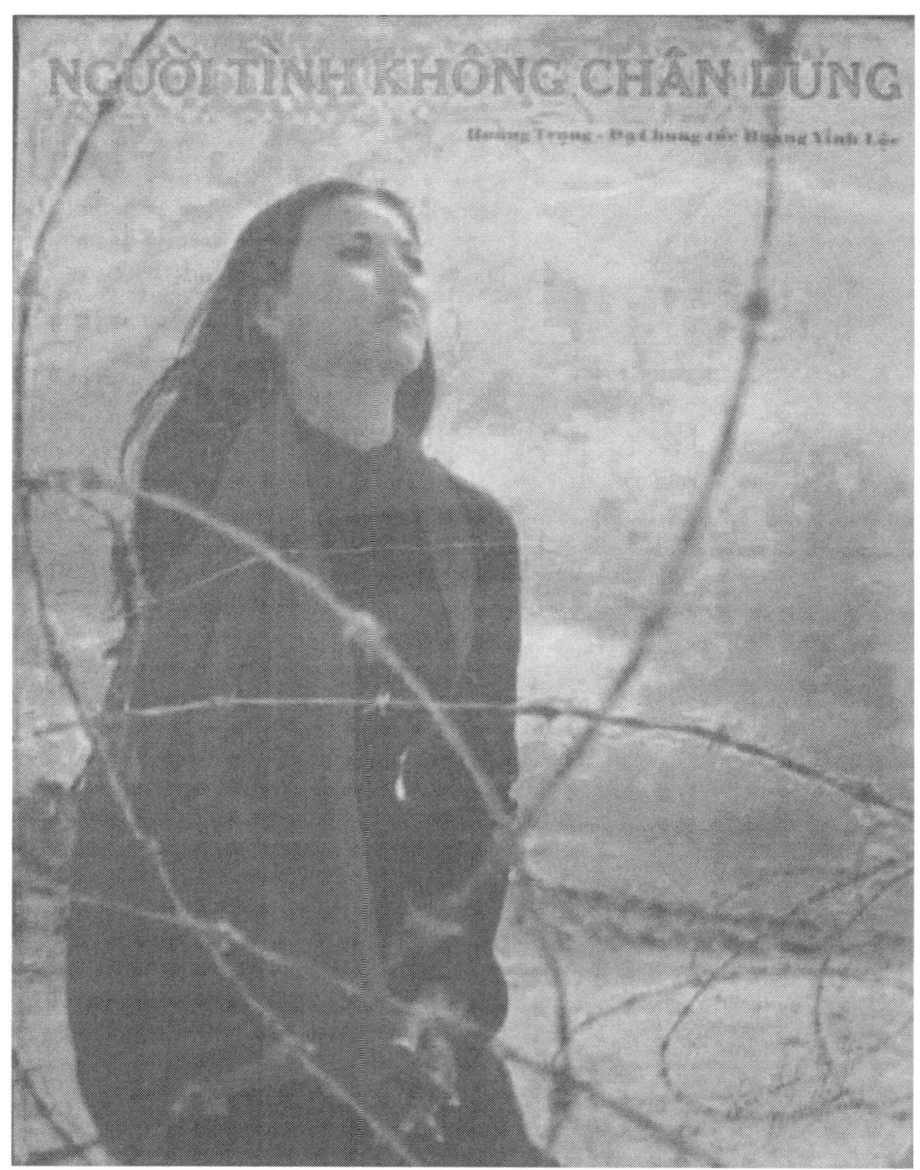

A still in the film "Người Tình Không Chân Dung" (The Faceless Lover), a production of Giao Chi Studio of Kieu Chinh who is also an executive producer and actor.

Kiều Chinh in "The Faceless Lover/Người Tình Không Chân Dung." Directed by Hoàng Vĩnh Lộc.

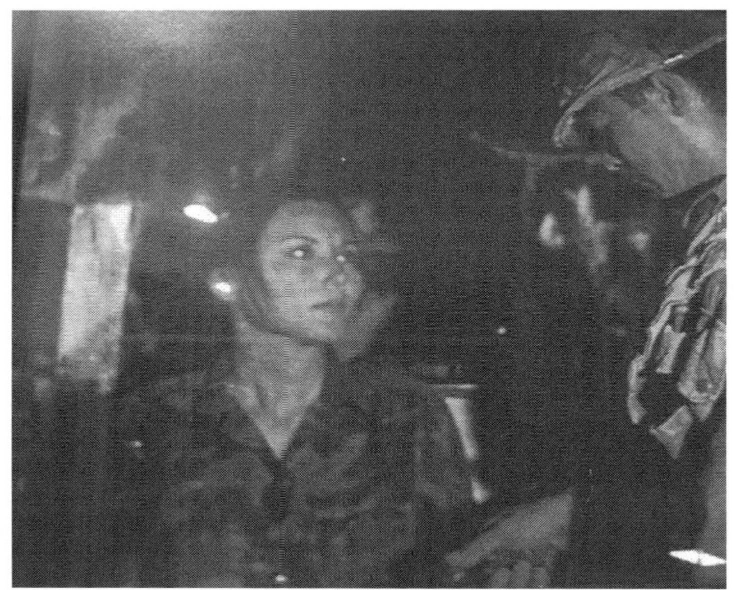

With Vũ Xuân-Thông
in "The Faceless Lover/Người Tình Không Chân Dung."

With Minh Trường-Sơn
in "The Faceless Lover/Người Tình Không Chân Dung."

Director Hoàng Vĩnh-Lộc and cast at the premier of "The Faceless Lover" at REX Theatre in Sài-Gòn. Kiều Chinh is at the microphone.

Kiều Chinh hugging two prizes, boards a flight for Saigon after winning two awards for the film "Người Tình Không Chân Dung" at the Asian Film Festival.

Poster for "Late Summer" directed by Đặng Trần Thức.

President Nguyễn văn Thiệu (second from left) presents Kiều-Chinh with the Arts and Culture Award. Director Thái Thúc-Nha is on the right

In evening dress at a reception.

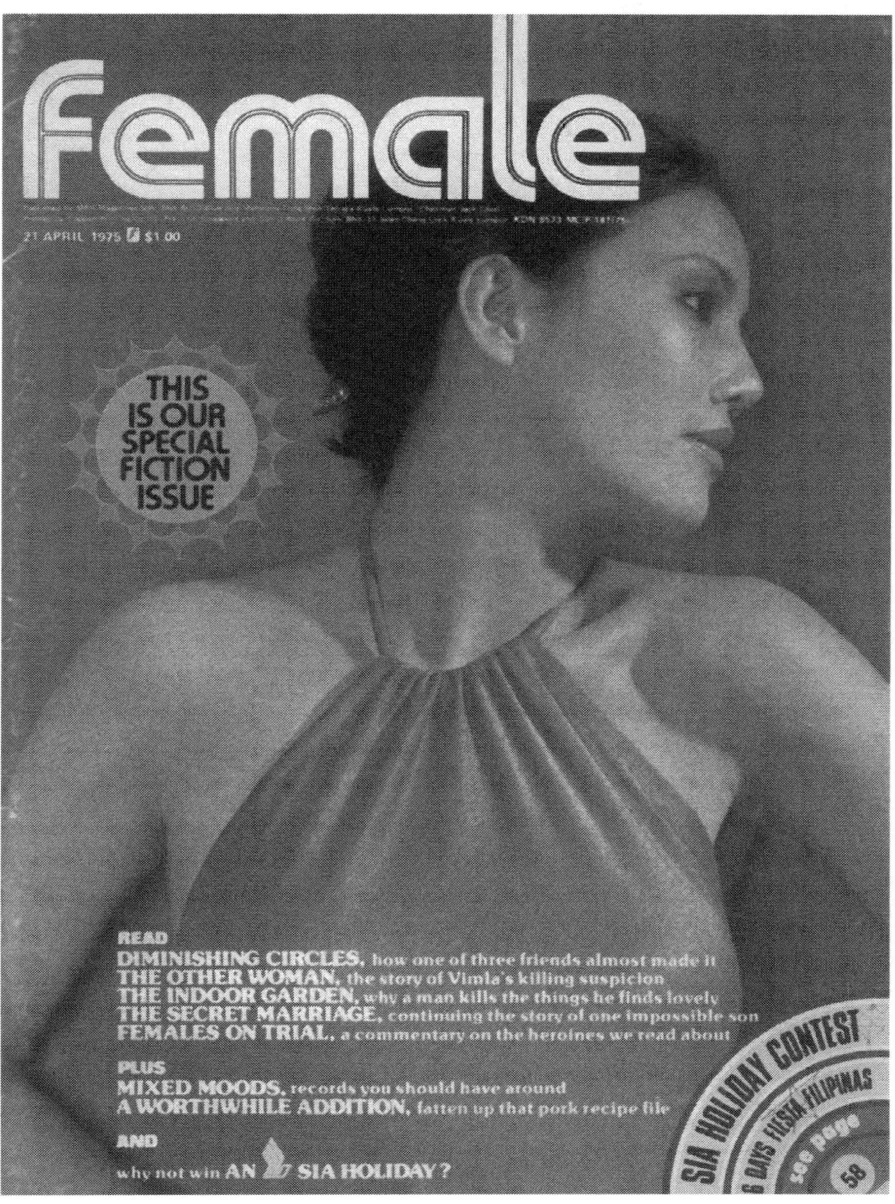

April 25, 1975 issue of Singapore's Female magazine featured Kiều Chinh on its cover five days before the Fall of Sài-Gòn.

PART III

Exile

The First Refugee

Ever since the U.S. started sending troops to Vietnam in 1965, many Hollywood celebrities came to the country as members of the USO Tour to help entertain service members. While in country, a number of them also appeared on the "Kieu Chinh TV Show" — Danny Kaye, Johnny Grant, The Hank Snow Band, Glenn Ford, Diane McBain, Tippi Hedren etc. Ten years later, in 1975, the host of that show became an exile with nothing but a few dollars and a small phone book. She was a stateless and homeless person, hopping around in the clouds hoping to find a country to take her.

I will never forget the moment I walked up to the immigration officer in Toronto as an asylum seeker. After stamping my passport, the man declared:

"Welcome! You are the very first Vietnamese refugee in Toronto!"

After finishing the necessary paperwork, I went with the children to brother Hoà's home. As I've noted earlier, Dr. Trương Như Hoà once was head of the Nuclear Center in Đà-Lạt in the 1950's. His wife, whom I call sister Mão, is my husband Tế's oldest sister. She was living in France for some time before coming back to work in Sài-Gòn. Afterwards she and her husband moved to Canada due to their work. They have three children: daughters Duyên and Mai, and youngest son Thế. It was very kind and thoughtful of them to let my children live and go to school in Canada while war was raging back home.

And now I had joined their family as well. My children and I roomed together in a small attic. I monitored the news from Sài-Gòn every day, worrying and wondering what might have happened to my husband and his family back home. I had no idea what I would do next. The children were still underage and I had no money. In just a matter of days, I had gone from a working professional with multiple film contracts all over Southeast Asia to an unemployed mother without even a bank account. The future looked bleak.

One early morning in May, in the bitter cold and windy weather of Toronto, I made my way to the government agency Welcome House to look for a job. I was given an old coat and $75 Canadian dollars. The lady who interviewed me asked:

"What is your professional skill?"

"I am an actress," I answered.

She gave me a sympathetic look and said quickly, as if to save me from further embarrassment: "We are not doing casting here." Then, pointing to a list pinned on a board nearby, she explained that those jobs marked with an "X" had already been taken.

I took a quick glance. All the light work that seemed to fit my physical stature were taken. On the last line I saw one that said "Cleaning after the chickens. Pay: $2.25/hour." Having no other choice, I signed up.

The work started at 6 a.m. each day. I had to get up very early and leave the house at 5 a.m., when the children were still asleep, to catch a bus to Salboro on the outskirts of the city. Once I got there, the workers gave me a pair of tall boots that reached up to my knees, a thick raincoat that reached below my knees, and a mask that covered most of my face. Thus protected, I was taken to where the water hoses were. These were not your garden variety hoses, mind you, but heavy-duty contraptions that resembled something firefighters might use. When the water was turned on, the pressure was so strong that if you weren't paying attention it would propel you forward and wrestle you to the ground. To avoid falling flat on your face, you would have to stand with your feet firmly planted and rather far apart. You would then walk very slowly and deliberately, grabbing the beast with both hands as you sprayed every inch of the chicken coop, swishing all the poops into one corner.

That was my first eight-hour a day job. Each day, I'd get into my safety attire, turn on the water, carry the hoses on my back, and use all my strength to spray off every nook and cranny of those chicken coops. The chicken farm was enormous. As I went from one coop to the next, the stench of chicken poops would be thrust up my nostrils, making me nauseous and dizzy at times.

My health deteriorated with each passing day. Not only was the physical work taking its toll, but psychologically I was always in a state of anxiety and uncertainty. I figured if I didn't get out of this chicken cleaning business soon, it would surely clean me up.

Alas, three weeks later I got news that my husband was able to get out of Việt-Nam on a boat and had made his way to Guam. He had to escape by himself under very arduous circumstances and thus could not bring his father who was nearly blind. My father-in-law stayed back with Sâm, the maid who helped me take care of my daughter Mỹ-Vân. It grieved me so to hear that Mr. Độ was left behind.

As I waited to bring Tế to Toronto after completing the sponsorship paperwork, I reflected on what a blessing it was that our family would be able to reunite when there were times I thought all hope was lost. The only regret I had was that my father-in-law could not join us.

Tentative Steps to Hollywood

Once the family was reunited, I began thinking about our future. We couldn't stay in my sister-in-law's house forever. I decided to say goodbye to the chicken farm. Using money saved from cleaning chicken poops, I started making long distance calls to the U.S., hoping to get some help from former colleagues.

The first person I called was Burt Reynolds, my co-star in *Operation CIA*. He wasn't home.

The second person was Glenn Ford. Not home, either.

The third was William Holden. He wasn't there, but I was able to talk to his ex-wife. She told me they'd been divorced, then gave me the number of his agent and said he'd know where Bill was. I excitedly called Bill's agent, only to be told he was on a hunting trip in Europe and wouldn't be back for another month.

By this time I had only $15 left. Out of desperation I called a person whom I'd met only once in 1965, ten years before, when she was a guest on my TV talk show in Sài-Gòn. Her name is Tippi Hedren, she was the lead actress in Alfred Hitchcock's classic *The Birds*. It was a really long shot, I was using the last few dollars from my savings to call someone I barely knew.

From the other end, I heard: "This is Tippi. Who is this?"

I was shocked and surprised. Tears began rolling down my face. I spoke slowly and clearly so she could know who I was:

"Tippi, this is Kieu Chinh. Kieu Chinh. Vietnamese actress. Sài-Gòn, Vietnam. Do you remember me?"

"Of course! Of course! Oh my God! Where are you?"

"I can't talk for long. I'm running out of money. Can you call me back at this number ...?"

"Don't cry! Don't cry! I will call right back. Everything will be OK!"

Three days later, I received a telegram, accompanied by a letter and a plane ticket from the organization Food For The Hungry. The telegram specifically stated that an invitation was "*extended to the actress Kieu Chinh to the U.S. to attend the opening of Hope Village in Sacramento: the first camp for Vietnamese refugees in the U.S.*" The word "actress" suddenly reminded me of who I was, even though it was used simply as an excuse to get me a visa into the U.S.

On the flight from Toronto to Sacramento, I reminisced about my first trip to America in 1968 for a film project about the life of Doctor Tom Dooley, the humanitarian physician who worked in Southeast Asia and became controversial for his CIA affiliations. I had the chance to meet many great artists in the dazzling world of Hollywood. I was invited to the opening night of *Doctor Zhivago* — directed by David Lean and based on a book by Boris Pasternak; the film eventually won five Oscars. At the post-screening party at 20th Century Fox studio, I was asked for a dance by the movie's lead, Omar Sharif, and also by Adam West — aka Batman. Memories of Hollywood splendor started to sparkle in my head.

It was dark and cold by the time I landed in Sacramento. Tippi looked like she'd been waiting for me for a long time. We hugged each other tightly, laughing, crying, unbelieving. I really can't describe all the emotions of that moment. In her arms I felt like a young girl who'd been hopelessly lost in the wilderness but who'd finally been found by a loving and caring older sister. At the same time I felt a weight had been lifted and someone had given me a set of wings. I was flying higher and higher. The sky opened up with a blinding light. I was reborn.

The first question she asked me was: "Where's your luggage?!" I shook my head and said all I had was a small bag containing two sets of clothes, on a pair of shoulders that was not too old yet heavy with burden. Tippi squeezed my hands hard. I sensed she understood and empathized with my situation — homeless, jobless, penniless!

After a long, anxious trip that ended with a warm and reassuring welcome from an older sister, I had no problem at all falling asleep that night. The next morning, Tippi drove me to the opening ceremony for Hope Village. The place used to be a large hospital that took up an entire hill, far from any residential area. By 1975, the hospital was abandoned and empty, so the government turned it into a temporary shelter for about 500 Vietnamese refugee families, the first group to resettle in California. The camp was run by Food For The Hungry whose chairman was Dr. Larry Ward, someone who was passionate about addressing hunger in Vietnam. Tippi Hedren was the vice-chair of volunteers.

The event began with a solemn flag ceremony. After many weeks being tossed around from place to place, I couldn't contain my emotions when I saw the flag of South Vietnam on American soil. After the "Star Spangled Banner" was played, the yellow flag was raised. We all stood and sang our old anthem. More than a few raised their hands in military salute even though they were in civilian clothes. The unexpected appearance of the yellow flag and the singing of the anthem brought many of us to tears. I was among them. It was like a miracle.

I was next introduced to say a few words. Standing on a small, wooden makeshift podium, I said: "My fellow countrymen, welcome. And thank you, America. Thank you for opening up your arms and your hearts to us, letting us make this our new home..."

I recognized a few familiar faces in the audience like General Chức and Lt. Colonel Lê Xuân-Vinh. Among people I had known were dentist Nguyễn Bá Khuê, journalist Đỗ Ngọc-Yến, female novelist Trùng Dương. We were so happy to see each other in Hope Village as camp mates, as exiles, as refugees. Nobody had any idea what the future would bring, but for me it was a very memorable encounter.

I stayed at the camp to help Tippi with daily tasks such as food service, cleaning the kitchen, distributing clothing and other necessities, interpreting for those who couldn't speak English, helping people fill out paperwork, etc. I was kept busy. So many people were calling my name. It was tiring, yet at the same time I felt rewarded for contributing something meaningful during my first days in America.

After we left Hope Village, Tippi took me to her house to stay with her. Every day she drove me to various agencies to get the necessary permission to stay in the U.S. Her daughter, Melanie Griffith (Oscar-nominated actress in *Working Girl*), had just moved out to live with her boyfriend, actor Don Johnson. So I got to stay in her room.

I wore Tippi's clothes and shared in all her daily activities. It was Tippi, with the assistance of William Holden, who helped me become a member of the Screen Actors Guild (SAG) and took me to all the gatherings so I could familiarize myself with the working environment of Hollywood.

I should also mention that as soon as he got back to the U.S. from his European trip, Bill Holden sent me an enormous bouquet of roses, more than a hundred flowers, with a note: "Welcome to America. Make this land your home."

Tippi also helped me find a place to stay. She rented a small apartment that was big enough for me and the rest of my family, whom she also sponsored. The apartment was in North Hollywood and was completely unfurnished. After handing me the key, she gave me $20 and said she'd be back.

Alone in the empty apartment, I suddenly felt lonesome and lost. I didn't know what to do in this cold, silent space. I understood what Tippi said, that eventually I'd be reunited with my husband and children. But at that very moment all I could feel was incredible emptiness and nostalgia. I was so homesick I wanted to cry. I kept pacing around the empty apartment in my own loneliness. Finally I decided to leave.

I had no idea where to go. I just knew that I had to get out of that chilly, empty place for awhile. So I locked the door and started walking. I wandered aimlessly from one street to the next. I walked through the busy traffic and into the afternoon sunlight. I walked among the trees and against the wind. I walked inside my loneliness, feeling a chill coming from within. I wanted so badly to scream out loud: Where are my loved ones? My father? My brother? My husband? My children? Why is everybody so silent?

I kept on walking until I noticed the street lights had come on. My legs were tired and my stomach growled. The feeling of exhaustion was like a reminder, telling me: "Never forget! Never forget that these are just the first steps in the life of an artist in exile!"

I walked past several fancy restaurants with white tablecloths and well-dressed patrons. I told myself that such places weren't for me anymore. My glory days were long gone. The reality was that at this very moment all I had was the $20 that Tippi gave me. Even if I wanted to, I couldn't afford to eat in those restaurants. And so I kept walking. Finally, I saw a McDonald's. On the window was an advertisement for a hamburger meal with french fries and a drink for just $2.00! I walked in. The place was noisy and crowded. I stood in line behind a young couple. They were talking in rapid birdlike sounds. They held each other in their arms. They kissed. They couldn't care less that there was another world beside theirs. They ordered. Then came my turn.

I took my tray of food and found a table in one corner where I could observe people. This was the first time since coming to America that I had dined alone. And the first time eating in a McDonald's! A country song was playing but nobody listened; folks were busy talking in a language that I was not fully familiar with. I felt like I didn't belong, like I was an alien from another world.

Halfway through the hamburger I suddenly had a craving for a bowl of *phở*. The image of the famous Flying Ship *Phở* on Lý Thái Tổ Street popped out of my head as though it had been waiting a very long time to do so. I was reminded of those Sunday mornings when Tế and I took our children there. I remembered the familiar faces we saw at the various *phở* places in Sài Gòn on weekends. I remembered the unmistakable smell and the cacophony of voices requesting more onion here, more hot pepper there.

Après phở we usually went over to the alley nearby for some coffee. It wasn't a real café, just an outdoor space next to a large tree where the owner had strung up a few tarps to shield customers from the sun and rain. Everything was simple, from the small oven for boiling water to the child-size plastic tables and stools. Customers had to seat themselves and make sure they were seen by the owner to order. The coffee, needless to say, was superb — even better when enjoyed with friends and loved ones.

Amidst the noisy atmosphere and the drowned out country tune, I suddenly wished I could hear "Love Song" by Phạm Duy:

I love my mother tongue, since the day that I was born.
The lullaby my mother sang, the lullaby I'll carry on.
My mother tongue! Four millennia of joys and pains
Through the ups and downs of our history.
My mother tongue! From the day I was in a crib
Has become the language of my soul, my homeland.

I tried not to cry as I whispered "*my homeland*" to myself in the middle of a McDonald's, all alone in a strange new land.

When I got back to "my" apartment, I saw that there was a "bed" in one room. Actually, it was just one of those mattresses one would find by a swimming pool. It was covered by a white sheet. There was even a pillow. But best of all was a lovely letter that Tippi left on the bed, wishing me "good night and sweet dreams."

I was awakened quite early the next day by loud knocks on the door. My first group of visitors was Tippi's mom and several of her lady friends. They gave me some pots, pans and kitchen utensils. I spent the whole day hosting visitors. Dr. Larry Ward followed the older ladies with a moving truck. The men brought in a refrigerator, dining table, beds, and an old couch. In just one morning, my empty apartment was transformed into a comfortable home with all the things a small family would need.

Tippi came by in the afternoon. After surveying my new place, she said: "Chinh, looks like everything's ready for your family reunion!" Not knowing what to say, I put my arms on her shoulder. Tippi turned around and gave me a big hug, telling me everything would be fine according to God's will.

And just as Tippi predicted, Tế and the children arrived not long after that. We began a new life. In fact, this was the first time since our marriage that my husband and I had a place all to ourselves, a real family home with just the five of us.

Through the years, Tippi and I have remained as close as real sisters. We have been by each other's side on many different occasions, in many different events. When Tippi was honored with a Hollywood star on the Walk of Fame, I was invited to speak. I was also asked by Melanie Griffith and her husband Antonio Banderas to wish Tippi well at her 80th birthday party. When Hollywood made a documentary about Tippi's life, I was asked to participate. When Camp Shambala where she was living and raising lions was destroyed by a storm, I came to help her. And when Boat People SOS and the Vietnamese-American Nails Association held an event to honor Tippi Hedren in Washington, D.C., I was invited to tell her story from 40 years before.

I have reserved a whole section to talk about Tippi, my incredible sponsor, in Part V of this book.

Movie Career Restart

Finally, with invaluable assistance from Tippi Hedren and William Holden, I was given a special entry into the Screen Actors Guild (SAG). I also was represented by the most respected talent agency in Hollywood — William Morris. But that didn't mean I could automatically become a Hollywood actor or join its working world. There were other obstacles for an Asian actor in America.

The first time I met my agent, I was advised to pick an American name to make it easier for people to call me. But I refused. I wanted my name to be Kieu Chinh. Just Kieu Chinh. No matter where or when.

Early in my life as an exiled artist I was interviewed fairly often. In one such interview by a TV station in Los Angeles, I told the host that the most important thing for me at the time was to find a job. I explained that since I was sponsored into the U.S. by an individual and didn't come as a war refugee, I was not eligible for any government assistance. One of the people who saw that interview was Father John P. Languille, head of U.S. Catholic Charities (USCC). Seeing that I could speak English and that the organization had a program to help Vietnamese refugees, he contacted the TV station and asked them to let me know that he had a job lined up for me should I want it. I guess he didn't realize that the "job" I was referring to was as a movie actress.

It was a difficult decision for me. With a regular eight-hour a day job, I wouldn't be able to go to auditions. And if I got the part, how would I be able to take time off to act? In the end, I decided to take the job anyway. But I asked Fr. Languille for a special concession — that he'd let me take time off for auditions and, if chosen, to act. Not only was he happy to oblige, he even hoped I'd get back to acting full-time soon.

Once I joined USCC, I discovered that the legendary Vietnamese singer Jo Marcel and musician Nam Lộc were already working there. Soon after, my husband Tế also joined. Then came actor Lê Quỳnh and several others.

Our daily tasks revolved around helping new refugees resettle. As their numbers began to rise, so did the amount of work we had to do. We split off into different units. I worked with Sister Susan to take care of newcomers. Later I was transferred to Sister Cahill and became a permanent employee instead of a contractor. My work was related to a federal program called Indochina Refugee & Immigration. As such, I had to travel often to Sacramento to attend meetings in the Governor's office.

Later on I also had to go to Washington, D.C. as a member of the U.S. Immigration Advisory Board.

All through that time, I began making forays into the world of Hollywood. I soon learned that auditioning was a tough business. Every time there was a casting call for an Asian role, dozens of actors would show up — Chinese, Japanese, Korean, Filipino, Indian, Malaysian, Indonesian... You name it. My agency sent me to all these auditions, of course. Compared to the hyphenated-American actresses born in this country, it quickly became obvious that English was not my strength. Competing against them was not easy. As a matter of fact, in all my previous 18 years of making movies in Vietnam and Southeast Asia, I'd never had to audition. Not even once!

In September, 1975, three months after arriving in the U.S., I landed my first role: a sales clerk in a cigarette shop in Chinatown. It was in the TV show *Joe Forrester*, a police drama, and my character had exactly two words.

I was told to show up at the studio in Burbank, Stage 21, at exactly 10:30 a.m. To avoid complications, I took an early bus and got there an hour ahead of time. I waited until 11:30 but the studio was still closed. About 15 minutes later a pickup truck stopped by. The driver stuck out his head and asked:

"Are you Kieu Chinh?"

"Yes."

"Come on up," he waved. "I'll take you to the location."

It was only then that I realized we weren't shooting at Stage 21 but on location. I climbed onto the back of the pick-up truck and sat on the bed. It was the costume truck; it took me straight to Chinatown. A section had been blocked off and set up. Onlookers loitered around. An assistant director was using a bullhorn to tell the crew what to do. The main actors were still sitting in their named chairs in a roped off area in the back. My driver brought me to the changing area so I could put on my costume. Then I was told to stand outside the roped area and wait until called.

About an hour later it was time for lunch. I saw people line up in front of a food truck with a menu. The smell of hot food made me hungry. I got in line and waited. A third-level assistant director (a gopher, basically) came and whispered to me that this was the hot food truck reserved for the main actors and technicians. He pointed to a long table on the left that had stacks of white foam boxes and said those were cold lunches for the extras.

Finally by 4 p.m. a pretty blond told me to follow her to the filming area at the end of the street. She asked in a friendly voice:

"Have you memorized your line?"

"Yes, I have."

"Don't be scared or nervous. Whenever you hear 'Action!' just start talking normally. The most important thing is don't look straight into the camera."

My part took only a few minutes in front of the camera. All I had to say was "Yes, sir" when the main character went into the shop and ordered: "Give me a Pall Mall."

When the director called out: "Action!", for some reason I became frozen and just stood there after the main character said his line.

The director yelled loudly: "Cut! Take two!"

The assistant director walked over and told me to respond right after the question and to look happier because a customer had just walked into the store.

After finishing the scene, I walked back to the area where the main actors were sitting. The lead actor, Lloyd Bridges, quickly came over to me, gently put his hand on my shoulder and said softly: "I know who you are."

I looked up at him and turned away. Tears welled up in my eyes.

When I got home that night I could still feel a lump in my throat. I told everybody what happened. My children tried to comfort me: "Forget it, Maman. Forget that you're an actress. Forget that profession."

Should I forget it? Should I just walk away? The questions kept swirling in my head as I tossed and turned in bed that night.

I knew that I would feel that lump in my throat many more times, but I also knew I could not forget it. I would not ... quit!

In the days and weeks that followed, I kept auditioning. I landed numerous small parts for a variety of TV shows like *Police Woman* with Angie Dickinson, *Lucifer Complex* with Robert Vaughn, *Switch* with Robert Wagner, *Cover Girl* with Jane Kennedy etc. None required real acting; they were just short appearances. The money I earned was hardly worth it.

Meanwhile, news from Việt-Nam was dark and bleak. My

father in the North was ill. My father-in-law in the South didn't have any money. I had to scrimp and save every penny just to be able to help out a little. Very little.

In the middle of 1978 I received the worst news of all, a telegram from Hà-Nội: Dad had died. All the hopes I was clinging to all these years were now completely buried. I would not see my father ever again. I was utterly destroyed.

My biggest regret was that I couldn't help him. I couldn't send enough money or medication to alleviate his suffering when he needed it the most. Neither was I by his side when he breathed his last. It didn't matter any more what I should say or do. Everything was too late.

One fall evening in 1977. Tippi called and asked me to go with her to a reception hosted by Universal Studios to celebrate their new blockbuster *Jaws*. How could I say no to my dearest friend, Tippi?

It was an elaborate party held at one of the top notch hotels in Beverly Hills. Many famous people were there, from actors and directors to producers and journalists. I can't remember who all I met that night, but a few days later I got a call from my agent telling me that the producer for M.A.S.H. wanted to invite me in for an audition.

I was very surprised. So was my agency. Typically, agents for unknown actors like me are the ones who have to be constantly on the hunt for roles for their clients. It's almost unheard of for producers to call up a talent agency and ask for a specific actor. Which was why my agent told me to immediately call him and let him know how the audition went.

And so I did. I called him as soon as I got home.

"Who did you meet there?"

"I only met two persons. Burt Metcalf and Alan Alda."

"Alan Alda?! Do you know who he is?"

"No, I don't. Who is he?"

"Oh my God! Don't you watch TV?"

My agent had no idea how poor we were. I couldn't save enough to send medicine to my Dad, how could I afford a TV!? How could I possibly know who Burt Metcalf or Alan Alda was?

"So what did they ask you?" He probed. "Did they ask you to perform? Were there others auditioning, too?"

"Nobody asked me anything about my acting experience. It seems like they already knew. They just asked me a bunch of unrelated questions like how things were in Vietnam? What was I doing? Had I settled in? Things like that. I didn't have to perform anything. And there were no others there for the audition. Before I left, they handed me a script and asked me to look it over. They said if I liked it, then the lead female role was mine."

"I'll be darned," he exhaled. "You landed a role without even having to audition! Guess I'd better get working on your contract..."

It turned out that at the Universal party someone had noticed me and done some research on my background. It was Burt Metcalf, executive producer for M.A.S.H. He must have seen me standing by myself in a corner, lost among the stars of Hollywood.

M.A.S.H. was a leading TV sitcom at the time. It revolved around a group of American medical personnel at a military field hospital during the Korean War. The producers felt it was time to introduce a light romance between the main character, Hawkeye (Alan Alda), and a local beauty. As they were working on the storyline, fate brought me to that party. Thus the script was touched up to include a love story between Hawkeye and a Korean woman.

Those were the best days of my career since arriving in the U.S. My chair sat next to Alan Alda's and had my name on it: Kieu Chinh. The main female role was a Korean woman from a wealthy family of noble lineage who'd lost everything due to the war. All she had left was an ailing mother who needed medicine but none could be found. So she ventured to the American field hospital to ask for help. Hawkeye, the medical doctor there, agreed to help her. In time the two developed an affection for one another. But eventually the ailing mother died, and the woman faced a difficult choice: stay there with her lover, or go back to her hometown? In the end, she chose to say goodbye to him.

Alan Alda, in an interview in a newspaper article as well as on Johnny Carson's *Tonight Show* had this to say: "She's so talented. There must be a place for her in Hollywood, somewhere." (This quote was later reprinted in *TV Guide.*)

On the movies front, after a number of trivial parts, in March 1981, I finally landed a rather significant role in a film called *The Letter*. I played a Chinese woman who was a love rival of actress Lee Remick in a tragic three-way relationship based on a story by William Somerset Maugham.

Some people, including producer George Eckstein and me, were initially surprised by how director John Erman chose me for this role without an audition. John Erman later explained that when he made the movie *Green Eyes* in 1977 he already intended to have me in the lead role opposite Paul Winfield. The movie was to be shot in the Philippines but unfortunately at the time I had neither a passport to travel outside the U.S. nor the necessary permit to work in the Philippines. So the role went to a Filipino actress instead. Erman regretted very much not having me in that film. He told me that: "For sure, we will work together in the future once we get the chance."

That is why John saved the role of a Chinese woman for me in *The Letter* even though I couldn't speak a word of Chinese, and it wouldn't have been hard at all to find an actress in Hollywood who could.

After *The Letter* and *The Children of An Lac*, I got to play a variety of roles in some of the more popular TV shows at the time such as *Lou Grant, Matt Houston, Santa Barbara, Cagney and Lacey, Hotel, Dynasty* etc.

Early in 1986 I returned to the Philippines to act in, as well as serve as consultant for, *Hamburger Hill*, the Vietnam war movie directed by John Irvin. I appeared very little in front of the camera. However, I was there for the entire shoot as a technical adviser. I advised on casting, helping choose locals to be extras; I advised on costumes, from Vietnamese *áo dài* to the conical hat, and even the wooden shoes. I also advised the crew on how to build the set for an open market, a village road, a bunker... and on any dialogue in Vietnamese.

The movie told the story of the fierce battles between American and North Vietnamese forces to wrest control of a strategic hilltop in the Central highlands near Laos. One night, the North Vietnamese Army used human waves to attack the hill and nearly wiped out the entire U.S. unit, only to be pushed back the next morning by bombing runs that opened the way for the Americans to retake their position. On and on, and back and forth, the fighting went. After each attack, piles of bodies were strewn all over the hill. Rockets and bombs then finished the job by mincing the corpses into ground meat, giving the hill its grisly but descriptive name.

In the end, the American forces were able to vanquish their foes and take control of the hill. But once the enemy retreated, military commanders saw there was no reason to stay. And thus a lush green piece of land that was so violently contested and which cost so many lives from both sides became a burned out forest on a barren hill that reeked of death. Finally, the Americans abandoned it, too. The film depicted the total meaninglessness of war.

In *Welcome Home* in 1989, I played a Cambodian woman who was the wife of an American G.I., played by Kris Kristofferson. This time, I had the great fortune of working with famed director Franklin Shaffner, who had won two Oscars for Best Director. He had directed some epic movies like *Patton* and *Papillon*. He was known for his ability to get his actors excited about their roles. Working under him gave me such joy.

Looking back at all the memories, both happy and sad, I just want say a heartfelt "Thank you" to all the directors, actors and fellow professionals I've had the privilege to work with. I'm very happy and proud that I've been able to stay with the film world for over 60 years — six decades! — on a long journey from Vietnam to Hollywood.

I thank you all.

Looking Back

Vietnam House

After years living with and taking care of my in-laws under the same roof, I finally had a home to myself as a result of the life-changing events of April, 1975. For the first time, my husband and I became inseparable partners in building a new life for our family. And even though the children were still teenagers, they also contributed.

After school, my oldest daughter Mỹ-Vân worked part-time in a pharmacy. My son Hoàng-Hùng worked as a box-boy at the local Alpha Beta supermarket. Even the youngest Cường, only 14 at the time, earned money delivering newspapers; he was so proud to show me his first check. To me, all the efforts and teamwork everybody put in was a reward more meaningful than anything else. Even though we were struggling financially, we had each other and we were happy.

Both Tế and I worked at the Los Angeles branch of the Catholic Charities (USCC). Together with several prominent members of our community such as Dr. Hoàng văn Đức and professor Trần văn Mai, we created the Vietnamese Association of California, the first community organization in the country. I was given the role of vice-chairwoman. Our first major event was the Tết (Lunar New Year) celebration in Los Angeles in 1976, with the participation of composer Phạm Duy, a giant in Vietnamese 20th century music, and the poet Cao Tiêu.

We also formed the Vietnamese Artists Association whose members included musical composer Hoàng Thi-Thơ, actor Lê Quỳnh, singer Jo Marcel, songwriter Nam Lộc, and many others. The first music show we put together for our compatriots was a resounding success.

I created an activity center called "Vietnam House," where we held the first Mid-Autumn celebration for little children, complete with an *áo dài* fashion show. The building was used daily as an office to assist students and other newcomers to the country. "Vietnam House" also participated in demonstrations to help boat people, organized welcoming parties at LAX airport to receive Amerasians, and took part in many other community events.

All in all, even though in the first few years in exile I was consumed by the need to survive as a family, I still tried to make time for community activities. Through them, I could feel that I was still Vietnamese and was not severed from my roots.

Film Conference in UCLA

One time, I attended an important conference at UCLA that explored movies with Vietnamese themes. The guest speakers' table was divided into three sections. To my left were four representatives who came from Vietnam, including the head of the Film Bureau in Hà-Nội. In the middle section sat I, the lone representative of the movie industry in South Vietnam prior to 1975. To my right were four representatives from Hollywood, one of whom was famed director Oliver Stone (*Platoon, Heaven & Earth*). It was standing room only. Many had to stand outside the door because the place was packed. There were UCLA students, American and Vietnamese media organizations, even the *Los Angeles Times*.

After some struggle, one Vietnamese TV crew made their way inside. As soon as the female reporter saw me on stage, she went back outside and told the crowd, which had many Vietnamese students and refugees from Orange County who came to protest the presence of the delegation from Vietnam, that "Ms. Kiều Chinh is sitting at the table with the communists!"

The crowd immediately went into a vocal frenzy. Police with K-9 units had to help establish order. As the conference went on, the noisy crowd outside continued protesting.

Despite all the commotion, we carried on our discussions in a professional and serious manner. The protesters, on the other hand, had no idea what was going on save one hasty and faulty statement by a clueless reporter.

After the meeting, we were led outside through a different door to avoid the unruly crowd. The next day, the *Los Angeles Times* printed a story on the event which included this statement by Nguyễn Thụ, head of Vietnam's delegation: "No one has taken Kieu Chinh's place in Vietnam. I don't think anyone can."

Người Việt (*The Vietnamese*), the largest Viet language newspaper outside Vietnam, had a story on the front page about the event. In it Dr. Võ Tư Nhượng, who had been in the room from the beginning, remarked that our community was lucky to have Kiều Chinh at the table to represent South Vietnam's film industry, otherwise it would have been strictly a conference between Americans and the communists.

Thanks to the accurate reporting and statements by people like him, the truth ultimately prevailed and any misconceptions sowed by that reporter were eventually dismissed.

In 1988, I was invited to be a judge for the Hawaii Film Festival, which screened films from all over the world. It was the first time I saw a film made in North Vietnam, *When Will October Come (Bao Giờ Cho Đến Tháng Mười),* directed by Đặng Nhật Minh.

As a judge, one had to watch many films in a day. The panel of judges sat in the front row. I was truly overwhelmed when *October* came on. It had been so long since I saw a film in which all the actors spoke Vietnamese.

Then came scenes of the countryside — a child flying a kite on the levee, an ailing father in bed with a mosquito net draped over it... I thought of my father, and tears just started flowing. As the lights came on after the end, Director Đặng Nhật Minh stood up for the Q&A session. Looking straight into my eyes, he asked:

"What did you think about this film?"

"Thank you, director. This film made me miss Việt-Nam, miss Hà-Nội."

The film ended up winning a prestigious award. Years later, every time I went back to visit Việt-Nam, Minh and I always met. One time, as we strolled around Hoàn-Kiếm Lake, Minh said to me:

"I hope we can make a film together before we die."

"Yes," I answered. "I've always wanted to make a film in Hà-Nội before I die. It's where I was born and where my parents are buried."

Family Matters

After decades of sharing a living space with my in-laws, it was the first time we lived by ourselves. Just the five of us. All three of our children were attending North Hollywood High School. Tế and I had a steady job at USCC. Occasionally I took time off to act. It was the happiest period in our family.

Thanks to everyone putting in the effort, after a few years we were able to buy our own house -- a newly built four-bedroom home in Montebello. Even though I still felt like an exile, our road seemed to be getting a bit straighter and smoother. Mỹ-Vân finished nursing school. She asked for permission to marry her long-time friend since Sài-Gòn, an engineer named Đào Đức-Sơn, eldest son of Dr. Đào Đức-Hoành.

And then, just when I was feeling hopeful, thanking God each night for a stable home, a stable job and three wonderful children, terrible news came crashing down: Tế was having an affair!

There were signs, of course. Unusual schedules. Missing family dinners. Everybody at work knew. His friends, even Lê Quỳnh, tried their best to dissuade him. No matter. He confirmed to them: "I will never abandon Chinh. But I can't leave the other one, either."

That seemed to quiet everyone. When I heard that confirmation, I immediately knew what I was in for. I knew I no longer had the patience I once did. My circumstances had changed. My in-laws were gone. I had faithfully kept and executed the promise that my Dad asked of me: *"Don't do anything to shame me before Mr. and Mrs. Độ."* I never did anything that my Dad would be ashamed of. For decades I took care of my in-laws as though they were my biological parents.

Before then, my children were too young to understand and I didn't want them to grow up without a father. But they were grown now. And so I called a family meeting with my children to come up with a group decision.

One evening, I went with my son Hùng to see Tế's youngest brother Hiếu, to explain the situation. I also talked to a niece of mine and her husband. Finally, I came to the decision which my children all supported — just let go. In truth, it was a decision to liberate not just me but our family as well.

I let my attorney Dave Garen, a friend of Tế's, take care of everything. One Sunday afternoon Dave came to our house to talk to Tế and explained to him all the legal details. Tế waved off his friend: "It doesn't matter. Whatever, just tell me where to sign. I'm busy and must leave right away."

Tế didn't show up in court. Only Dave Garen and I were there. The judge explained that according to California law the man would have to pay his ex-wife $300 a month until she remarried, and pay child support for each of the children $300 a month until they reached 21 years of age or stopped going to school. Dave told me to accept it. I shook my head and said:

"No, I don't want to take money from Tế. He wouldn't have enough to live on if he had to pay us like that." I continued, "Having to separate from my husband after 25 years is painful enough already. I never thought it would happen to me. But now I just want to give him his freedom and let him live his own life."

I can still remember the suffocating atmosphere in the courtroom that day. The judge picked up his gavel, he paused to give me a long look then brought it down: "Done!"

I started crying. Dave helped me up and guided me out of the room. I walked with him down the long corridor of the Los

Angeles courthouse like a zombie. My body shivered as though I was suffering from malaria. Tears couldn't stop falling.

So that was it. "Done!"

Although we were divorced, Tế still stayed in the house with us. The two of us just didn't stay in the same room. He could do whatever or go wherever he wanted. Indeed, many people didn't even know we were divorced. Sometimes we even received wedding invitations addressed to Mr and Mrs Nguyễn Năng Tế!

I still loved Tế, my first love. I kept wondering how he would live. Who would cook for him? Not to mention all the things that I used to do for him all those years, even the littlest thing like sewing a button, ironing his shirt, making sure he wore the right shoes etc. But after a while I decided that I had to sell this house — this home of happiness that we all worked so hard for, otherwise we'd never be able to break out of the current situation.

After making a $30,000 profit on the house, I split it three ways. One third went to Tế, one third to me, the rest to my two youngest children. Around this time Hoàng-Hùng had just graduated from college with a degree in Engineering and got married. His wife, Nguyễn Bích-Trang, is a dentist. I used half of their portion to help pay for their wedding. The other half I used to buy Cường a new car because he was starting college at California State University at Northridge. I used my portion as down payment to buy a small home in Studio City where Cường and I lived. It felt quite deserted with just the two of us around.

This was a really difficult period for me psychologically, because ever since leaving my father in 1954, I had always lived in a large household. Now I must keep myself mentally balanced so that Cường could at least get a semblance of a family atmosphere. I saved up some money to buy him a piano. Cường loved it. He had played the piano since he was five years old and later studied under Mr Nghiêm Phú-Phi, head of the Conservatory of

Music in Sài-Gòn. Ever since we left Việt-Nam, Cường switched to playing the guitar because we didn't have a piano.

Besides music, Cường also loved tennis; he was a pretty decent player on his school team. His weekend activities were mainly playing tennis and entertaining the folks in nursing homes with his guitar on Sunday mornings.

Studio City is near many film studios in Hollywood but was far from the Vietnamese communities in Orange County. Cường and I had a very peaceful time living there. I kept telling myself: "Try harder! Try harder to adjust to a new reality. Your life has turned a new page, a new chapter." But even so, it took me fully three months to get over my lost love and come to terms with fate.

Tế, on the other hand, used his portion of the money to take a trip to Paris. There he met an old friend, Brigitte Kwan whom he had known since before 1975. He later was able to bring her over to the U.S. and married her.

I still consider Tế a friend. I didn't want my children to lose their father just because he and I were separated. I'd invite him and Brigitte over whenever we had birthday parties for the children or death day celebrations for my parents-in-law. On the altar in my house there are portraits of both his parents' and mine.

Little House in Studio City

It was a small house, but a big decision. To me, choosing to live in Studio City was a deliberate decision to remain in the film industry for the rest of my life.

Though little, the house was cute and comfortable. It sat high above ground, with wooden floors and a steep roof that resembled an English bungalow. Farmdale is a low traffic street lined with tall shade trees. It was so quiet that sometimes, if you paid attention, you could hear a leaf drop on the pavement like the sweet sigh of a lover missing her rendezvous.

After moving in, I also added a touch of Việt Nam to the place and named it "My World."

Beneath the weeping willow in the front yard I placed a large stone. Next to it was an old wooden post with a sign that says "My World." In the backyard I planted bamboo, peach blossom, grapefruit, banana etc. Outside my bedroom, underneath the veranda I hung a hammock.

It was a three-bedroom, two-bath house. Tuấn Cường and I took up two rooms. The third bedroom looking out to the street was converted into my home office. The family room and kitchen looked out to the backyard. The living room had a fireplace and a little nook which served as the music room. Tuấn Cường liked to play the piano there. Next to it was a long couch where I loved to sit, looking out through a low window at the weeping willow sallying in the wind, listening to my son play.

We had many wonderful years here. Cường attended Cal State in Northridge nearby. An art and music lover, as well as a tennis buff, he chose to study filmmaking. On weekends we'd go see a movie together then hang out at one of the many cool coffee shops like Café Moustache or Café Le Figaro on Melrose. On Sundays, my daughter Mỹ Vân and her husband would drop by. They had a handsome firstborn, my first grandchild, named Stephen Dao, who was the joy of our family. We got together often, and shared many happy moments here.

Even though Studio City was far from Little Sài-Gòn where most of my friends lived, they still came to visit me often. A most frequent guest was author Mai Thảo whom I first met in Sài Gòn in the '60s and mentioned in Chapter II. "My World" hosted many gatherings of well-known Vietnamese composers, writers, painters, playwrights, poets, singers, musicians. It was here that the famed trio Thăng Long — brothers Hoài Trung, Hoài Bắc, and sister Thái Thanh — reunited and sang for the first time outside Vietnam after Thái Thanh successfully escaped. Many of us couldn't hold back our tears when they sang "Longing for Home," a song about leaving the North and living in the South written by the their brother-in-law, Phạm Duy, Vietnam's most prolific songwriter who was also present in the room.

Among the younger crowd who came to "My World," two in particular became close friends of mine — the poet Trần Dạ Từ and his wife Nhã Ca, author of the harrowing *The Mourning Headband for Huế* about the 1968 Tết massacre which won a National Book Award in South Vietnam. Their daughter Hoà Bình later became absolutely instrumental in the making of this memoir.

The old sign post "My World" became a favorite picture-taking spot for visitors. Some even made different names and signs for my place and nailed them to the post. I have hosted so many people here that I can't name them all. Three that I must mention are actresses Tippi Hedren, Ina Balin, and writer Alison Leslie Gold (author of *Anne Frank Remembered*.)

Reporters from *People Magazine,* the *Los Angeles Times,* and the *Orange County Register* have visited "My World" as well. A *New York Times* article stated that "This is a Vietnam house, far away from Vietnam." Director Patrick Perez also came here to shoot when he made the documentary *Kieu Chinh: A Journey Home* for Fox TV, which won two Emmy Awards.

The Proposal

In those days, I used to work with the United Way. We often had fundraising dinners at a private home near the Bel-Air Hotel on Sunset Boulevard. It is an enormous house with expensive furniture and artwork. The front and back yards were vast open spaces that made the whole place seem like an oasis in the middle of the city.

The owner liked to show me around and explain the various interesting facts about the house. He also introduced me to many people in his upper class circle of friends. He was a successful person, very polite and spoke little.

One time our working group met in his office in a high-rise building also on Sunset Blvd. Looking out the window, I was suddenly reminded of one of my favorite movies, *Sunset Boulevard* — directed by Billy Wilder, starring Gloria Swanson and William Holden. In his office hung a large autographed photo of actor Anthony Quinn plus many movie posters. It was then that I realized our philanthropist also was a film producer whom I hadn't known about, even though we'd been doing charity work together for some time.

It was also here that I met his daughter for the first time. She had just come back from London to visit her father. A few days after that encounter, I was very surprised to receive a handwritten letter from him. It read:

Dear Kieu Chinh,

My Dad used to tell me, if you meet a beautiful woman whom you really like, move quickly. Don't let the opportunity slip away because it's very hard to meet someone like that.

Ever since I met you, I've been thinking a lot about what my Dad said. However, I don't want you to misunderstand that I'm asking you out for a date.

I understand Eastern cultures enough to know that I must show respect to the person I like. I am writing this letter to formally ask you to marry me, not for us to be dating like boyfriend and girlfriend.

I hope you don't interpret this letter as an unwelcome advance but rather a gesture of respect toward a very decent human being.

Respectfully yours,

The marriage proposal caught me completely off guard. I had to explain to him that I had just been divorced after a 25-year marriage, that I still had not gotten over the shock and was still going through a grieving period. More importantly, I was living comfortably with my youngest son and had no intention to remarry.

He wrote me a second letter, suggesting that if I accepted his proposal then after the wedding he could arrange for my son to go study abroad, in any country of my or his choosing — like France or England, as his daughter was studying in London at the time.

He invited Cường and me to dinner at his house to meet him and his daughter. I politely declined.

Afterwards, I received a large bouquet of roses from him, but I decided not to respond. Soon after, I traveled to the Philippines to do a movie and visit the refugee camp which I mentioned earlier.

Uncle Nghị Came to Studio City

My mother's oldest brother, Docteur Van Nghi, as I've mentioned before, was a renowned physician living in France. One year, he was invited to a conference organized by UCLA to speak about acupuncture to an audience of physicians from all over the world. Even though the organization had arranged hotel accommodations for my uncle, he chose to stay at "My World" with me instead. It was the first time I had the chance to live with him in the same house. We spent many precious hours talking and sharing stories.

It was as though I got to live with my mother again, the mother I lost when I was only six years old. Every day I went to the conference with him. He delivered his lectures in French which were then translated to various languages for the different groups of participants, each of which had its own set of headphones. I was filled with pride seeing how much my uncle was revered by his peers, especially by those from Việt Nam.

Uncle Nghị was invited often to dinner by other participants, but he usually declined except for a few times the group of Vietnamese doctors asked him. Most of the times, however, he preferred to dine alone with his niece. That was when I had the chance to learn about the genealogy on my mother's side of the family.

One night, with a cup of tea by the fireplace, he told me about my mother and father. He and my Daddy Cửu were classmates at Bưởi High School. Born in 1909, he was one year older than my father and they were very close friends. One time he invited my father to his parents' home in Gia-Lâm, Gia-Quất, across the river Hà. It was there that his friend Cửu met his sister An. All members of his family, including his parents, really liked my father.

After a period of getting to know each other, it was Uncle Nghị who recommended that his sister should marry his friend.

The wedding was a grand and joyous affair. My Dad's father was very happy to have a well-mannered daughter-in-law from a well-educated family. The newlyweds were well liked and respected by their in-laws. My mother's two younger brothers really looked up to my father.

After getting his medical degree in 1935, my uncle left Việt Nam and went to China to study acupuncture. After that he moved to France. He later married a French woman; they had four children — one daughter and three sons. The family lived comfortably and owned several vacation homes around France.

His daughter, Christine Nguyễn Recours, is herself a well known French surgeon. She later co-wrote some books with her father on medicine and acupuncture as well as textbooks for medical students. Several of my uncle's books have been translated into 16 languages. He didn't forget to bring me some as gifts.

Because he left Việt Nam when he was so young, Uncle Nghị said he always had a deep yearning for the home country, especially for his younger sister — my mother. He was already in France when my mother was killed by a bomb. That's why when he saw me he became very emotional. For him, it was like seeing his own sister again after so many decades being away from home.

For years, Docteur Van Nghi was vice-chairman of the International Acupuncture Association and chairman of the European Acupuncture Association. Many prestigious French magazines featured articles about him. In particular, *Paris Match* and *Le Monde* once wrote about how during World War II he used acupuncture in place of anesthesia before operations because there was a shortage of anesthetic medications.

On one remarkable occasion, my uncle and his daughter performed a brain surgery without using any anesthesia. The operation was recorded live; it created a huge sensation in the medical world not only in France but all over the globe. Dr. Christine Nguyễn and Dr. Nguyễn Văn Nghị instantly became recognized as rare talents in their field.

Before leaving the U.S. to return to France, Uncle Nghị asked that I take him to a lawyer. At the office of attorney Ngoạn văn Đào in Los Angeles, he signed paperwork giving me the copyrights to all of his books that are published in the U.S. I'm sure this unexpected surprise decision stemmed from the love for his younger sister who died an untimely death.

The short amount of time we spent together helped us learn so much about each other. I began to understand why all the Vietnamese doctors at the conference really looked up to my uncle and always treated him with a sense of reverence which a world-renowned physician like him truly deserved.

The day before he left, Uncle Nghị asked me to make a simple dinner at "My World" in Studio City so he could invite some Vietnamese physicians he knew. After the meal, as we sat around the table having tea and exchanging laughter, my uncle turned serious and announced to those present:

"Look everyone, my niece is living alone, and I can't be here to take care of her. So I'm asking for your help. I'd like for her to have a husband. If any of you knows someone who's qualified, please help make that happen."

I was both stunned and amused by my uncle's unexpected announcement. Everyone turned to look at each other, then at me. And finally at the only two bachelor doctors at the table!

The Accident

Fate is a Cruel Thing

I pray that this never happens to any mother. Even now, looking back on it I still feel like a woman lost in a cemetery for months without knowing her way out.

It was the evening of April 18, 1984, one day before my daughter Mỹ Vân's birthday. I was awakened by the annoying ring of the telephone in the middle of the night. A strange female voice was on the other end:

"Is this Mrs. Nguyen?"

"Yes, it is."

"Your son, Cuong Nguyen, was in an accident. He's in the UCLA emergency room right now. You need to be here to sign some papers."

My heart stopped. I sat straight up and ran out to the car, not even bothering to change out of my night clothes. I was in total panic mode. One minute too late and I might not see my son again! Which way to UCLA? Where's the Emergency Room?

"Oh God! Please Lord! Hang on, Cường, Man is coming!" (Man [mahng] short for Maman for Mom in French, is what my children call me.)

I drove like a mad woman. Anyone who's driven on the twisty Laurel Canyon road along the hills of Studio City knows how dangerous it can be going full speed at night — one slight mistake and you can fly off the cliff. But it was the only way from my house to UCLA.

Once I got to UCLA. I still didn't know where the ER was. After driving around the empty campus without anyone to ask for directions, I finally found the entrance. Before I could see my son, the people at the front made me sign all kinds of paperwork, promising I would not sue them in case the operation was unsuccessful because the patient was unconscious.

My whole body shakes. Just tell me where to sign. Here? Yes. OK. I just want see my son. Here, too? OK...

I run after the nurse who's holding the stack of paper I've just signed. The door opens. Cường lies there motionless. His clothes have been burned. His legs are blackened, leg bones protruding. Blood is everywhere.

"Cường! My son, can you hear me?"

I run over to him but someone holds me back:

"You can't get close to him. Your son is badly burned. You have seen your son. Now we need to get to work. Please leave the room."

"No! I won't go anywhere. I need to be by my son."

"You won't be able to handle what we're about to do. Please leave here so we can start quickly."

"No, please," I start begging. "Let me stay. I can handle it. I have to be by my son at this time. I have to..."

I grab the side of the bed, dry eyed.

"Please let me stay. I will handle anything!"

The lead physician turns away from me and looks at his assistant. A nurse pushes forward a table full of medical implements. They immediately start working. The big light is pulled down nearer to Cường. I can now clearly see my son's face. It is black with smoke. His eyebrows and hair have been singed.

They slowly cut away his shirt and pants piece by piece; there's no way to undress him because the heat has seared everything into his flesh. My body starts shaking; I try to suppress it for fear of getting kicked out.

They cut. And cut. And cut some more. I begin to see flesh. Cường's skin has been badly charred! The hands have burned to the point you can see bones sticking out. His pant legs have turned into charcoal almost, buried into the flesh and mixed with blood. They pick out one piece at a time. Then they start cutting into the flesh itself, the burned portions, one small morsel at a time. I strain to look at my child; I see blood running from his femur bone. Tears begin to come out but I force myself to swallow them back. I try to remain absolutely still:

"Dear God! Dear Buddha! Dear Jesus! Save my son, please! Please!"

Cường's legs have no skin now, only flesh and bones. Now the doctors turn to his arms. The skin on his arms has been similarly seared. Black as an overcooked piece of steak. After the arms are complete, they move to his hands. The fingers have curled up. They slowly stretch them out one by one and start cutting out the burned parts. Blood starts oozing out. The fingers are much harder than the leg bones, so they work slowly and meticulously. They move forward no more than a centimeter at a time, and blood comes out at every touch. The assistant stands ready with a towel to absorb any running blood. I feel like it's my own skin that's being peeled, my own blood that's dripping. The room is quite cold, yet beads of sweat flow from my forehead.

My God! Flesh has been cut out of his hands. And from each finger too. I start praying to anyone I can think of. Dear Jesus, Buddha, mother, father... Please help my son get through this, please!

I grab the railings as my body begins to rattle and my knees want to give way. My eyes remain wide open so I don't miss a single second of my son's existential battle with Death. I don't know what's pushing me through, keeping me from turning away as they cut my son into pieces.

I can't remember how long the cleaning operation took. I just recall that the head physician turned around and said they had to pause after they finished drying up the blood on the remaining flesh and bones because my son had gone into a coma. They could not use anesthesia on him because in this situation it could cause the patient to never come out of coma.

Two nurses transferred Cường to another bed that had just been brought next to the operation table. They draped a white sheet over him. On the operating table was a messy pile of bloody skin and flesh. Cường was taken to another room. I asked to follow but this time they were adamant:

"Your son will be in Intensive Care. It is a sanitized room to keep your son safe from contamination since he's in a coma."

Another nurse tried to sound sympathetic:

"You should go home now. We'll call you about his conditions if needed."

"Can I sleep on the floor by his bed?" I begged even though I knew the answer.

"Absolutely not," she responded. "You cannot be here now. Visiting time is tomorrow."

"Let me stay at the hospital," I pleaded as though in a daze.

"I'll be in the waiting area." They all looked at me with pity, not knowing what to say.

There wasn't anyone in the Emergency Room that night. It was so cold and uncomfortable. Too exhausted to care if anyone might see me, I lay down on the floor and curled up into a ball. It was only then that I began to cry.

I cried and cried, letting all those pent up emotions out, opening up a floodgate of fear, frustration and loneliness. I lay on the floor all night.

It wasn't until the next morning that I called my two other children to let them know what happened. The hospital didn't let Vân and Hùng in until 9 a.m. We had to wear face masks, and each person was allowed to see Cường only for a few minutes.

Cường lay motionless. His eyes were closed. Since I couldn't touch him, I just whispered, hoping he could hear me:

"Hang on, Cường. Try hard to wake up, son. Wake up..."

That afternoon my children came back to see their brother again. They told me:

"Go home, *Man*. You need to home to get some rest. You can't stay here like this forever."

But how could I leave? How could I rest when my whole being was on fire?

By the second day, Cường was still unconscious. Doctors closely monitored his progress. I hung around the waiting area just so that every now and then they'd let me come in to look at Cường for a few minutes. Vân and Hùng brought me some fresh clothes, a sweater, a scarf, and my little phone book. I also asked them to stop by the house to add food and water for Bogie, Cường's pet shih tzu.

In the middle of the second night, I was jolted out of my exhausted sleep by a loud bang. I opened my eyes and saw a large stranger looking down at me. I was so frightened because I didn't know what was happening. It took my brain a few moments to remember that I was at a hospital — and why. The man told me he had to vacuum the floor. I tried to explain that I needed to wait here because my son was in a coma, but he didn't seem to understand. Finally, he told me to go wait in the ladies' room.

By the third day, Cường still was not moving. His face looked almost bloodless behind all the tubes and tapes and wires. I didn't know what else to do but pray. "Please Jesus, please Buddha, help my Cường live through this. However he survives is fine, as long as he's alive, dear God."

Through prayers I began to feel closer to Jesus, to Buddha. So I kept on praying. The days in the hospital felt so long, the nights felt even worse. Worrying for my son's life while fighting a lonely battle against this horrendous hurricane took its toll on my body and spirit. There were times I thought I would break down.

Sometimes I turned to my father: "Daddy, I can't take this anymore. Help me father. Please help wake Cường up. Please..."

I remember calling my long-time friend Mai Thảo. About two hours later, he showed up with another friend of ours, Đỗ Ngọc Yến, and the Buddhist monk Thích Mẫn Giác. I started to cry when I saw my good friends come in. Not allowed in the ICU, they stayed in the waiting area to be with me. Mai Thảo kept pacing nervously around the room, mumbling "Good grief... Good grief..."

Yến came back early the next morning to bring me some Vietnamese breakfast and a hot cup of Vietnamese coffee. I thanked him but could only take the coffee because I had no appetite.

I became so concerned about what might happen to Cường, especially after hearing the doctors say they'd have to operate on him because some of the tendons in his hands were burned through. They'd also have to remove the dead flesh so that it wouldn't spoil and infect the rest of the body. But they also said they wouldn't be able to do that until Cường came out of the coma. And nobody knew when that would be.

This latest news caused me to panic even more. I stayed up all night praying, simply because there was nothing else I could do.

When I came in to see Cường on the fourth day, he was still lying there motionless with his eyes closed. I looked intensely for any discernible movements on his face or body but didn't see anything. So worried and tired, I sat down on the floor next to his bed. I gently took one of his bandaged fingers, put it in my hand and kept it there for a long time. I think I might have fallen asleep. All of a sudden I heard Cường's voice, as though in a dream:

"*Man*, oh *Man*! Where are you, *Man*!?"

I jumped up and shouted: "I'm here! *Man* is right here!"

At that moment I noticed that his finger was slightly moving. So excited, I immediately pushed the alarm button. A doctor and a nurse rushed in.

Cường started to mumble, as though he was in a half dream state: "Where are you, *Man*? Where are you? How come I can't see anything?"

The doctor lifted up his eyelids and examined with a flashlight. His eyes were red as blood pudding. Just as quickly, Cường passed out again. They took him to another room but did not let me follow.

As I anxiously waited outside, my heart started pounding; I thought it could explode at any moment. Time passed very slowly, it seemed, while my prayers sped up. I called on anyone who crossed my mind: "Dear Jesus! Dear Buddha! Dear Dad! Dear Mom! Please get Cường through this... Please!"

The door suddenly opened and the doctor walked out. I ran after him. He told me Cường had come out of coma and was alert. He said that fortunately we now had time to use anesthesia on him to scrape clean the dead flesh before it became infected.

"Scrape clean the dead flesh..." the sound of that was like a dagger in my heart.

The doctor also said they'd have to transfer Cường to another hospital that specializes in burns. Where my son had been the past few days was just an emergency care facility while he was still in a coma. Long term care and recovery would have to be done in a different facility where they have the proper equipment to take of patients like Cường. He needed more intensive operations and procedures such as skin grafting, tendon reattachment, rehabilitation and so on.

The Decision

Cường was transferred to a hospital in Torrance specializing in treating burn patients. Here, again, I had to fill out a stack of paperwork. It was then that I realized Cường did not have health insurance!

After we moved to the U.S. from Toronto, Tế and I both worked and we bought insurance for the entire family. But that policy was now no longer in effect because we had been divorced, and Cường was over 21 years old and therefore no longer part of the family plan.

"What should I do? What now?" The questions kept swirling in my head until I realized that it didn't matter. The most important thing right now was to get Cường admitted. He needed to be treated immediately before infection set in. I'm not someone who's versed in insurance matters, but this was definitely not the right time to do research.

I understood simply that my job was to sign all these forms and be responsible for everything. I had a vague sense of concern about my current situation, but the more pressing issue at hand was Cường's survival — and the grueling days ahead.

The staff started with a thorough cleansing of his body. All the wounds, all the burned areas, all the loose flesh and leftover skin, were properly cleaned out. I was not allowed to stay at this hospital, but I was always there during visiting hours. That meant 8 a.m. to 5 p.m. every day. I watched Cường's progress every minute of every hour.

Every day, I followed the nurses as they pushed his bed to the operating room. It was gut-wrenching, helplessly knowing that Cường understood he was about to be "butchered" on that table. He always gave me a desperate look before the doors closed. It's impossible for me to describe those pleading, begging-for-help eyes. I could only assure him:

"Hang in there, son. *Man* will be right outside these doors waiting for you."

I kept the promise to myself to never cry in front of Cường. From where I sat I could hear his screams which always filled my heart with horror. I would run around asking the staff what was going on. They explained that they were doing skin graft that day. In my state of ignorance and confusion, I'd ask dumb questions like:

"But why don't you use anesthesia?"

"We do," they answered. "But sometimes the medication wears off and the patient can feel..." Annoyed by my questioning, one nurse said curtly:

"You must remember, this is a patient who's just come out of a four-day coma."

What she meant, as I understood it, was that doctors couldn't give Cường too much anesthesia for fear of a coma relapse from which he would never come out again. I could only hold my head in my hands and braced myself against that terrible sound. But sometimes his screams came from inside my head and heart.

Each evening, I returned to a house that was cold and empty save for Bogie, Cường's little shih tzu. Cường named him Bogie because he knew I liked Humphrey Bogart in *Casablanca* with Ingrid Bergman. When Cường first brought Bogie home, the cute puppy still had long hair covering much of his eyes and face.

Cường took Bogie with him everywhere, even when he went shopping at Beverly Center. He'd wear a trench coat with a large pocket for Bogie to sit inside, sticking his head out. People would stop him and ask to take pictures of the cute little dog.

When Bogie got bigger and could no longer fit in his coat pocket, Cường bought a backpack to lug Bogie around. They were like two inseparable hobos. Sometimes I called him "Humphrey! Humphrey!"

When I came home from the hospital, Bogie ran to the door, wagging his tail and blocking my path as though to ask "Where is Cường? Where is Cường?" I picked him up and walked to the music room and sat down on the floor next to Cường's piano:

"Listen, Bogie. Cường had an accident. He was badly burned and is in a lot of pain right now. He's in the hospital. He won't be home for a while. So it'll be just you and me here. Let's pray for him, OK?"

I sat there in silence. Bogie lay quietly in my arms. The house suddenly seemed dead, as if all the life spirit had been sucked out of it.

That night Bogie slept at my feet. I woke up in the middle of the night and gently got out of bed so as not to wake him up. I walked over to Cường's room. His bed was nicely made without a wrinkle. A guitar was laid across the pillow. I found myself talking to my son:

"Cường, are you sleeping well? It's very painful, isn't it? I know. I know how much you're hurting..."

I sat down on his bed and accidentally hit a guitar string. The sound woke Bogie up; he ran over and jumped up onto Cường's bed with me. I started to tear up again. We lay there until it was time for me to go back to the hospital.

Every morning, I would first feed Bogie, then make a big breakfast for myself so that I could last a whole day without eating. I brought with me only a hot cup of coffee and cream. Before leaving the house I always filled up Bogie's bowl with extra food and water. I spoke to him as though he were the only friend I had during this hellish time:

"I'm sorry, Bogie. I'm sorry you to have to be here by yourself all day without anybody to play with. Cường won't be here to walk you every day, either. So this will be our routine for awhile. I know you miss Cường. Me too. We both love him."

I had the feeling Bogie understood. He gave me a sad, dejected look as I closed the door.

My most critical decision at this time was to resign from my job at USCC where I had been working as a permanent employee for years. The job would have guaranteed me a pension and other benefits when I retired. I knew this was the "wrong" decision, but at that moment I had no other choice. Cường needed me every day!

I often experienced many strange emotions as I sat in Cường's room. He was wrapped from head to toe like a giant, immobile ball of cotton. One time, when I was about to doze off, I suddenly heard him call: "*Man*!" I came over. He gave me a deep, long look. His eyes were not as red as before. I so wanted to hold his hand but everything from his shoulders down was completely bandaged. Before we could say anything to each other, a nurse came in to take Cường to the operating room for more procedures. So I went back to waiting some more.

Every day we went through the same routines: First his arms got rewrapped and hung up, then the legs got rewrapped then hung up. I'd help him drink using a cup with a straw. I also spoon fed him soup. While doing these things I often thought about the active person he used to be, about his swift movement on a tennis court or his fast fingers on the piano keys. One day he said:

"*Man*, please bring me my cassette player so I can listen to music."

I could tell he was having a hard time being stuck here: "I'll bring it for you tomorrow. But you can only listen while I'm here, because when I'm not, you can't turn it off yourself."

Duck-webbed Hands

After a few days, Cường was transferred to the operating room so the doctors could examine the results of the skin graft. My heart jumped every time I heard him scream. I kept wondering: "What are they doing in there? Why is he being kept in there so long? Are there complications? ..." It was like sitting on hot coals.

After a few long hours, the doors swung wide open and Cường was pushed out. He was unconscious and motionless. His eyes were closed. I had to stop a doctor to ask. One said the skin graft results weren't great. The skin on the fingers became attached to one another, so instead of five fingers now the hand was just one big finger — a webbed hand that resembled a duck's foot.

He said that when Cường saw his own hand he let out a big scream. The operating team had to put him back on anesthesia so they could separate his fingers one by one and re-graft the skin.

I waited by my son's side for the rest of the visiting time, but he didn't wake up, so I had to leave. When I got home Bogie was so happy to see me. I put his harness on. It was the first time Bogie had gone outside since Cường's accident. On and on we walked, turning from one street to the next without any plan. I didn't want to go home. Actually, I was scared to go home. I was afraid of the silence. And the loneliness.

That night I could barely sleep, haunted by what the doctors said and the extra pain my son had to suffer. In the following days Cường became even more withdrawn, which worried me. Was he too tired? Too scared?

I picked out some more tapes of music that he liked to play or sing along to. "*Imagine*" by John Lennon. "*Bridge Over Troubled Water*" by Simon & Garfunkel, "*Green Fields*" by The Brothers Four, "*Magic Boulevard*", "*Maman*"... Songs that Bogie and I had listened to over and over at the house the night before.

I sat in a corner while Cường listened intensely with his eyes closed. After awhile I came over and saw that tears were coming out of his eyes. I understood. My son was worrying about how he would ever play piano or guitar again with his webbed hands.

One evening, after a long day at the hospital, I walked into the house with a heavy pile of letters which I'd been neglecting to take out of the mailbox. One big, thick letter immediately caught my attention. It contained the bills from UCLA. I nearly fainted: $14,200.

I started thinking about all the skin graft procedures at Torrance and wondered how much those cost. My question was eventually answered: $51,000. That brought my total liability to more than $65,000 — in 1984 dollars!

After scraping together all of my savings and the pay from my latest film project in the Philippines, I was able to come up with almost $10,000. I negotiated with the hospitals to let me make monthly payments after paying 10% up front. At the same time, I knew this situation could not go on. I was advised to end it, that I should let Cường go. After all, he was over 25 years old. As his mother, I was no longer responsible for him financially. Let the state take care of it; I should not sign any more papers.

From that day on, Cường was moved to Los Angeles County Medical Center — a public hospital. He no longer needed to be in the ICU because all the skin graft procedures had been done. But now he no longer had a private room; he was put in a bigger room which he shared with other patients with all sorts of ailments. Nonetheless, he was in the Burn Unit.

I still came to be with him every day, and Cường was always happy to see me. Knowing how hospital patients can feel stuck or abandoned if their relatives don't come to visit, I assured my son:

"Don't worry. I will be here with you every day."

Every morning, Cường was given a special "bath" by two muscular men. The bathing area is a cavernous room with about twenty above-ground rectangular pools. The pools were built in pairs; one had steamy hot water, the other one cold water with ice cubes floating on top.

Even though visitors were not allowed to watch, after much pleading the nurse let me come close enough to see them bathe my son from a corner of the room. One man picked Cường up by his arms, the other grabbed his legs and lifted him up, naked and all, and shoved his whole body down into the hot pool. He struggled and screamed in a most horrifying voice. The men were very strong. As Cường tried to wriggle from their grip, they pushed him down even more, leaving only his face above water. They kept him down for a fairly long while. Then they simultaneously lifted him up and dunked him in the ice pool.

By this time Cường had almost no strength left to resist. All he could do is scream and beg:

"*Man, Man*! Tell them to stop! Please!!!"

The two men worked like a machine — unemotional and precise. Cường couldn't take it anymore, he started cursing:

"Stop! Damn it! Stop!!!"

It was unbearable to watch. I pleaded to the men: "Isn't that enough already? I don't think my son can take it any..."

One of them cut me off: "You should be relieved, ma'am, that your son is struggling and can still feel hot or cold. If he can't, it means his nerves are dead. Then it's hopeless."

After several bouts of getting dipped in and out of extreme temperatures, Cường was taken to the medicating room. There they dried off his open wounds and applied different types of ointment and medication. It must have hurt so much because Cường was also yelling at these nurses. But they didn't seem to pay any attention to him. They worked methodically and carefully, slowly moving from one exposed area to the next. Each time they touched him,he would shriek in pain. All done, they bandaged him up and pushed him back out. He would give me a cold stare. I wasn't sure if he was angry with me or just too exhausted to complain.

It broke my heart to see my son go through that excruciating ritual every morning. But it had to be done. The doctors told me that these daily "baths" were critical in stimulating Cường's nerve endings. At the same time they helped clean out the ointment and medications applied the previous day, making it easier to put fresh medication on him.

I said to Cường: "Bear with it, son. That's the only way you can recover. It won't be much longer. Grin and bear it. Just grin and bear it."

I think he understood. After a few weeks, the bath procedure stopped. However, Cường still needed to be bandaged from head to toe. The only difference was his arms and legs were no longer hung up.

Rehabilitation

Eventually, Cường was able to sit in a wheelchair. Each morning after breakfast, a staff person would push him to the exercise room.

The chief nurse was a nice Filipino woman. She'd bring Cường a plastic bucket containing about a dozen wooden clothespins. His task was to pick each one up and clamp it to the top of the bucket. Once done, he had to unclamp the pins and return them into the bucket. He worked very slowly, struggling to get the finger muscles to obey. His facial expressions revealed a lot of frustration and pain each time he failed.

After the bucket, came the string-pulling exercise. A string was slung over a bar. Cường had to grab both ends and pull the string up and down like a see-saw.

He seemed to be making good progress when one day he suddenly said to me:

"I can't stay here anymore, *Man*. I can't get any rest. It's driving me crazy. Can you take me home?"

No matter how much I tried to persuade him, Cường adamantly demanded that he must go home. The reason, as I discovered, was that his bed was sandwiched between that of a young dude who was always playing his rap really loud and a half-crazy old woman who was always mumbling to herself, sometimes laughing or crying out loud. And so I had to ask a doctor friend to talk to the hospital staff to allow my son to be treated at home instead.

After much persuasion, they agreed. But before letting Cường go home, the hospital sent someone to my house to make sure it met all the requirements. Is it clean? Does it have air conditioning? Does it have a bathtub? etc. etc. Last but not least: It can't have any cats or dogs.

I had to take a crash course on how to take care of a burn patient: how to bathe him, how to apply medications, how to bandage his wounds and so on. On top of that, I still had to take care of all the household chores, including cooking dishes that had the proper nutrition to help speed up the healing process.

My two older children lived too far away. And they had their jobs, too, so they couldn't help much. One of my best friends, Diệu Lê, lived closer and was able to help me out more. Her three children really liked Bogie, and so when she heard about the pet requirement, Diệu Lê offered to take care of Bogie for us for a while. She said her children would love it.

I then hired some people to come and thoroughly clean all the rooms in the house, even the refrigerator. I bought fresh new groceries, with special attention to vegetables to make soup, plus many different kinds of fruits. In the car on the way home I explained to Cường that Bogie had to come live with my friend Diệu Lê. He didn't say anything. I sensed he was disappointed but knew he had to accept that as a condition for leaving the hospital.

Cường was so happy to be home. He could watch TV in his room and listen to music that he liked. It gladdened me to see him so happy. I felt like we had just turned to a new chapter in the book of our lives.

Home Nurse

From that day on I never left the house. I was at home 24/7 to take care of my son: bathing, changing bandages, applying medications, cooking, even feeding him since he couldn't hold a spoon by himself yet.

Whenever he slept or rested, I used the free time to prep food for the next meals. A lot of time was spent on cleaning and washing. I wanted to sleep on the floor next to his bed in case he needed me, but Cường refused to let me do that. So I had a bell wired up near his bed so he could alert me. My bedroom door remained open always.

One night I was awakened by a loud thud. I ran over to Cường's room and saw him lying on the floor. He needed to go to the bathroom but didn't want to wake me up. We ended up spending more time cleaning, bathing and all that not-so-fun stuff.

In spite of all the hardship, however, his being home also brought me many moments of relaxation in the spirit of love and friendship. Time seemed to go by faster; tasks weren't as stressful. I felt more comfortable, as well as more comforted.

One day Mai Thảo and Đỗ Ngọc Yến came to visit. Unlike the first time at the UCLA Emergency Room, this time they brought with them a beautiful vase of flowers with the message "Welcome Home" — and a big bowl of *phở*! My, oh my. It had been so long since I had had a such a simple pleasure as a bowl of Bolsa *phở*, with some of my dearest friends, too!

After spending months focused on nothing but my son's accident and recovery, I finally got a reminder from reality: I didn't have enough money to pay the bills. The electricity bill, in particular, was sky high because I had to run the air conditioner full blast even though we lived in temperate Southern California

My friend Diệu Lê offered to pay the mortgage for me, but I politely declined. She said in that case she could lend me the money; I declined that also. Finally, she made a tactful suggestion which I couldn't refuse:

"Khanh [her husband] has just won a major contract with the airport. With the extra income we decided to build a bigger house. We want to buy some new furniture, but we're not as good as you are with that sort of stuff. How about selling us the sindora wood dining table that you're not using for anything?"

Thus went the dining set. Then next month was the couch. The following month were my sheepskin coat and designer bags... Of course, my friend didn't really need any of those things. She just wanted to help.

As time went on, with the thoughtful and caring assistance of our friends, Cường and I slowly regained our footing. His health gradually improved and he could take care of himself once again, including bathing and feeding. Some of his friends dropped in to visit. Even his father Tế and his new wife Brigitte came. For me, these were all very good signs; Cường was on his way to a full recovery. I began to feel less anxious and more hopeful.

One evening, after dinner, I told Cường I needed to run to the store to get a few things and pick up some medication.

"Will you be OK at home by yourself," I asked. He nodded.

I came back about an hour later and didn't see my son anywhere. I saw traces of blood. Panicked, I ran into his room. He wasn't there, but there were shattered glasses and blood on the floor. I ran all over the house calling his name. My heart nearly burst open.

Grabbing a flashlight, I ran out to the backyard. Not a trace! I went around to the front of the house and began running northward, calling for Cường as I swept the flashlight around. Hysteria set in. I turned around and ran in the opposite direction. I shined light into every bush and at every tree, hoping to hear his voice. There was nothing but an eerie silence.

At the end of the street was a little bridge over a small stream that led to Ventura Avenue. In a sudden flash of light I saw a foot sticking out from under the bridge. It was Cường's. With all my strength I pulled him up.

Questions swirled as I helped him back to the house. Why did he leave? How long had he been lying there? Where did he try to go? What was his plan? Why the blood on the floor? If I'd been gone longer, or gone in a different direction, would he still be alive?

I tried to remain calm and asked him just a few basic questions, but Cường said nothing. I felt like the whole world had turned its back on me, leaving me to face an immense silence.

I led Cường to his bed:

"Lie down, son. Get some rest. I'll go boil some water."

A few minutes later I came back with a cup of tea, and fresh bandages which I'd just bought at the pharmacy. I gently wrapped up his bleeding hand. Neither one of us said a word. My heart bled, and I think his did too, as I wound the tape around his wounds.

Emptiness

Even though Cường's health was getting progressively better, he still had to take a lot of pain medication. Not only that, I still had to take him to the hospital every day for rehab.

Once his wounds started to heal, I thought about bringing Bogie back home so that the two of us could have a third "person" to talk to, or at least someone to share some affection with. Whenever I talked to Diệu Lê I always asked her about Bogie. Her answer was always positive, that the shih tzu was happy and well. But when I thanked her and asked to take Bogie back, she had to finally tell me the truth. Bogie had run away; they never could find him.

My guess is that Bogie tried to find his way home. We'll never know if he got lost, got picked up by someone or, worst of all, run over by a car. I never said a word to Cường about his dog, but Bogie would sometimes haunt me in my dreams. I had a vague foreboding that the storms of my life were not yet over, that a more sinister undercurrent was waiting to swallow me up. But I had no idea how drastically the time I spent taking care of my son had altered the course of my life.

After two years battling what must have been his darkest days, Cường finally made it back to the normal world. He went back to school. There were adjustments that needed to be made, of course, but for the most part he did fine.

I was so grateful for the blessings from the gods that helped me and my son survive this ordeal. I was so happy to see Cường regain his vitality, his joie de vivre. I especially wanted to thank all the doctors and nurses and therapists who worked so hard to give me back my son.

However, that period of time was a totally different story for me. I lived exclusively for Cường; I never spent any time on me. I completely lost myself in the caretaker's role. From the moment I woke up to the time I went to bed, every thought I had was about him. Everywhere I went, I worried about him. He even invaded my dreams, the only refuge I had left from that stressful reality.

Once he was well enough, Cường could drive himself around. Every night, after coming home from school, he would sit down at the piano and practice, playing his favorite pieces. It was also a way to exercise his finger muscles. I could once again sit by the fireplace and enjoy his music.

Soon after graduation, Cường found a job at CBS through a good friend of ours who'd been a cameraman with them for many years. Seeing that the storm was finally over, my friend Mai Thảo suggested to the composer Phạm Đình Chương that they should organize an event in my honor — "to make her happy," he said.

With the help of producer Phạm Chí Thành, "Kiều Chinh: Twenty-Five Years in Films" was expertly put together and took place in Washington, D.C. Mai Thảo insisted that Cường must play something in the show as a tribute to his mother. That seemed to really motivate him.

Cường chose, appropriately enough, the French song '*Maman.*' He practiced it day and night.

The show went really well and succeeded beyond everyone's expectations. Many friends and artists participated. Singer Ý Lan stole the show with her rendition of Đức Huy's "*And the Heart Is Happy Again*." It was also at this show that she and Cường met and fell in love. Not long after, Cường asked for my permission to move in with Ý Lan.

And so it was. One by one my three little birds had left the nest. I was happy for them, of course, but at the same time inside me there was an indescribable feeling of unease. All of a sudden I no longer had any responsibilities toward my children. I was no longer needed by anybody. I sensed very clearly that it wouldn't have made any difference if I went on — that is, if I lived or died.

The feeling of emptiness grew slowly by the day. It gradually spread through my veins and rose ever higher in my mind. It threw me into a vacuum of space where my spirit was drowned in a sea of meaninglessness. It sucked me into its heart and floated me along on an endless parade of dark, ominous clouds. I wandered aimlessly between the living and the nether world beyond.

Suicide

Since Cường left to live with Ý Lan, the house suddenly became empty. I had no one to talk to but my own shadow. I began to fear loneliness. I began to dread dinner alone at night; in fact, I changed my schedule to eat earlier when there was still daylight. I was afraid of sunset and the silence that came down with it which made me want to cry. I was frightened by darkness, and by sleepless nights staring at the black sky. Where was everything? Why was I surrounded by nothing but emptiness?

I was scared by the sound of the rain hitting my bedroom window, by the howling winds, and even by the pounding of my own heart. Storm water gushing down the roof made me think I was being buried inside a phantasmagoric tomb.

Some nights I would hear the front door open followed by the sound of Cường's footsteps on the wooden floor. But when I looked, there was nobody there. I began falling into a void with nothing to hold onto. I felt no one needed me.

Even my youngest child, the one whom I loved and cared for the most, didn't need me anymore. He had recovered his life and discovered his raison d'être. Did that not mean I had fulfilled my role as a mother? In fact, all three of my children were now fully grown. I could only pray that the gods kept an eye over them as they went through life. Even my ex-husband had started a new life with another woman.

I asked myself what I would do once I had performed all my duties. I had walked miles and miles on the roughest roads; many times I had fallen and had to pick myself back up again because I knew I was living not just for myself. But now that reason didn't exist any longer. It seemed that at the most fundamental level I had always lived not for me but for others.

I started to lose sleep. I began to have splitting headaches that were excruciating. My head felt like it would explode. The pain was so fierce that I would scream and bang my head against the wall. Alarmed neighbors called 911.

I remember there were two men who rushed into my house with a thick jacket that had really long sleeves. They put my arms through them then tied me up and took me to the hospital. They gave me morphine to help me sleep because I was screaming so much from pain.

When I woke up, I saw blurred shadows of several people watching me in silence. My eyes felt heavy with a piercing pain, causing me to scream again. My oldest son Hùng held my hand. My friend Phương Lan and her husband Dr. Nguyễn Gia Quýnh were also there. Hùng asked the attending nurse to give me more morphine but Dr. Quýnh advised against it, saying that I should not sleep too much while in this condition. But what could they do to help me through this terrible pain? While the physicians consulted with each other, Phương Lan took my hand in hers and gave me a gentle massage.

I normally took Valium to help me sleep because Tylenol PM had lost its effect. But since the hospital didn't have any Valium, they gave me Excedrin to alleviate what they called migraine headaches. In the beginning, I would take one Excedrin pill every night, then it was increased to two. However, the migraine headaches kept getting worse, so they went back to giving me morphine again. As I started to realize that my life had become dependent on drugs, I became even more dejected. Depression set in.

After a few days I was released as my condition stabilized. It was Christmas season. Farmdale was one of the prettiest neighborhoods in Studio City. All the homes around my house had put up their decorations. Christmas music floated in the air. I could hear my favorite song "*Silent Night*" coming from afar. It made me even more depressed. I walked around the empty house like a lost soul. Unlike previous years, there was no Christmas tree, no wrapped presents, no signs of a warm family gathering about to take place anywhere.

I stood by the window and stared for a long time at the neighbors' yards before turning around. What should I do? What should I say? With whom, and to whom? All was silent.

Sad and tired, I just wanted to lie down. But even while lying down I still could not fall asleep. Images of Dad, of my brother and sister kept appearing every time I closed my eyes. I wanted so badly to relive the happy days, to reunite with the people I loved. I missed my Hà-Nội. I wondered what Hà-Nội was like now. In my mind, it was a totally different world on the other side of the earth where my loved ones were either dead or hopelessly suffering. I wanted to go back, to call "Oh, Daddy!" I wanted to go home.

I can't remember how many nights and days I spent in that despondent state. I just knew that I did not want to let my children know. I didn't want them to worry. I wanted them to enjoy their families, their happiness. At the same time, I knew I had to get out of this situation as soon as possible. I didn't want to think about anything anymore. I didn't want to keep wandering aimlessly down this path with no purpose, day in and day out.

One night, while tossing and turning in bed I suddenly had the urge to have a long deep sleep. In a moment of delirious lunacy, I decided to take all the sleeping pills in the bottle. I don't remember what the drug's name was, but there must have been at least a dozen pills or more. With a full glass of water, I slowly popped them one by one, until the whole bottle was empty.

I lay down, and very soon my entire body felt like it was paralyzed while my mind immediately came alive. I thought about all the things I still needed to tell my children, and all the unfinished businesses I needed done. It occurred to me that I hadn't said goodbye to anyone! I thought I should call Hùng. I needed to hear his voice. I had to say at least something to him! Oh, my children, I need to hear your voices!

I tried to reach for the phone by the bedside, but I couldn't lift my arm. I struggled and struggled, but it was no use. I bent my knees and pushed my legs against the bed so that I could turn my body to one side. That helped put me closer to the phone. But now I couldn't remember Hùng's number! For some reason I couldn't remember any of my children's phone numbers even though I'd always known them by heart!

By the time I could reach the phone, my hand could no longer hold onto it. The phone slipped from my hand and just hung there. My mind, however, was very clear. I tried to talk into the mouthpiece, but my throat was too dry to make any sound. I mumbled: "Oh God, please let me speak to my children so I can say a few last words... I'm so sorry, children. I'll be gone soon. Love and care for one another. Vân and Hùng, take care of Cường for me... You know how much I loved you. All I wanted was for you all to have a healthy and happy life... Be decent. Be good, children. May our ancestors protect you. I love you... I kiss you..."

I wanted to hang on, to keep my eyes open. But it was too late; I drifted into unconsciousness. I felt like I was flying with the wind.

Just when I'm about to lose all consciousness floating toward another world, I suddenly feel a sharp pain in my left thumb. Someone is pinching me, it feels like a needle piercing through my heart. I vaguely hear Cường's voice coming from somewhere: "*Man*, wake up! Wake up, *Man*!"

His voice sounds like it's coming from the other world, calling me back. As Cường keeps shaking me, I hear a stranger's voice, a man: "She feels the pain."

Whose voice is that? I want to open my eyes to look but can't. I can't move a muscle. It's like my body belongs to someone else. I feel lifted off the bed. I hear Cường say: "She's cold!" Then I hear the ambulance sirens as I drift off again.

Somebody is lifting up my head and pushing it back. They open up my mouth. I feel a sharp pain inside my mouth. They're putting something down my throat. I reflexively stretch my torso out to receive this alien but painful object. They keep pushing it farther and farther down into my body. The pain makes me want to vomit.

What are they doing to me? I want to see so badly, but I can't open my eyes. Suddenly fluids start pouring out from my mouth, going down my neck then my chest. Finally, urine and feces come out from below my belly.

There are people talking all around me, but I can't make out what they say. Then all of a sudden, my eyes are opened. Cường is looking intensely at me. I'm in a hospital, sitting up in a big couch. There are two people in white coats. Are they doctors or nurses? One of them holds my head against the back of the couch, the other takes a big jar of liquid and pours it into a funnel that's connected to a tube that's been shoved down my throat. The tube is in quite deep, it hurts so much that tears involuntarily roll out. All the while Cường is holding my hand, encouraging me and praying for me.

I begin to recognize my surroundings — the people and the sounds. Someone's shouting something. The man in the white coat hands Cường the jar of liquid and runs over to a gurney that has just been pushed into the room. After Cường finishes pouring the rest of the jar into the funnel, the man comes over and slowly pulls out the plastic tube. Putrid smelling fluids spill out all over my clothes. I close my eyes and drift off again...

When I came to, I saw that I was in a room with white curtains all around. Hùng sat at the end of the bed, watching me. I had no idea how long he'd been there or how long I'd been out. When he saw me open my eyes, he jumped up and gave me a hug. Neither one of us said anything. Tears flowed as a deep sense of regret came over me. I had made my children so worried.

Hùng held my hand in his:

"We need you, *Man*. We love you!"

I squeezed his hand to acknowledge that I understood. I felt remorseful for having acted so selfishly. I only thought about running away from my own misery like a coward, without any consideration for others. My action frightened the children. I was irresponsible. I looked at Hùng, struggling to speak because my throat was so sore:

"I'm so... sorry... son."

The curtain was pulled aside, a young doctor and a nurse walked in. They said they needed to work. I squeezed Hùng's hand again:

"I'll be OK... Don't worry... Go back to work."

Hùng bent down and kissed me before he walked out. The nurse placed a glass of water with a straw on the table next to me then left. The young psychiatrist, notepad in hand, pulled up a chair and started his work. With a cold and detached tone, he asked:

"Your name is Kieu Chinh, 46 years old?

I nodded.

"Why did you want to commit suicide?"

I looked at the young doctor without saying anything. He continued, like a machine:

"I need a reason to put in the report."

The soundless voice inside my head spoke up: "*Reason? Why? My life? Where did I come from? I'm an exile! How could you understand?*"

Not hearing anything from me, the doctor continued, this time more like a command:

"In America, you have no right to kill yourself. That's against the law!"

The law?! Really... I looked straight into the young man's eyes: "I have nothing to report."

The doctor pushed his chair and stood up:

"Then you should know, ma'am, if you don't say anything then they can put you in a mental health hospital. It's up to you!"

I looked up at the ceiling. It was all white. The curtain was pulled closed again.

Tippi came to visit. She brought a bouquet of yellow roses and a copy of the *Hollywood Reporter*:

"Chinh, nothing's more important than your own life!"

We hugged. She continued:

"You don't belong in here. It's beautiful out there."

I don't know if Tippi had said anything to anyone, but the next day the doctor who came to see me wasn't that same young man but a woman older than me, beautiful and polite. She sat down on the edge of my bed, exuding the air of a caring older sister. She brushed aside the loose hair on my forehead with her hand then introduced herself:

"You're beautiful. I love you in M.A.S.H., I love M.A.S.H. Alan Alda is terrific, isn't he?"

I smiled at her last statement. She spoke in an easy-going manner, with a friendly demeanor that made me feel like we'd been friends forever. She came back again the next day and took me to her office, which wasn't very far from the hospital. It sat on the top floor of a four-story building. I was taken by surprise as I walked in. It was like entering a forest. All the walls, and even the ceiling, were painted with trees and plants and flowers of different kinds. The window looked out to tall pine trees. Furniture was sparse at best.

She pointed to a long couch and asked me to lie down to rest. Then she turned on some soft music which sounded like it was coming from far away. She pulled her chair next to the couch and asked me if she could record our conversation, that way she wouldn't have to bother with taking notes. She started off by talking about herself first:

"When I was young I dreamed of becoming a movie star. But I'm not as lucky as you who get to live the life of an artist. I was raped and then went crazy. After many months living like a mad person, not knowing what to do and experiencing too many failures, I decided to change myself and my life. I went back to school and got a degree in psychiatry. From that day on, I merged my life with the lives of others. Today I have the chance to merge it with yours. So share it with me."

I looked out the window. Pine trees swayed in the wind. The music transported me to the past...

The next day, she came to pick me up at my house. We had breakfast at a small café. Then she took us to the ocean. We strolled on the beach, listening to the waves.

"Our lives," she explained, "are like these tiny grains of sand. The waves wash over us then go away... then come back again." Before taking me home, she said: "Live. Breathe while you still can. Find meaning when you can still feel the wind."

I'm so thankful to all the people who do their everyday jobs with all their hearts and all their conscience. It wasn't until much later that I learned that on the night I attempted suicide, Cường got in a fight with his girlfriend and decided to come home. He was the one who saw me unconscious, who called the ambulance and saved my life.

One night, as I sat by the fireplace with a glass of wine, I came to the realization that from now on there would be only me in this house. I had no choice but to accept that.

I decided that I'd turn the page and write a new chapter of my life. I decided to rejoin the battle.

Return to Southeast Asia

The Children of Anlac

On January 24, 1980, I flew to the Philippines with the film crew of *The Children of Anlac*. This was the first time I left the U.S. to go back to Southeast Asia. Before reaching the Philippines, the pilot announced over the telecom that the plane was flying above Sài-Gòn. I tried to look down but saw nothing but clouds. My homeland was right down there, hidden behind a curtain, yet I had no way to visit it.

I had many fond memories of the capital city Manila. It was here that I was honored and celebrated in 1968 after starring alongside Leopoldo Salsedo in *Destination Vietnam*. Because it was the first movie made in the Philippines by Paramount Pictures, the actors were given an elaborate reception. As soon as the filming was finished in Việt-Nam, Tế and I flew to Manila to attend a press conference with Director Rolf Bayer. And when the film opened in theaters, I was invited to the Philippines again, this time as an honored guest of the Department of Defense.

I'll never forget that military parade, replete with helicopters overhead dropping leaflets like confetti. Leopoldo and I stood in a topless army Jeep with mounted machine guns on the way from the airport into town. Thousands lined the streets of Manila to cheer us. Now, not even twelve years later, I was returning to Manila as an exiled artist. We arrived quietly and in total obscurity.

Children of Anlac is a story by American actress Ina Balin about her experience at an orphanage named An-Lạc in Việt-Nam during the war. Balin came there to adopt three children. My job was to play a modest role in the film and serve as technical adviser. It was an emotional experience for me as we recreated scenes from before 1975 with the orphans. The main actors included Ina Balin, Shirley Jones and Beulha Quo.

The following are some excerpts from my diary during my first return trip to Manila since April 1975.

Les Miserables of José Fabella

January 28, 1980

Before returning to Manila I was told there were thousands of Vietnamese living in a camp called José Fabella. So I made a mental note to set aside a day to visit my compatriots at this camp. After four straight days of working, I finally had a break on the fifth and decided to spend that whole Thursday at José Fabella.

When I got there I quickly realized it wasn't so much a camp as a slum on the outskirts of the city. At the time of my visit, there were just over one thousand Vietnamese living there, the majority of whom were women. These people didn't receive any government assistance because they didn't come as refugees.

During the war, the Philippines was one of the countries that sent service members to fight and work in Vietnam. These were women who either married Filipino soldiers or escaped with Filipino nationals when Sài-Gòn fell in 1975. Once in the Philippines, many of them were later abandoned for a variety of reasons: family situation, financial hardship, personal feelings and so on.

Without money, work, a place to live or proper papers, these women were not allowed to stay in the city but were moved to José Fabella. To support themselves and their children, or in some cases also their elderly parents whom they'd brought with them, the women had to take on any work available, including the oldest profession of all.

I fell speechless at the decrepit scene that greeted me. Tattered shacks propped up under the relentless tropical sun. Ragged children crawled on dirt floors while haggard old men and women sat watching, soulless and motionless.

A young mother rushed over to me with a baby in her arms: "Please help me, ma'am. I don't have enough money to buy milk..."

An old woman clasped her hands in a praying motion: "Please miss, I can't hold out much longer. I am sick and need money for medicine. Can you help me..."

I stuffed a $20 bill in her hand. She started kowtowing before me. I couldn't hold back the tears as I tried to get her up. Had I known sooner, I would have brought more than the $100 and a few pesos I had on me. But even if I had more cash, no amount would have been enough.

January 29, 1980

The next evening, after a long day on the set, I immediately left at 5:30 p.m. and rushed back to José Fabella because I heard there was a murder the night before: a sixteen-year-old Vietnamese boy was shot dead by a Filipino man.

I visited the victim's family and listened to their sad story — one among too many sad stories in a diaspora community dispersed all over the world because of war. They told me that the night before two Filipino men came into the camp to buy sex and then refused to pay. The poor woman's son chased after the men with a baton, demanding money. The two men ran away but returned later with a gun and shot the boy dead.

I held the shaken mother in my arms as we both cried. I knew I didn't have much to offer by way of help. And that realization hurt me even more. I didn't tell them this so I don't think they knew, but a working actor like me, beyond our regular salary, was given only $75 per diem, enough for three meals a day: $15 for breakfast, $25 for lunch, $35 for dinner. I'd eat breakfast at the hotel to save $15; I even stashed away pieces of pastry to eat later. On the set, I ate as much as I could of the free lunch provided by the contractor, always grabbing an extra banana or a piece of bread to bring back to the hotel for dinner. I then used the money I'd saved up to give to the old people at José Fabella or to buy presents for the kids when I visited them on weekends.

As technical adviser for *Children of Anlac*, I suggested to Producer Jay Benson that we should use real Vietnamese in the minor roles and as extras. I also told Jay about José Fabella and proposed that we hire some of those people as helpers. Jay happily agreed.

I contacted General Tobias, whom I'd known twelve years earlier when we filmed *Destination Vietnam*. He was in charge of the refugee program and also happened to be a close confidant of the first lady, Imelda Marcos. He helped me secure the necessary work permits.

One day. Jay and I went to José Fabella to select the people we needed. Once that was done, each day we sent a bus to pick them up every morning and return them to camp at night. Those hired were so happy, not only because they got paid but also because they could eat for free!

Among those chosen from José Fabella was a 12-year-old girl named Lài. She always followed me around while I was on the set. Lài was very intelligent and likable; she also worked hard and fast. We always sat next to each other on the set and she became my little friend.

When we had only two weeks left, Lài asked me to adopt her so she could go to the U.S. and study. I tried to explain to her that the adoption process was very difficult, especially for someone like me who wasn't even a U.S. citizen.

The day before I said goodbye to my young friend, I knew it would be nearly impossible for us to have a meal together again. Lài was somber. I was heartbroken. I hope she found a way to get an education and start a new life that I believe she deserves, one that's better than *Les Miserables* of José Fabella.

Bataan, Island of Boat People

Sunday, February 24, 1980

I was invited to go with the First Lady of the Philippines, Imelda Marcos, to visit Bataan, an island that housed a large

Vietnamese refugee camp. At the time there were roughly 7,000 people on Bataan, located about 70 miles from Manila.

General Tobias, who worked in the Presidential Palace, organized the trip and asked me to come along. He said the people in the camp had already been told I'd be coming with Mrs. Marcos. The General also told me that the number of boat people had been on the rise and the refugees were facing many problems. Mrs. Marcos wanted to go there in person to see how she could help.

We flew in Mrs. Marcos' private helicopter and got got there around 3 p.m. The sun was red hot. From afar, the island looked like a tiny boat that was on fire in the middle of the ocean, flashing brightly lit sparks. But once we got closer, I realized that the flashes were thousands of corrugated metal roofs, tents and other temporary shelters.

The chopper touched down in the middle of the camp, kicking up a terrific storm of red dust. Hundreds of people immediately swarmed the landing zone. Some people recognized my face and started calling my name. We were instantly surrounded. Mrs. Marcos' guards had to start blocking people off. I stepped away from the First Lady in order to get closer to my people. Some grabbed my hands, others cried tears of joy, asking me all kinds of questions. Many asked me to tell Mrs. Marcos that they needed this and that. Some handed me letters and asked if I could mail them to their relatives for them. The same scene repeated at each of the camps on the island. The crowd following us kept getting larger and larger.

We walked past a tent where a woman inside was calling out to me and furiously waving her hand. Mrs. Marcos stopped and asked her what she needed. The woman sat still even though everyone had earlier been instructed to stand and greet the First Lady. Mrs. Marcos' assistant and a reporter asked me to tell her to stand up.

After I translated the message, she stood up slowly and tried to explain while looking very embarrassed: "Ma'am, I'm having my period. But we don't have any pads so I was afraid to..." As she spoke, a swarm of flies flew up and then settled back down on the piece of newspaper the woman was squatting on.

By the time we finished distributing the clothes and packages to the island residents it was nearly sundown. On my walk back to the helicopter, I saw a scraggly man standing alone, looking like he was lost. As I approached to ask how he was, he gave me a blank stare then suddenly hugged me, crying:

"Forgive me, darling. Please forgive me..."

Someone came and gently extricated the man from me. Another person explained:

"Please excuse him. He's not well. Everybody here knows. He was a South Vietnamese soldier. His young wife was pregnant and was afraid to make the escape trip. He begged her to come with him. Their boat was intercepted by pirates in Thailand, his wife was raped and left for dead. He usually doesn't say much, but every now and then he'd go crazy, especially when he sees a woman. He thinks they're his wife and tries to apologize."

I watched in anguish as the man limped slowly toward the sunset.

After our three-hour visit, representatives from each camp gave me a list of requests, in Vietnamese, to give to the First Lady. I also had a sack full of letters that I'd promised to buy stamps for and mail off. It was quite heavy.

We lifted off just as the sun was setting. As I looked down through the vortex of red dust, I could see people running after our helicopter waving goodbye. Their figures became smaller and smaller.

My heart sank when I realized I was flying toward land while my people were still stuck on Bataan like prisoners banished to some deserted island. Even though the sack of letters they entrusted me with was heavy, it was nowhere near as heavy as what was inside my head and my heart. The things I just heard. Images I just saw. Despite the deafening noise from the rotor blades, I still could hear the pleadings from the boat people and the sobs from that poor man. I saw my teardrops hit the bag of letters I was holding.

As promised to Mrs. Marcos and to the people on Bataan, I made a detailed list of essential items that were needed. Even though the list was already quite long, I didn't forget to include tampons for women.

Back to The Fatherland

Going Home

Here it is, at last! I'm setting foot on home soil!

The air was hot and steamy like a sauna. Yet I couldn't have felt happier walking down the steps of the airplane and into that familiar heat.

The moment I stepped into Nội Bài airport — in Hà-Nội where I had left 41 years before, I could spot my brother right away among the crowd of waiting people. At the same time, I had the feeling that I was seeing my father as well since my brother resembled Dad so much. Every cell in my body seemed to explode at what my eyes saw, something I'd thought only existed in my dreams.

My brother was much older, of course. His hair was graying and he looked gaunt. Though lines of hardship were etched on his face, I could tell he still was my brother Lân.

He was wearing a nice, white shirt, and holding a bouquet of red roses. He ran toward me and we hugged. His body shook as though the emotions were too overwhelming. He lifted me off the ground and kissed me. We clung to each other for a long time, afraid to let go lest we'd be separated again.

"Oh my God," I whispered in his ear. "It's really you, brother Lân!"

"Chinh, oh Chinh!" His voice choking, "I've been waiting for you for so long."

I didn't know if I was laughing or crying, I only knew that my brother refused to let go of my hand. I was so happy to see that, despite years of suffering, his hands were still strong, just like the ones that led me through the happy streets of my childhood once upon a time.

His wife, Lan, and their daughter Loan, also came. On the way back from the airport neither one of them said a word, out of respect for the overwhelming emotions my brother and I were experiencing. We talked non-stop. Story after story poured out from the unfathomable well of our decades-long separation. My brother, like me, had been desperately waiting for this day. And it had finally arrived.

As soon as I'd made the decision to return, I told my brother about it right away. I told him which places I wanted to visit and whom I wanted to see. "Don't worry about a thing," he assured me before he left my hotel that evening. "Everything has been arranged exactly as you requested. I will be here at 8 a.m. tomorrow and we'll go to Sơn-Tây to visit Dad's grave."

I was wakened in the middle of the night by the rain. I looked at the clock: only 3 a.m. The pattering on the window panes was unmistakable. That's it! Hà-Nội rain! It's not similar to the rain in any other place I've been to; it sounded strangely familiar.

Looking down from my window, I could see the street lamps in front of the Sofitel dimly reflected by rainwater. I wanted to pinch myself: Am I really in Hà-Nội? Am I dreaming? No, I'm wide awake!

Then a memory returned. It was a rainy night like this. Dad walked me under his umbrella to see *Les Plus Belle Années De Notre Vie (The Best Years of Our Lives)* at the Philharmonic Theater on the other side of Hoàn-Kiếm Lake.

Another image also came back: the house on 10 Lê Trực, shaded by the ylang tree and scented by its beautiful fragrance. I wondered what had happened to all those places.

The stream of memories steadily flowed like a silent movie. It took me back to my childhood days at Kim-Mã Estate and then rolled forward all the way to the day brother Lân left to join the resistance, when he left Father and me behind in that empty house, anxiously awaiting our fateful voyage.

The Cemetery

My niece Loan and her husband Truyền had prepared everything we needed for our cemetery visit — incense, flowers, joss sticks, fruits. Yên-Kỳ cemetery lies in a mountainous region in Sơn-Tây, about 60km northwest of Hà-Nội. My father, mother and youngest brother were all buried here. On the way there I felt so anxious. After all, I was about to see my father, or at least his grave, very soon. Even though it was just his grave site, I had never seen it before.

The cemetery was quite large. Rows and rows of graves lined up all the way to the horizon. My first impression was that the place looked unkempt and neglected. Tall, dried grasses grew everywhere. Many tombstones were leaning or falling over. I didn't see any spent joss sticks. I thought to myself, maybe their relatives were dispersed, or perhaps were themselves dead and gone. It reminded me of a supernatural belief that the living and the dead are connected by a sacred link. But at this moment, standing before this depressing looking cemetery, I thought differently. I saw that the severance between the two worlds had reached its ultimate conclusion. There was no sacred link. Nothing to be remembered. Just pain. Searing pain. Like dying before living!

My father's grave had just been rebuilt. My brother explained: "We were very poor when Dad died. His grave was just a dirt mound with a temporary tombstone." Apparently my brother fixed it up just two weeks before my return. He didn't want me to see it in such a sad state.

I hastened over and put both hands on the tombstone. It was like I saw Dad in front of me and I was holding him. "Daddy, it's me. It's Chinh." I knelt down and talked through the tears, "I have come back, Daddy." I apologized to Dad for not being at his side when he most needed me.

My brother placed a hand on my shoulder: "We both were at fault, Chinh. But my fault was much greater than yours."

I don't know how long I stood there in utter silence. Images from the past gushed out like an angry waterfall, flooding my mind. My heart hurt, I felt like something was constricting its blood flow, causing it to beat out of rhythm. Agony. Torment. Angst. A paroxysm of indescribable feelings.

The time eventually came to leave. My brother and I knelt beside Dad's grave. I kissed it and whispered: "Farewell, Daddy. I love you."

On our way back, my brother made sure we drove by Hoả Lò prison. He said: "Dad spent two years here, Chinh." Then he continued, "After that they transferred him to a different place."

I stared at it — the infamous "Hà-Nội Hilton" where many American prisoners were held, most notably John McCain and Pete Peterson. (McCain later went into politics and became a senator, while Peterson became the first U.S. Ambassador to Vietnam after the two former enemies normalized relations in 1995; I'm honored to have met them both.)

Growing up, I never heard or knew anything about this prison. What I saw before me now was a high stone wall with barbed wires at the top. At each corner was a tower. The gate looked gloomy, morbid and cold. I was told the prison that once held my father was being destroyed to build a five-star hotel, save for a few cells preserved for tourists.

"Can we go in to see it?" I tugged on my brother's shirtsleeve. "I want to see where Dad was held."

"No," he shook his head. "They've kept a few cells, but how can we know which cell Dad was in? Besides, they won't let us go in. I'm taking you now to see our old house."

As we drove off, the ear-shattering noise of hammers and construction machines continued to pound inside my head.

Our Old House

"There it is," my brother exclaims. "Do you recognize it?"

It is late afternoon. We're standing on the side of a street full of shops and stalls. An old woman is selling crab noodle soup nearby.

"Look closely," says my brother. So I look, but still couldn't see anything familiar until he points to a corner behind the little shops: "See the iron gate?" Oh my God! Yes, the iron gate, where we said goodbye 41 years ago!

My eyes burned. The gate was still there, albeit very misshapen and rusted, but at least it had survived. It was there, but it was not what it once was. The front of the two-story villa had been transformed into a row of seven or eight little shops, selling everything from sandals to birdcages.

How could I ever forget this place; it was our home for many years.

"After you left, Chinh," my brother continued in a monotone voice, "our house was confiscated. They let a dozen families come live in it." The way he said it made it sound like this was just a trivial piece of data that had absolutely no emotional value, a common turn of fortune that everybody had to accept without complaining.

We walked past the gate and entered the courtyard. I suddenly stopped. Here was where we put the ping-pong table. I could still hear the click-clacking sounds, the conversations, the laughter. Youthful faces reappeared — "Tall" Hiệp, "Dark" Trường, Khuê, Tế... my brother's ping-pong buddies.

We asked the owner for permission to go up the stairs to the second floor. The owner was actually a young girl whose parents were not home. She gave the two strangers a confused look then nodded her head.

The creaky old stairs led me back to a past that appeared to have been totally lost. The once spacious living room was now cluttered with beds and things. I felt like I'd just stepped inside an abandoned house where everything had dissolved into a murky twilight zone. There was no trace of my childhood anywhere. The moldy and run-down walls had erased everything except the evidence of poverty and decay that those who came after us had left behind.

Standing in our old room, I could feel memories rush through like waves crashing on the shore of my tender soul. They reappeared before me. The person who'd left here four decades ago and vanished without a trace was standing here now.

Does the shadow on the wall recognize me? "Yes, I do," answers the shadow. "We are one, aren't we?"

That's right, memories don't get wiped clean. They just go to hide in a corner of your heart — a safe and secure bunker.

I can't recall how long I stood there letting my mind drift back into the past, but in the end I had to leave. I had to leave this place again because it never really belonged to me in the first place, only the memory of it perhaps.

The young girl silently came and stood behind me. I turned around and asked where she slept. To my surprise, she pointed to the old spot where I used to lie in bed looking up through the large window at the ylang tree as it reached toward the sky, where I used to let my imagination fly off to the dreamland of youth.

It was through that old window with peeling paint that I lived my happiest days, with mornings full of birdsong up in the canopy, calling me to join them outside. They were begging me to come out and bathe in the sunrise, when the scent of ylang was still lingering in the air after the dew had evaporated. And I'd be led to believe that the ylang's fragrance would not go away until after I'd had the chance to fill my lungs with its delightful smell.

I was too young then to understand, of course, that dreams and reality were parallel paths that rarely come together. And in countries constantly at war like mine, those paths were not only rough but full of calamity and death as well.

Before I left the room of my childhood, I looked at the little girl as if I was looking at the shadow of my youth. I secretly wished that her dreams would eventually come true.

Dad's Best Friend

Today, I went to see an old friend of my father's — Mr. Ngọc Giao, who also was my godfather when I was a young girl. Before the country was divided, Mr. Ngọc Giao was a prominent author whose books were bestsellers at the time. He and many other poets and artists used to hang out at our house in Hà-Nội. My father was closest to Mr. Ngọc Giao, who after the communist takeover was not allowed to publish anything anymore.

At the time of my visit, uncle Giao was living in a two-story house hidden away in a small alley. His oldest son greeted me at the door. When we entered the living room, he turned around and said: "My father put on his best clothes and has been pacing around all morning waiting for you."

Mr. Ngọc Giao, 86 years old, appeared at the top of the stairs in a suit and tie with long, silver hair. He opened wide his arms, took me in and cried.

"I have waited years to see you, Chinh," he said as he gave me a good look over. "Take a look at this," he pulled from his pocket an old photo. It was a picture of me at 14 years old. On the back was my handwriting: "To uncle Ngọc Giao, Dad's best friend."

After a few minutes of greetings, he led me upstairs to his private room and told me to sit down on the wooden bed next to the window.

"That's where your father used to sleep," he told me. "When your father first got out of prison he just wandered around, hungry and poor. One stormy night he came here secretly and asked for some food."

He pointed to the bed: "Your Dad slept on that side, I slept on this side."

I sat down on the bed and put both hands on the cool slab of wood. So this was where my father once lay. A sharp pain pierced through my heart, I couldn't stop crying. Teardrops fell onto the wood where my father slept.

Uncle Giao placed his hand on mine in silence. I looked up:

"Do you know why Dad was in prison?"

With a real sadness in his voice, he began:

"In those days life was very hard. It was terrible. Many people didn't have jobs. Your Dad was one of those. Every now and then someone might hire him to work on their farm, but most of the time he had to work at public construction sites. One time, after a long day of labor, while he and a few others were eating at a roadside stall, your Dad saw several gigantic banners across the street that read '*Nothing is more precious than Independence, Freedom and Happiness,*' and '*All citizens unite to build a better life.*' Your Dad said to his friends at the table: '*What freedom? What happiness? People are suffering and starving. Where in the bloody hell is this happiness?*' The owner overheard it and reported your Dad to the security police. They came and took him away for a few years, nobody knew where to."

Uncle Giao also said that after my Dad was released he only had a little nook under the staircase of a house on Lê Trực to sleep overnight. "Your father didn't have much to eat because in those days only regular citizens were given ration cards. Since he was an ex-convict, he couldn't have one. It was a gruesome time, you wouldn't be able to imagine it," said the writer. "My wife had to sell sweet rice to support the family. I told your father that every morning I'd save him a small bag of sweet rice and leave it in the alley behind the house. And so every day your father walked a few kilometers here to secretly take the rice near the trash can and quickly got away before he could be seen by our neighbors, which would cause trouble for us."

I was speechless. My godfather tried to assuage me: "The most important thing you need to know, Chinh, is that your father was a decent and honorable man. I am very proud to have been his best friend."

He took my hand and continued: "After a while your father

stopped coming to get the rice… I'm so sorry that I couldn't be with my friend when he died in 1978."

"Your father always told me that he loved his youngest daughter very much. He said he understood your soul since you were a baby, and he predicted that you would be an artist because since you were a child you had shown that you loved beauty and the arts. The last time I saw your father, he said he hoped he could live to see you return, but he was afraid he would not be able to survive the illnesses that were ravaging his body. He requested that if I saw you, to tell you everything. *'Tell her that I tried to live a clean and upright life because I thought of her. Tell her to write down everything that happened to our family, to our generation.'*"

"I have waited many years for you," my godfather continued. "Now that I've been able to relay to you what your father asked me to, I can wait in peace for the day I get to see my old friend again in another world."

Brother and Sister

I reserved my last night in Hà-Nội for family: dinner at my niece Loan's house with her husband Truyền. Loan is my brother's oldest child; she also has a younger sister named Liên living in Sài-Gòn.

I had oftentimes wanted to ask my brother about Dad, and about his own experiences as well, about what happened to them through those dark years. But then I'd put it off. We were so glad to see each other that I didn't want to reopen the wounds, thus I always set my queries aside.

As previously planned, the following day my brother would come with me (and James Kimsey) to Quảng-Trị, Huế and Sài-Gòn. In Quảng-Trị we'd join the Vietnam Children's Fund delegation which included Terry Anderson who'd flown in from New York, and Sam Russell, VCF's director in Vietnam. We would inaugurate VCF's first school — at the 17th parallel, which during the war was the demarcation line.

Unlike the last time I said goodbye to Hà-Nội without my father or brother, this time brother Lân and I held hands as we sat together on the plane. When it took off, we put our heads to the window and looked down at Hà-Nội. Both were overwhelmed with emotions. Forty-one years earlier, had we had each other and Dad with us, our lives certainly would have turned out very differently.

In Đông-Hà, it was arranged for us to share a double-bed room in the local guesthouse. Late that night, after a business meeting with VCF, I came into the room and was touched to see my brother sleeping soundly with one hand on his forehead just like Dad used to do.

At 7:00 a.m. the next day, we went to the opening ceremony. The school building has two stories with 12 classrooms. It was purposely built near what was once the Demilitarized Zone (DMZ) to commemorate all those who died in the war.

VCF representatives included: American journalist Terry Anderson who was once taken hostage in the Middle East, Terry was a co-founder and co-chair of VCF like me; James Kimsey, a veteran who fought in Vietnam; plus a few other VCF members.

A new sign had been erected with the school's name: Lewis B. Puller, Jr. It was so named because not far from there was the location of a bloody battle in which Lewis lost both of his legs. For those who don't know, Lewis Puller Jr. was a legend among Vietnam veterans. Son of the most decorated Marine general in U.S. history, Second Lt. Puller volunteered to go to Vietnam. In a battle in Đông-Hà, an enemy mine blew up his legs and heavily damaged his arms. Back in the U.S., Puller obtained a law degree and wrote "*Fortunate Son: The Healing of a Vietnam Vet.*" The book won a Pulitzer Prize in 1992. President Bill Clinton even invited Puller to work in the administration, but he declined, citing the desire to devote his full time to veteran-related projects.

After helping found the VCF, it was Lewis who volunteered to go back to Việt-Nam, this time in his wheelchair, to the old battlefield in Đông-Hà. And with the help of other veteran friends in VCF, he came up with the plan to build the first school here.

Just as the project was underway in Quảng-Trị, a terrible tragedy struck. On May 12, 1994, Lewis shot himself in the head at his home in Virginia. After 26 years of fighting the excruciating pain from his injuries, he could not take it anymore. Lewis Puller Jr. was 48 years old.

About 200 villagers were there to witness the opening of the Lewis Puller Jr. School. Also present were local officials and students in their white and blue uniforms. In my speech, I said:

"... To me, you the students represent the hopes for the future of Vietnam. I hope and pray that you all do well in school and can live free and happy in a peaceful world..."

I also repeated this message when we cut the ribbon and planted the commemorative trees. I truly felt inspired seeing a brand new school arise from the land that was once the dividing line between North and South. I also didn't forget to thank our sponsors, contributors, and especially the former combatants who came back to lay the first bricks to build a new future for children of war.

After the ceremony we drove to the ancient city of Huế. That afternoon I went to visit Thiên-Mụ Pagoda where 38 years earlier I played a Buddhist nun in my very first movie role, kicking off my film career.

"Are you Kiều-Chinh the movie actress?" The man selling incense sticks asked as I walked down the steps to the street below. Seeing the look of surprise on my face, he beamed:

"I remember you. I knew you from the days you were making the film. You bought incense from me every day."

I made *Bells of Thiên-Mụ* in 1957, nearly four decades ago. Apparently this man and his family had been selling incense sticks at the pagoda all these years!

On our last night in Huế, our group took a boat trip on the Perfume River that included a live performance of Huế's traditional imperial music and a poetry recitation. Sitting next to me, my brother seemed quite taken by the atmosphere, I think he'd never experienced anything like this before. At the end of the program, each guest was given a small paper boat with a candle to light and release into the river while making a wish. My brother and I simultaneously lit ours.

I asked him: "What was your wish?"

He stared for a long while at the fleet of paper boats, with their candles bobbing playfully on the water, before answering in a soft voice: "I wished that after this trip you'll return soon, and stay longer."

We landed in Tân-Sơn-Nhất at 11 a.m. the next day. Sài-Gòn 20 years after was so different, so changed. There wasn't a parcel of empty land anywhere. Mixed among the tin roof homes were new houses with red tiles. Billboards crowded high above, competing for your eyeballs. In the streets, vehicles of all types were fighting for every inch of roadway. The city center was full of smoke and noise. There were people everywhere wearing all kinds of fashion and styles. Some even had mobile phones in hand.

As I was walking along, a legless man on a self-made skateboard rolled toward me.

"Sister," he said, "I'm an invalid from the South Vietnamese Army. Could you help?"

My heart broke. The image of the handicapped vet haunted me all the way back to the hotel.

I went to our old apartment near the Phú-Thọ racetrack, but the new owner didn't let me in. The woman closed the door to my face when she learned that I was a former resident now living in the U.S. who just wanted to take a look at some old memories.

On my last day in Sài-Gòn, my niece Liên and her husband Luân made a memorial meal for her grandfather so that my brother and I could pay our respects to Mom and Dad; it was also a farewell dinner for me. After dinner, I finally had a moment alone with my brother. We went up to the little attic on the third level of Liên's house on Pasteur Avenue.

"I've been coming here to be alone," he opened up. "This little room is my private world."

I looked around. It was a narrow room, with barely enough space for a small bed and a dresser. It opened to an even tinier balcony where one could stand and look out at the city.

We sat on the bed, flipping through three albums containing family pictures. The story began with a yellowed photo taken at Kim-Mã Estate of my brother as a young boy in a velvet suit and fedora hat, held in Dad's arms.

"You know, I've been wondering all these years," I gently began, "about where you went that night after we parted. Where did you ride your bicycle to, where did you sleep, what were the following days like?"

"I went with 'Tall' Hiệp to Bắc-Ninh as part of the Patriotic Students of Hà-Nội Movement. We went into a jungle camp to join the resistance."

"Did you know Dad stayed to look for you?" I asked. "When did you see Dad again?"

"It wasn't until almost a year later, in October, 1955, that I was able to come back to our house on Lê Trực to see Dad..."

My brother paused, finding it hard to continue. "But, the situation had changed by then... Maybe... Tĩnh has told you, that when I came back Dad was already in prison..."

Neither of us said a word. I looked into his eyes.

"Did you become a foot soldier, go to the front, or join the Party?"

"You have to understand," he answered, "that not everyone could join the Party or the military..."

We flipped to the page that had a picture of Dad riding Phi-Mã. Next to that was a picture of Dad in a trench coat visiting Hạ-Long Bay with some friends. I pressed on.

"After he spent two years in Hoả-Lò and then was transferred to Lào-Kay, Yên-Bái, were you able to visit him?

"I could visit him only once."

I asked my brother how Dad looked and what he was doing in prison.

"When I visited Dad for the last time, he was very thin, his eye sockets were really deep... his fingers were full of scratches... He worked in the group making bamboo products. He had to cut and split bamboo to make baskets and so on. That's all I knew. After that came my turn to be arrested. I spent one year in Hoả-Lò. Then three years of hard labor."

Suddenly he took my hand in his and said, "I think that's enough, Chinh. I can't answer any more. It was a time of war. Tragedies befell many families, not just ours. Forty years of agony cannot be told in one night. Please don't ask me any more questions. Everything is past. You're leaving soon. Just know that we always love one another, and that's enough."

I left my hand in his and answered in a very calm voice: "I understand. But please allow me two more questions. I need to know how Dad died — who was with him and what he said at the last moment."

"It's impossible to tell you all the hardship and changes... Dad was sick, poor, hungry... I got out of prison... Life was so hard. I had to do all kinds of work to survive. Pushing ox carts, selling my own blood... It was very tough, Chinh. Dad died in 1978 of dysentery... there was no medicine... and no one was by his side. He lay in bed sick. That morning I went out to buy some rock candy so Dad could have something to eat with rice congee. When I came back he was already dead."

After a long pause, my brother bowed his head to wait for the second question. Keeping my emotions in check, I continued:

"What did you have to do in prison?"

"I did anything and everything to survive. Making sandals from used tires. Melting wax to make candles..."

I suddenly thought of the candles on the paper boats that we released on the river along with our wishes. I pulled my hand from my brother's and hugged him. I kissed the tears rolling down his cheek.

"I will come back. I hope next time sister Tĩnh and her children will be able to come too. We will visit Mom and Dad's graves together, our children will know their cousins."

I stayed up until 2 a.m. packing and then went to the airport at 5 a.m. When I got inside the terminal, I turned around and saw my brother running toward me. I ran back. We placed our hands on the glass pane. I looked at my brother and cried.

One day in 2004, I was in New York for a VCF conference. After a day-long meeting with VCF staff, we had a nice farewell dinner. While we were toasting the latest milestones and successes, my phone rang. It was bad news; my brother had died. I turned ashen, put my glass down and immediately left the table. Terry asked what was wrong. I cried: "My brother in Việt-Nam is dead."

Terry hugged me: "I'll walk you back." He draped his arm over me as we walked back to the hotel.

"Oh my brother Lân, why? After the time we three siblings met in France you said you wanted to come to America once. I had done all the paperwork, dear brother. All you had to do is wait for the day. And now that day will never come. Oh my brother!"

Old Friends' Reunion

Toward the end of my first return trip to Việt-Nam, twenty years after the war had ended, I flew from the North to the South to visit Sài-Gòn and some of my old friends. My first meal was at the home of painter Đằng Giao. His wife, Chu Vị Thuỷ, is the daughter of the author Chu Tử. It was a most delicious home cooked meal. The house was beautifully decorated with artwork.

At that dinner, I met many old friends like author and songwriter Nguyễn Đình-Toàn, military writer Minh Quang and artist Nguyễn Hải-Trí, better known as Choé [chwair]. We talked non-stop. So many questions to ask, so many stories to share. We were like excited kids.

When I left, Choé walked me out to the alley, not wanting to say goodbye. Six months after I had come back to the U.S., I received a package from him — a portrait of me big as a tabletop. The painting is decidedly abstract. Apart from a pair of eyes, the artist threw paint all over the canvas in a seemingly random fashion. He wrote: *"The lady was gone. All the artist could remember was her eyes and his own mixed emotions."*

A few years later, Choé lost his eyesight. After a lot of effort by his family, he was allowed to come to the U.S. for an operation. He gleefully announced the news and promised that once his eyesight was regained he would visit his friends and pick up the brush again. His wife accompanied him to America. Shockingly, Choé died only a few days before his operation. His wife had to accompany her husband's body back to Việt-Nam.

One year after Choé's passing, I had the chance to go back to Việt-Nam and light some incense for my friend's first death anniversary with his wife and children.

Twenty Years of *The Joy Luck Club*

The Joy Luck Club (*JLC*) is a film based on a book with the same name by Chinese-American author Amy Tan, who also co-wrote the screenplay with Ronald Bass (Oscar-winning *Rainman*.) The Disney-produced movie was directed by Wayne Wang. At 139 minutes long, it was the first full-feature Hollywood film about World War II set in China, in the Guangzhou area near the border with North Vietnam.

Both the book and the film are still considered one of the most successful literary and film products by Asian-Americans. The book became a bestseller in its first year, was translated into 35 languages and recreated on stages all over the world. The film earned $17 million at the box office in its first week. It was listed by the National Board of Review Awards as one of the best movies in 1993. It also set sales records when released in home video format. Due to its widespread popularity, I sometimes was pleasantly surprised by the response to the film as I traveled around.

For example, in 2007, I was invited to be a keynote speaker to open the West Virginia Book Fair in Martinsburg. After the Q&A session in which I fielded many questions about *The Joy Luck Club*, I walked around to check out the exhibits. Suddenly, a tall young man stopped me and smiled sheepishly. He introduced himself and said:

"I'd like to thank you for clarifying something I've always wondered about in the film."

In the Q&A session, his question was how did I prepare myself to play the mother, Suyuan, as she was about to abandon her two children. The 20-year-old student from Africa told me he was studying film and acting at the film school in Martinsburg. He explained that his mother was Chinese and he used to watch a lot of videos with her. It was *The Joy Luck Club* that got him interested in filmmaking. Ever since he was a kid he'd always wanted to write a book and make a film about his mother and his family. That was why when he saw the actor who played Suyuan he just had to work up the courage to talk to her.

The encounter with that young man from Africa reaffirmed my belief that the story of *The Joy Luck Club* transcends the geographical and cultural barriers of China, or even Asia. In my mind, being able to inspire a new generation is the most rewarding gift for an artist and a work of art. The beautiful smile from that young man — and from many others whom I've met through the years — to me was the best "real life award" for the film.

The Fellowship of The Joy Luck Club

With sixty-four characters and sixteen major roles, the film brought together a large group of people who maintained a close friendship during and after the filming, with many official and unofficial gatherings full of fun and laughter. One memorable occasion occurred on a September day in 1993.

We were together again for the Telluride Film Festival. Frank Vrecheck, famous Hong Kong filmmaker and CEO of Pacific Rim Films, invited our group to a horseback riding trip through the beautiful Colorado mountain country. At one point, I decided to separate myself from the group and rode my horse alone up a hill. Cool wind blew through my hair and my shirt. It reminded me of my youth when I rode with Dad and uncle Phúc through his orange grove in Bố-Hạ. And of the time I played a princess escaping on horseback as the capital was attacked in *The Evil Within*, shot in India in 1972. And of the horse I left behind at Cercle Hippique on Nguyễn Du Street after April 1975. And of Sài-Gòn.

I stopped on a hillside and looked up at the brilliant clouds in the clear blue sky, laughing at myself for yet another birthday wandering alone — this time in a real wilderness.

That evening, as the cast and crew were milling about the hotel chatting, Director Wayne Wang asked everyone to gather around. All four mothers and four daughters from the film were there. Also present were author Amy Tan and her husband Louis DeMattei, Ron Bass who co-wrote the screenplay, and Janet Yang the producer. Once everybody was situated, a birthday cake was unexpectedly produced and everybody sang "Happy Birthday, Kieu Chinh," followed by hugs and kisses.

Holding the cake in my hand, with a single flickering candle signifying another year older, my heart was filled with gratefulness for the love and friendship we had developed, for the beauty of art, and for life itself.

The Fellowship of *The Joy Luck Club* also manifested itself on many other occasions. Like at the film's premier in Santa Monica where we were invited to a wonderful reception attended by some of Hollywood's biggest names such as director Oliver Stone and actor Richard Gere. Our exceedingly gracious host for that evening was none other than the lovely Annette Benning, wife of actor Warren Beatty. She gave our cast and crew her most special attention.

After Los Angeles came Orange County, home of Little Sài-Gòn. Recognizing this as an event to honor the Vietnamese actress in the film, the *Orange County Register* reserved the entire front page of its October 1, 1993. edition for just a photo of Kiều Chinh taken by Bruce Strong.

Among those who played the mothers, France Nuyen (Ying Ying) and Lisa Lu (An Mei) came to an event celebrating "Kieu Chinh: Forty Years in Film" in 1997. Lisa even gave me some beautiful jade stones. In 2006, thirteen years after the film's release, my children and I flew up to San Francisco to attend an event honoring Amy Tan who still calls me her second mother.

At the 2006 San Diego Film Festival where I was presented with a Lifetime Achievement Award, Ming-Na Wen spoke and called me "Mom" just like she did the first time we met. "Thank you, Mom," she said, "for sharing your talents, and for paving the way for Asian actresses like me."

Characters and Actors

The Joy Luck Club centered around four mothers and four daughters but required sixteen different actors to play them through various intersecting time periods. Auditions took place at several locations — New York, San Francisco, Hong Kong, Shanghai. Over 5,000 people took part, including many well-known names in the industry.

After being selected, I had a meeting with the production team which included director Wayne Wang, screenplay writers Amy Tan and Ronald Bass, and producer Patrick Markey from Disney.

Since I had never played mah-jong before and couldn't speak a word of Chinese, I was afraid that I'd be asked to learn these things quickly. But Wayne assuaged my fears by explaining that everyone in the room already knew who Kiều-Chinh was and what she was capable of. Someone even mentioned an interview I did with Richard Bernstein after I played a Cambodian mother in *Welcome Home*, the last film by the late Franklin Schaffner.

Bernstein's article emphasized the traumatic elements in the life of a refugee actor from Vietnam as she first lost her mother, then later her father because of war. The full-page article, "Art Meets Life for a Vietnamese Artist," calling me someone who brought real-life emotions to the big screen, ran in the *New York Times* in 1989 — the same year that the book *The Joy Luck Club* was published.

At the meeting, I was asked if I could choose one of the four mother characters — three alive, one dead — which one would I want to play? I said each character was different, but the one I loved the most and would fit me the best was Suyuan Woo, the dead one. Amy Tan broke into a big smile; everyone in the room nodded in agreement.

All the actresses who played the mothers were accomplished Asian stars, already well-known in the film world. Our large cast worked together nonstop for four weeks in San Francisco where much of the movie was filmed. Last came the few scenes with Suyuan and her babies which were much trickier to do because they had to be filmed behind the Bamboo Curtain in communist China.

The plan was that the production team would go in first to get everything set up. I then would fly into Guilin to meet them and do the evacuation scene. After that we all would fly up to Shanghai to rendezvous with Ming-Na (June) to film the final scene where June was able to recognize her half-sisters through the image of their deceased mother Suyuan.

But my flight from Hong Kong to Guilin ran into a major storm. The pilot had to make an emergency landing at a small airport somewhere in Guangzhou to wait for further instructions. The feel of a communist small town was palpable as stern-looking security policemen paced back and forth keeping a close eye on us.

After several hours of waiting, passengers were told to line up to get a pack of instant noodles. Then we had to go to another line to get a cup of warm water that wasn't even hot enough to cook the noodles. But that was still better than starving, since nobody knew how long we'd be stuck there.

By midnight, it was announced that we would have to stay overnight. We all lined up again as security called our name one by one so that they could take us to an inn. The place was more like an abandoned housing unit in the middle of nowhere, with rows of small rooms dimly lit by dirty old light bulbs.

And thus my first night in faraway Red China was spent alone in a dinky little room, listening to the wind howl and the rain shake a leaky, creaky window. It was also very cold, I recall. The sound of water crashing down on the roof reminded me of so many people and things. I thought of my father. I thought of my mother. I thought of my childhood. I called out to Dad! All through the stormy night I found myself calling my Dad. Sometimes I heard him calling me. At times I saw myself living at Kim-Mã Estate. Other times I saw myself alone and terrified in a different storm from another time. The images drifted in and out of my consciousness until I heard a loud knock on the door telling us to get ready to go back to the airport.

It was daylight; the storm had passed.

The Scene

On the flight to Guilin after the storm, I sat next to a young man wearing a red shirt that said "Film Crew." Seeing that I didn't speak Chinese, he switched to English and told me that he was going to Guilin to do a movie. He said if I needed work, he could hire me. He promised that not only would I be paid, I would also be fed three meals a day. He said the producer needed 2,000 extras, so anyone could get a job. Before we landed, he even handed me a piece of paper with instructions on where to go and reminded me that work would start the next morning. I thanked the enthusiastic young man, wished him well and said I hoped to see him again.

At the hotel, everyone was so relieved to see that the only main actress for this shoot made it ashore safe and sound. After a substantial lunch and meeting with the U.S. crew, we all went to work. Amy Tan, Wayne Wang, Patrick Markey and all the technical staff spent all afternoon getting everything ready for the shoot the next day. Wayne paid attention to the smallest details. Before we adjourned, he reminded the costume department to make sure they had soft blankets and heating pads to wrap around me because it would be very cold working outside all day.

When we arrived at the location the following morning, there already were fires, smoke and convoys of armed "Japanese" troops standing by. Thousands of extras in '40s clothing were sitting around waiting. My young friend in the red "Film Crew" shirt was busy directing people. When he saw me standing across the street, he waved me to come over. Seeing that I didn't move, he tried to run over. But before he got there, the assistant directors came and gave me the wheelbarrow with the baby twins and began going over the instructions. Director Wayne Wang gave me a hug and wished us all a successful day of shooting. I didn't have time to explain to my red-shirted friend who looked a bit confused, but I hoped he understood.

Because it was a crowded scene, Wayne had to deploy four different film crews with four separate cameras to capture all possible angles. As the fire and smoke began to rise, the trucks started rumbling down the road. Wayne yelled: "Action!"

I push the wooden wheelbarrow with two babies through the crowd of panicking evacuees. The Japanese trucks come crashing through. I can see people's possessions scattered by the side of the road. Houses are burning...

We march from one village to the next, from one hillside to another. On and on we walk. The sun begins to set. At last the wheelbarrow breaks and I fall down. I put the twins in my arms and struggle to stand up. I push on. One step after another...

The evacuation scene was much more elaborate and much bigger than I had imagined. Besides all the fires and smoke and Japanese soldiers and Chinese extras and so on, it was the breathtaking backdrop that was impressive. The jagged limestone mountains in the background gave the whole scene a fantastical quality that could not have been created by human hands. I finally understood why we had to shoot here, and nowhere else.

After we finished, I came over and congratulated Wayne for pulling off such a magnificent feat. He thanked me, but said that the hardest part wasn't to capture noisy crowds, but silence. That would be the next scene where Suyuan left her two children behind. He said we would have to go farther and earlier to catch the sunrise. The filming would be harder and the acting much more demanding.

We left very early the next day, bringing with us heaters and tarps to shield us from the bitter wind. It was a long drive. We got there about 5 a.m., and the sun had not come up yet. The technical crew, which had arrived a few hours before, were just sitting there. They said they couldn't do any prep work because the big tree where we planned to shoot the scene had been surrounded by villagers armed with clubs and other farming tools. I could hear people yelling from afar.

From that direction our producer, Patrick, appeared. He said he showed them all the necessary paperwork approved by the authorities, but the villagers said that we should go to wherever those authorities were to do our filming. This tree, they said, belonged to the village, and only they could authorize its use. Patrick said they basically wanted money — a few thousand dollars. They even charged a fee for the cars and trucks parked in front of the villagers' houses.

Back and forth the haggling went without any progress. The sun had risen quite high. It was no longer possible to get the shot with the sun's rays on the tree roots at an angle that the director wanted. Wayne said that without that light, there would be no filming.

Suddenly, the weather changed. Dark clouds appeared out of nowhere and rain began pouring down on us. Patrick draped a piece of nylon over me and led me down a slippery red dirt road to the car. We left in the shivering cold and rain. After a full afternoon of negotiations, a final price was agreed upon for the use of the tree.

We returned early the next day. Once again, Patrick helped me down the dirt road to the spot. Curious villagers stuck their heads out the window as we passed by. When we reached the tree, everything was ready. Cameras were in position, and everyone was ready to roll. But now we had to wait for sunlight to hit the right spot.

I walked through the sequence of Suyuan in my head — war came, fires and bombs everywhere, the twins were placed in a wheelbarrow, Suyuan pushed her babies in the crowd, the wheelbarrow broke down. And now she comes to this spot. All her strength is gone. She knows she's about to die. A nicely dressed man walks by. She holds her babies up, begging for help. The man walks on. She looks at the tree. It alone will not abandon her. She gives her babies to the tree before passing out.

That was the entire flashback scene by the mother, Suyuan. But for just those few minutes of screen time, we all had to spend so much time and effort. As for acting, there wasn't much by way of dialogue. Just two words. To call for help for her babies, and at the same time, to say goodbye to them. It was in Cantonese; I had it down pat.

Another cold breeze blew through, but it still wasn't time. And how would we know when the right time would be? There was no way to calculate these things. The director had to get there early enough to set up everything and wait. Why was that ephemeral sun ray so critical? I remembered what Wayne said to me on the first day — the difficult part wasn't to film the noisy crowd, but the silence.

I asked Wayne how he wanted me to act in this scene. He said I already knew what to do: "Just act in the Kieu Chinh way." And then, with a serious tone he instructed: "The last words don't have to be in Cantonese. Use any language you choose. Also, the cameras will already be rolling. As soon as the sunlight hits, begin. I will not call 'Action!'"

All around us, everyone became silent. Wayne was silent. I was silent. I could almost hear my own heartbeat. It was quite cold. My breath was steam.

Beyond the limestone mountains, the first few rays start to appear. I become Suyuan. I pick up my babies. A man walks by. I hold them up to him, begging in Cantonese for help. The man keeps walking. I look up at the sunlight, asking the tree to protect my babies. As I place the twins down on the ground, I suddenly hear Dad's voice calling me. My tears start flowing uncontrollably. and a gut-tearing voice suddenly screams out from the depths of my soul: *"Con ơi!"* (My child!)

My body keeps shaking. I grip the roots hard with both hands for support. My eyes open wide, trying to see my babies through the tears.

I remained motionless on the ground for what seemed like an eternity. There was no sound of "Cut!" And then I felt an arm around my shoulders. I knew it was the director's. I tried to stay calm:

"Do we need another take?"

"No. No need." Wayne answered. "There's nothing more that could be done."

It sounded like he was not talking to me but to himself.

Late that evening, while I was in a tired, deep sleep, I was awakened by a knock on the door. It was Amy Tan. She gave me a hug and asked why I wasn't downstairs, the cast and crew were celebrating and wondered where I was. I told Amy I was exhausted. She took my hand, insisted that I should go down to the restaurant and have a drink to say goodbye to Guilin. I shook my head and said I was too tired.

Amy put her hand on my forehead and exclaimed: "Why are you so warm? You have a cold!"

"Yes. Since last night. I was shivering and sweating all through the night. I could hardly sleep."

"Why didn't you tell us sooner so we could take you to a doctor? And you had to get up so early this morning too!"

What could I tell her? After all the things that happened the day before, how could I look into Patrick's and Wayne's eyes and tell them to give me a day off because I was sick? Thousands of people had been mobilized. Hundreds had been working day and night to get ready. If Suyuan stopped for one day, all those people would have had to stop with her. And what about all the shoot schedules, all the flight schedules? I had to act strong no matter what.

Amy said she would call a doctor, but I told her I'd already taken some Tylenol.

"All I need, really, is some rest. Tell everyone not to worry and have fun. Tomorrow we leave for Shanghai."

Paris

The Joy Luck Club was a big success, indeed. After a strong showing at the box office in the first week, Disney Films flew Amy Tan, Ming-Na Wen and me first-class to Europe to attend more opening events. From Charles de Gaulle Airport in Paris we were taken directly to the Ritz Hotel. I picked the suite named Chopin because it reminded me how, as a young girl studying piano in Hà-Nội, I used to daydream about the love story between the romantic composer and his muse George Sand.

The next day was all work. The three of us spent the entire morning in a press conference held in the Coco Chanel Room, fielding countless questions from behind a table, with a Disney representative and secretary present. After lunch and a brief respite, we went over to the next room to tape some TV interviews — individually first and then all three of us. We didn't finish until 5 p.m.

The next day, while Ming-Na went off on her own, Amy and I went to visit Le Louvre nearby. Amy only had two hours, but I stayed until the museum closed and still wished I had more time. Of course, I had to see the Mona Lisa and her enigmatic smile. I also bought a small statuette of Chopin, which I planned to place on the piano in "My World" in Studio City.

My favorite place at the Ritz Hotel was perhaps the Hemingway Bar. It was just a small drinking spot but full of Hemingway-related paraphernalia. In one corner sat an old typewriter, and next to it a newspaper with a photo of the writer on the front page; in another was a WWII-era record player. Framed photos of Ernest Hemingway at different stages in his life were everywhere. At the end of the room, far from the bar and darker than usual, was a small table with two black leather couches next to it. A painting of an older Hemingway hung on the wall.

I walked in. Seeing that I was alone, the host asked if I would like to sit at the bar. I looked around. Most of the tables were taken. I pointed to the small table in the dark and asked if I could sit there. "Bien sûr," the old man responded. He led me to my table and explained: "Monsieur Hemingway used to sit here every time he came."

He handed me the drinks menu embossed with a picture of a late-period Hemingway with a full beard. It was a beautiful photo; in it he looked very manly, very artistic — the same Hemingway as in the painting on the wall. White Russian Cocktail... Hemingway Scotch Whiskey... Cognac...

"May I have a dry martini, please."

"Bien sûr, madame."

The place wasn't completely full, but there was hardly an open table. People conversed in deliberately soft tones, giving the bar a friendly yet warm ambience. The martini was brought out; even the napkins had Hemingway's name on it. As I sipped my drink, I thought about all the characters from Hemingway novels that had made it to the big screen. Spencer Tracy in *The Old Man and the Sea*; Tyrone Power in *The Sun Also Rises*; Rock Hudson and Jennifer Jones in *A Farewell to Arms*; Gregory Peck and Ava Gardner in *The Snows of Kilimanjaro.* Heroic characters in great movies that mesmerized me once upon a time, yet how tragic that such a literary genius had to kill himself when he was barely 60 years old. I knew that I had to visit this place again in the future.

While in France I also visited the Martell Cognac distillery at the invitation of its owner, Patrick Martell. I had met Patrick several times before when he came to Los Angeles and always received a card from him every Christmas.

Patrick sent a car to pick me up at the Ritz on the morning of January 10, 1994. It was a big, black Citroën, chauffeured by a man wearing a suit and hat. The road into "Martell Village" was very picturesque; tall trees lined the sides in equidistance, lush green fields spread far as the eye could see.

An enormous sign that said "Martell" signaled we were close. The car stopped in front of a mini-chateau. A suited man opened the door and took my bag. A middle-aged lady wearing a long black skirt touching her heels was standing on the steps waiting for me. Patrick appeared from behind the steps; we hugged and greeted. He then turned to the lady and explained that she would be taking care of me during my two-day stay. She led me into the house, with its beautiful wooden staircases.

At 7 p.m. she met me at the bottom of the stairs and took me to a room for some aperitifs. A server came in with a tray of tasting glasses and gorgeous-looking bottles; the spirits therein were excellent as well. After dinner, we went over to the "tasting room" where I had the chance to sample some more cognac.

The next morning, I came down for breakfast right at 8 o'clock as planned. There were already three other men at the table; Patrick explained they were company employees. After breakfast, we went on a tour of the village. About three thousand employees worked here, not counting family members. From the fields I was taken to the building where glasses and bottles were made, then to the distillery itself. Finally, we stopped at the cellar. It was a large warehouse with hundreds of wooden casks. A service person carried around a tray with several samples for me to try.

The air in the village was fresh and clean. Every now and then a gentle breeze would carry a subtle scent to complement the cognac as I brought a "ballon" glass to my nose. It was an indescribable sensation.

Before I went home, someone already had packed me a large box containing many different kinds of cognac. But there was a special package that Patrick handed to me personally. It was wrapped in blue velvet, and inside was a custom-made bottle with a gold neck on it which was inscribed: "*To Kiều Chinh - January 11, 1994 with compliments*" Signed: *Patrick Martell.* Accompanying the bottle was a passport holder inscribed with: *Cognac L'Or de Martell.*

After three days in the City of Light, we took off for Rio de Janeiro to attend the Brazil Film Festival where *The Joy Luck Club* would be screened. Thank you, *JLC* Family. Thank you, Disney Films, for a wonderful trip full of great memories.

Journey From The Fall

It wasn't until thirty years after I left Việt-Nam in 1975 that I had the opportunity to be in a Vietnamese film made outside of Việt-Nam. The cast and crew were all part of a younger generation of Viet-American filmmakers.

Journey From the Fall was directed by Trần Hàm and Nguyễn Lâm, and produced by Alan Vo Ford. It was filmed mainly in Thailand, with some indoor scenes shot in California. I played the role of a black-toothed grandmother. Together with her grandson (Nguyễn Thái-Nguyên) and her granddaughter (Diễm-Liên), they escaped by boat in search of freedom. Her son (Nguyễn Long) stayed behind and spent years in re-education camps. He later died together with a fellow inmate (Mai Thế Hiệp).

In order to stay in character I had to keep my teeth blackened, like a traditional North Vietnamese woman, for the whole day while we shot. This meant I could only eat once in the morning, before make-up, and not be able to chew anything for the rest of the shoot. But that was a very small price to pay.

During the time in Thailand, I could not stop thinking about Dad and my brother Lân, especially when we shot scenes of the communist labor camps. But the scenes at sea were toughest, both physically and emotionally. I thought about the millions who tried to escape by boat, many of whom never made it to the shores of freedom (some estimates have put their number at at least half a million, but we'll never know). I also thought about the thousands of girls and women who were robbed, raped and killed by pirates. It made my heart ache.

The filming was exhausting at times. Some people were seasick and started vomiting, making the set even more realistic than we had planned. In one scene, I had to walk from one end of the boat to the other with my "grandson." The boat was bobbing and the bottom was very slippery; I was so afraid of falling into the water. I called out: "I'm so scared. I can't swim!"

Lâm Nguyễn assured me: "Don't worry, Ms Chinh. I will make sure you are safe." As soon as he said it, Lâm jumped into the ocean — to catch me in case I slipped and fell. What a sweet young man, bless his heart! These are talented individuals who belong to a new generation of artists. They truly give me hope for Vietnamese films in the future.

After the film's release, I had the chance to travel with the team to various screenings throughout the country. *Journey From The Fall (Vượt Sóng)* was extremely well received. It won 28 awards in total at multiple film festivals, including Best Actor for Nguyễn Long at the Newport Film Festival. At the Sundance Film Festival it was shown four times — a record.

After the first screening at Sundance, as soon as the lights were turned on an older man came over and knelt down in front of me. With tears in his eyes, he said: "Thank you, Kiều Chinh, for making this film. Thank you for saying for us the things we've been wanting to say but couldn't."

I, too, was crying.

Twenty Five Years of Filmmaking

In 1983, I returned to France. A number of friends organized an event called "Kiều Chinh, 25 Years of Filmmaking." Needless to say, it was an emotional reunion with many people whom I had not seen since 1975. Like the owner of Cosunam Films, Mrs. Gilbert Lợi. I also met many actors and directors, as well as classical guitarist Lê Thành Đông.

Most special of all was a superb musical program produced by the renowned Vietnamese music scholar Trần Quang Hải and traditional opera singer Bích Thuận, with the participation of many well known traditional musicians.

I was so moved when they presented me with a plaque to commemorate and show appreciation for my contributions to the art of filmmaking for the past twenty-five years. It was heartwarming to see that so many people showed up in the audience. I also cherished the opportunity to reconnect with many people whom I had not seen in such a long time.

Best of all, I saw my sister Tĩnh and Uncle Nghị again. This time he introduced me to a student and protégé of his named Đ. upon whom my uncle heaped compliments and praises. He said he wanted me to marry Đ., a nice and decent intellectual who had never been married before. For his part, my uncle said he would take care of the wedding and even gift me a house in Paris. Uncle Nghị said he wanted me to have a more comfortable life, which he believed I deserved.

Not long after I came back to the U.S., Dr. Đ. flew to California to visit me. He formally asked me to marry him and proposed that I could live half a year in Paris and the other half in the U.S. with my children.

The conditions were very reasonable and agreeable. Unfortunately, my heart was not in agreement. My sister Tĩnh later told me that Uncle Nghị was very disappointed that I did not follow his advice. Perhaps my uncle didn't understand what I wanted.

PICTURES
PART III
Exile

The ancestral altar at the house still has the photographs venerating parents on both sides of the family

The family is reunited for the first Christmas in America at the apartment in North Hollywood.

The marriage ceremony of the eldest daughter Nguyễn Mỹ Vẫn with Đạo Đức Sơn, the eldest son of Dr. Đào Đức Hành

The marriage of the eldest son, Nguyễn Hoàng Hùng with Nguyễn Bích Trang, who is the second daughter of pharmacist Nguyễn Hùng Chất

Mother, daughter, sons and the two dogs (Polo and Bogie) in the garden behind the house in Studio City.

Stephen Đào hugs and kisses his grandmother (KC)

Bogie

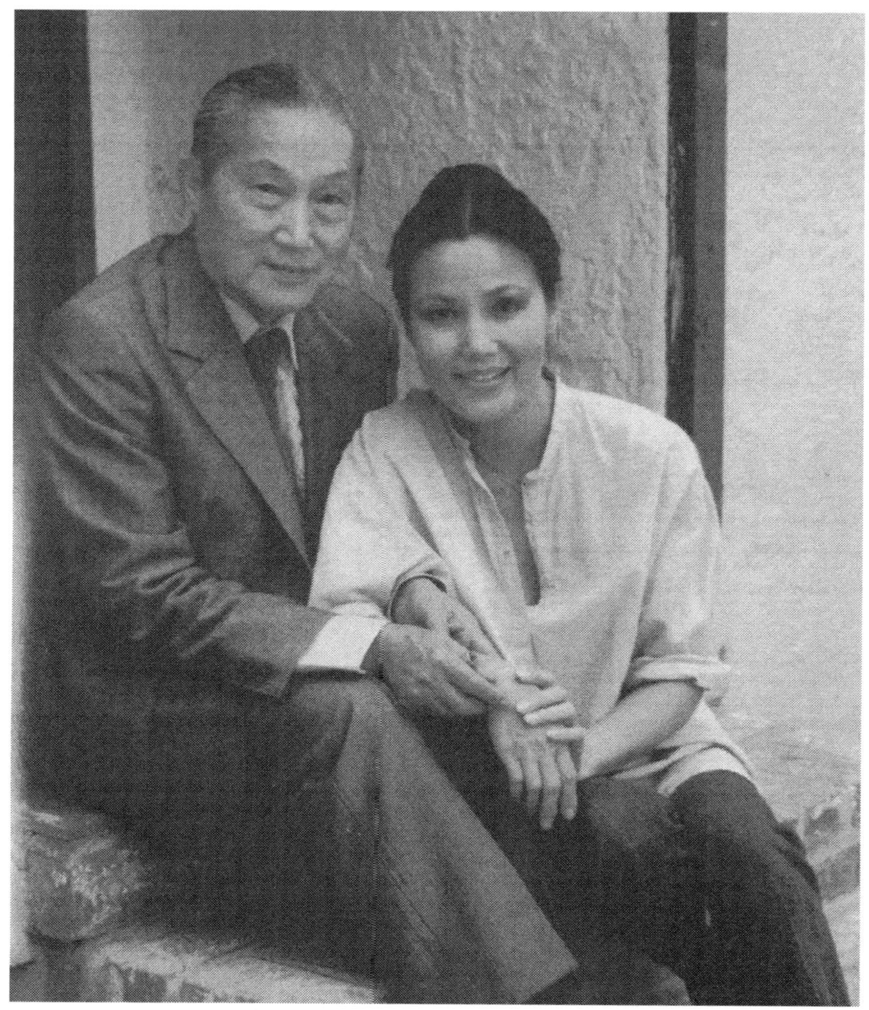

With Dr. Nguyễn Văn Nghị, who is my mother's brother. He came from France to visit his niece, at her home in Studio City.

Kiều Chinh and her sister Pauline Tính kiss each other with effusion, after so many years of separation.

My sister Tính's two children, David and Lysa, went to the train station in Marseilles to greet their aunt Chinh.

Family dinner at my sister's house. From left to right: Jean Claude, David and his wife, Christian, Chinh, and my sister Pauline Tĩnh.

Lân, Tĩnh và Chinh meet again for the first time in Marseilles, France.

Hoàng Hùng flew to France to meet his uncle Lân.

The sisters Tĩnh, Chinh with the four children of of uncle Nghị, the medical doctors Luc, Johan, Patrick and Christine.

Family reunion in France with my sister Tĩnh and the children of Uncle Nghị on the wedding of David (the son of my sister Tĩnh)

In joy brother and sister embrace after 41 years of separation.

Full of emotion Kiều Chinh touches her father's grave and burns an incense stick in his memory

A corner of Hỏa Lò prison.

Looking through the window bars into a cell in Hỏa Lò prison (Hanoi Hilton)

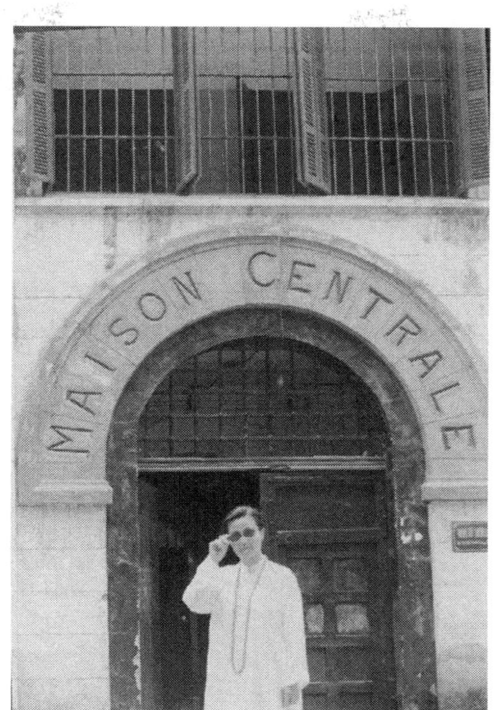

In front of the entrance gate of Hỏa Lò prison (Hanoi Hilton), where my father Cửu and my brother Lân were imprisoned.

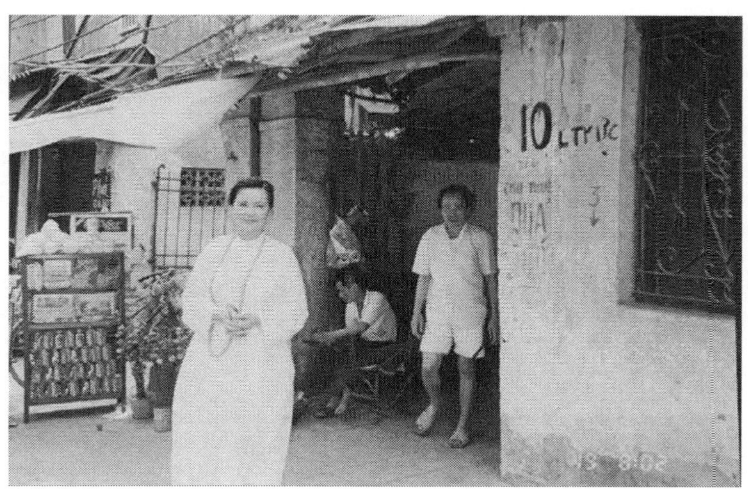

Returning to the old house at No. 10 Lê Trực Street, Hà Nội, where everything has changed.

With my godfather, the writer Ngọc Giao who is also an old friend of my father.

With my uncle, Ambassador Nguyễn Văn Quang reunited in 2000.

Visiting my uncle, Dr. Nguyễn Văn Thành in Hà Nội.
(Photo by Daniel A. Anderson, Orange County Register).

With the poetess Ngân Giang the day of my return.
She looks at the lines on the hands of her niece from yesteryear.

The directors, Lê Mộng Hoàng and Lê Dân and actress Kim Cương came to pick me up at Tân Sơn Nhất airport.

Touching reunion after 20 years with artist friends. From left to right: the painters Đằng Giao and Chóe, Kiều Chinh, the writers Nguyễn Đình Toàn, and Văn Quang.

Tuấn Cường's wrecked car, dismantled and burned.

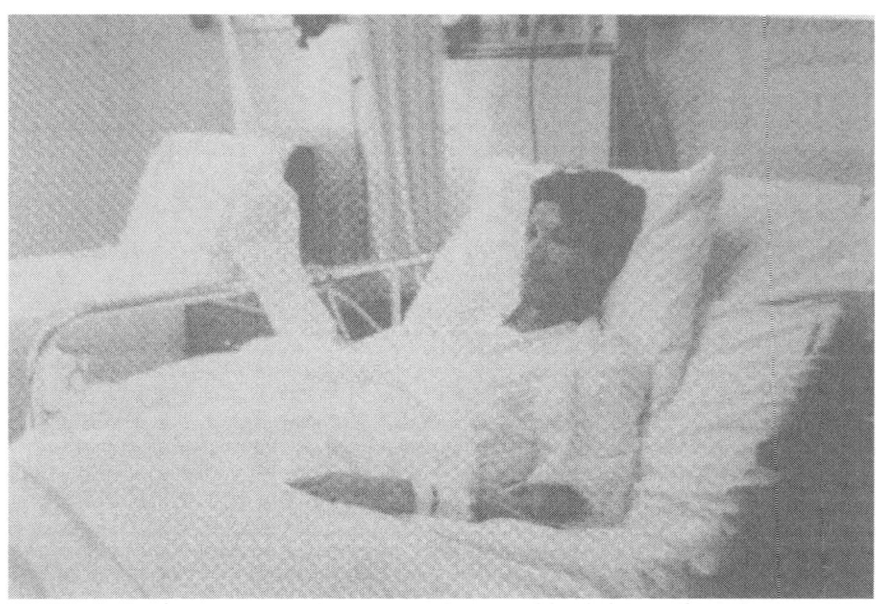

Tuấn Cường is lying on a hospital bed, his right arm hanging in the air

Tuấn Cường và Kiều Chinh kính thăm Thiền sư Thích Nhất Hạnh tại Lộc Uyên.

From left to right Tuấn Cường, Kiều Chinh, TouTou Lê Nam, Ý Lan.

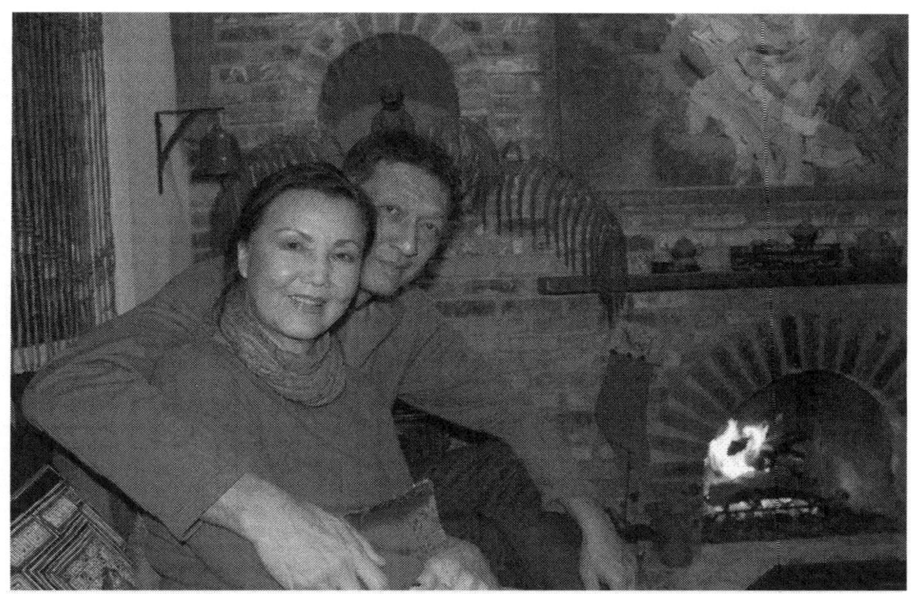

With my son Hoàng Hùng beside the warm fire of Christmas

Tuân Cường takes picture of his son, Nguyễn Lê Nam with grandmother Kiều Chinh

The Luân-Liên couple . Liên who is Lân's daughter, is visiting Kiều Chinh's family. From left to right: Cường, Vân, Liên, Chinh Luân et Hùng, in front of the house in Hungtinton Beach.

Celebrating Tuấn Cường's birthday with uncle Tony Lâm Quang, grandson Lương Minh Châut, Ý Lan and her children.

Big family reunion at Kiều Chinh's house: Elder brother-in-law, Nguyễn Giáp Tý, sister-in-law Mão and her children from Toronto, Tế and Tuyết, younger sister-in-law Kiều and her son Nguyễn Chí Tôn.

Big family get together to celebrate Nguyễn Năng Tế's eightieth birthday

With four beloved grandchildren: Stephan Đào, Aimée Nguyễn, Nguyễn Lê Nam, Jean-Paul Nguyễn

Stephen Đào (maternal grandson), graduate of Chapman University

Jean-Paul Nguyen (paternal grandmother)
graduated from MSOE University

Jean Paul Nguyễn, engineer graduating from MSOE University Photo taken with Kiều Chinh, his paternal grandmother, his father Paul Hùng Nguyễn and his mother Jan Bich Trang Nguyễn.

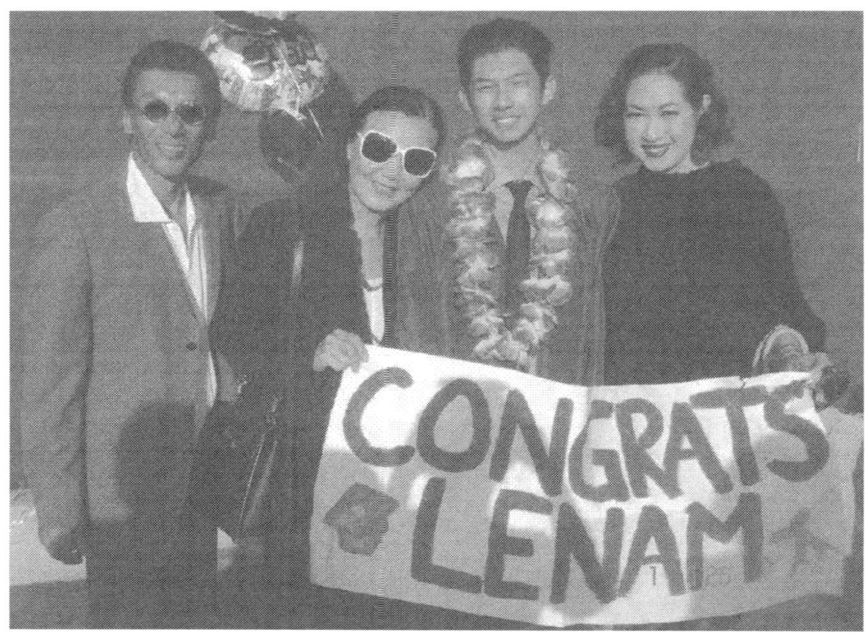

Tuấn Cường and Ý Lan celebrate the graduation of their son, Nguyễn Lê Nam in the presence of Kiều Chinh.

Aimée Nguyễn (paternal granddaughter) graduated from UC Berkeley.

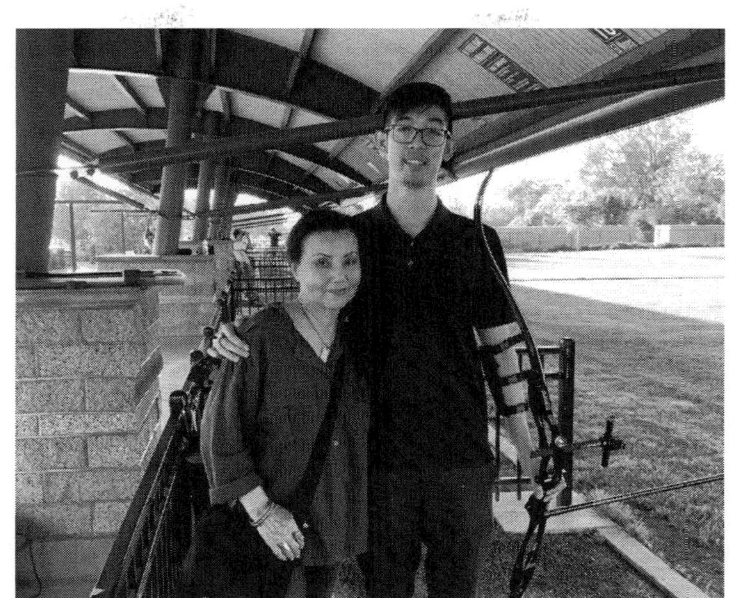

Archery practice on days off, with grandson Jean-Paul, who is also my coach.

On the archery range.

Movie Career

The chair named Kieu Chinh on the Hollywood studio

A special photo gathering Hollywood's ethnic minority actor-friends. Kiều Chinh is seated in the front row on the left.

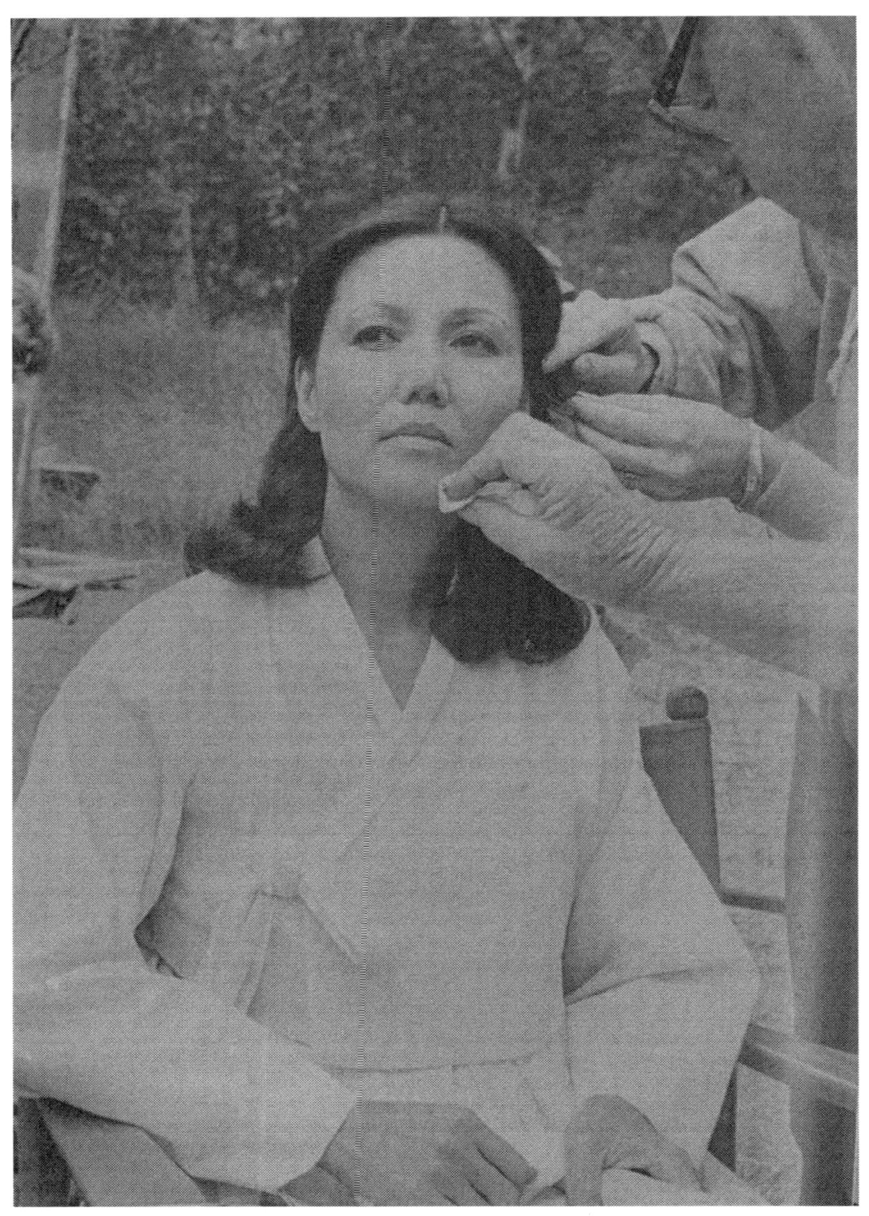

Makeup on the Hollywood set for the TV show M.A.S.H.

With actor Alan Alda in the television series M.A.S.H, 1977

A scene from the film "The Letter" starring actress Lee Remick.

With actor Ricardo Montalban in the television series Fantasy Island.

With actor John Forsythe in the television series Dynasty

With Gurinder Chadly, director of film "What's Cooking"

TV interview with Richard Chamberlain

Kiều Chinh, technical advisor on the set of the movie "Hamburger Hill".

Kiều Chinh, on the set of the movie "Hamburger Hill" (Getty Images)

In "Call to Glory" produced by ABC Television, Kiều Chinh plays the role of Mrs. Ngô Đình Nhu. First Lady of the Republic of Vietnam, the Japanese actor S. Shimoto, in the role of President Ngô Đình Diệm and Greg Nelson, the role of an American officer.

Kiều Chinh playing the role of a Laotian mother, leading her children on an evacuation in the film The girl who spells "freedom"

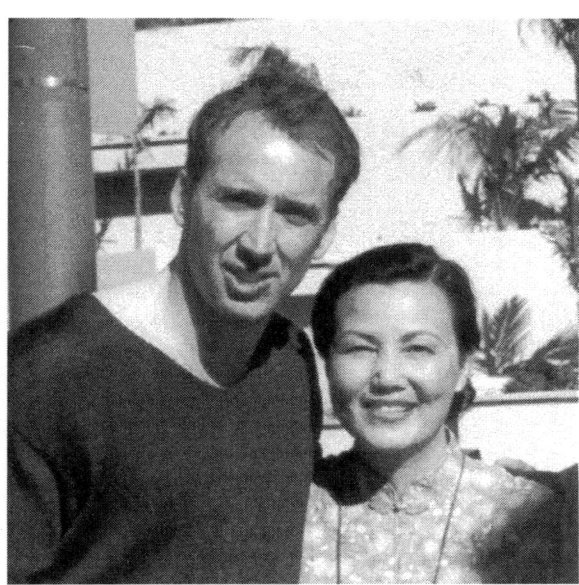

With actor Nicholas Cage in the movie "City of Angels"

Cambodian actor Haing S. Ngor and Kiều Chinh, who play the role of a couple in movies and on television, are friends in real life. A doctor turned actor, he received an Oscar for his role in the film The Killing Fields

A scene from the movie "Welcome Home", directed by Franklin J. Schcffner and shot in Malaysia.

With actor Kris Kristofferson in the movie "Welcome Home", shot in Malaysia and directed by renowned director Franklin Shaffner.

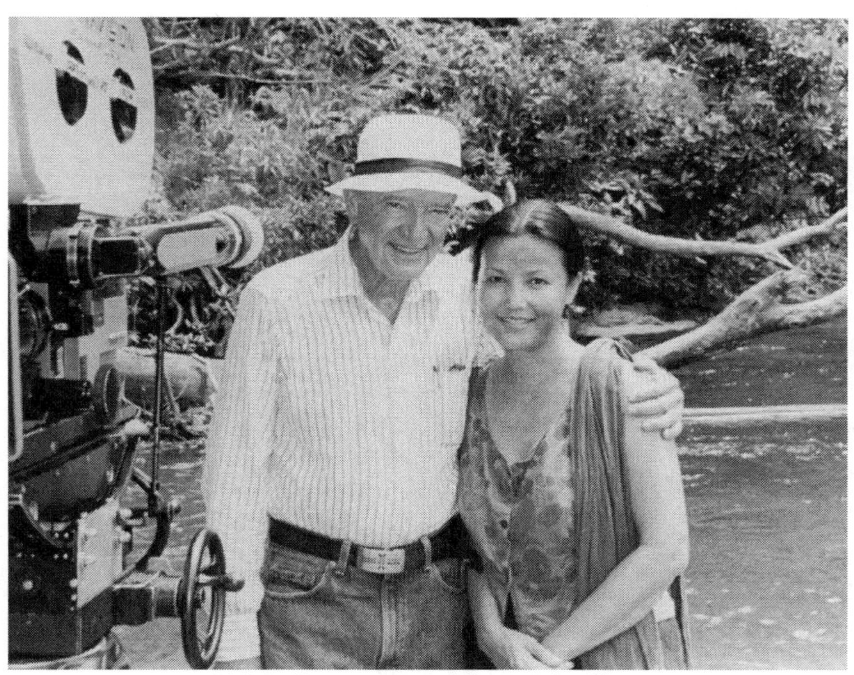

With director Franklin J. Schaffner on the set of "Welcome Home"

With director Wayne Wang on the set of "The Joy Luck Club" in Guilin, China.

A scene from "The Joy Luck Club": Kiều Chinh as Suyuan, the mother who had to abandon her two young children in the flight from chaos.

In pairs, the mothers and daughters of "The Joy Luck Club".
From left to right: Kieu Chinh, Ming-Na-Wen, Tamlyn Tomita Tsai Chin, France Nuyen, Lauren Tom Lisa Lu, Rosalind Chao.

The Joy Luck Club team at the Sundance Festival.
A pleasant surprise awaits : a birthday cake for Kiều Chinh.

Ming Na-Wen, Amy Tan and Kiều Chinh at a press conference in the Coco Chanel Room at the Ritz Hotel in Paris

With writer Amy Tan, author of the novel The Joy Luck Club, at the Louvre Museum in Paris.

Film star Tippi Hedren and Kiều Chinh at the premiere of "The Joy Luck Club" in Hollywood.

Kiều Chinh with Richard Gere at the Arman Hammer Museum, Westwood, after the premiere of "The Joy Luck Club" movie.

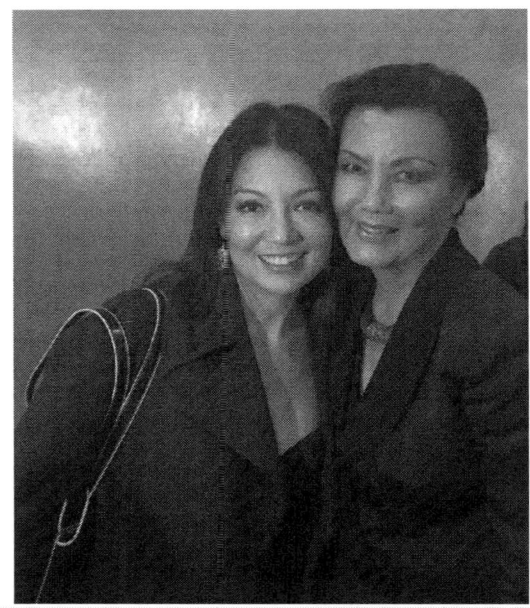

With Ming-Na Wen playing the daughter of Kieu Chinh in the movie "The Joy Luck Club"

Janet Yang (producer of The Joy Luck Club), Kiều Chinh & actress France Nuyen

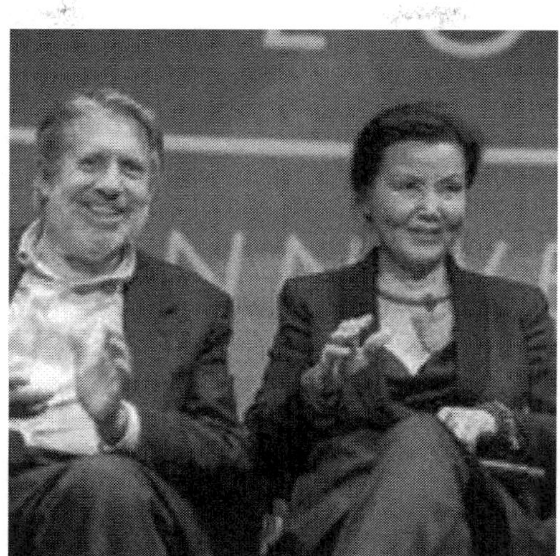

On the stage at TIFF with Ron Bass
(Oscar winner screen writer)

A part of the family of The Joy Luck Club, from left to right: Janet Yang (producer), 1 friend, Russel Wong (actor), Amy Tan (author), Kiều Chinh, Lauren Tom (actress), Ron Bass, Wayne Wang (director)

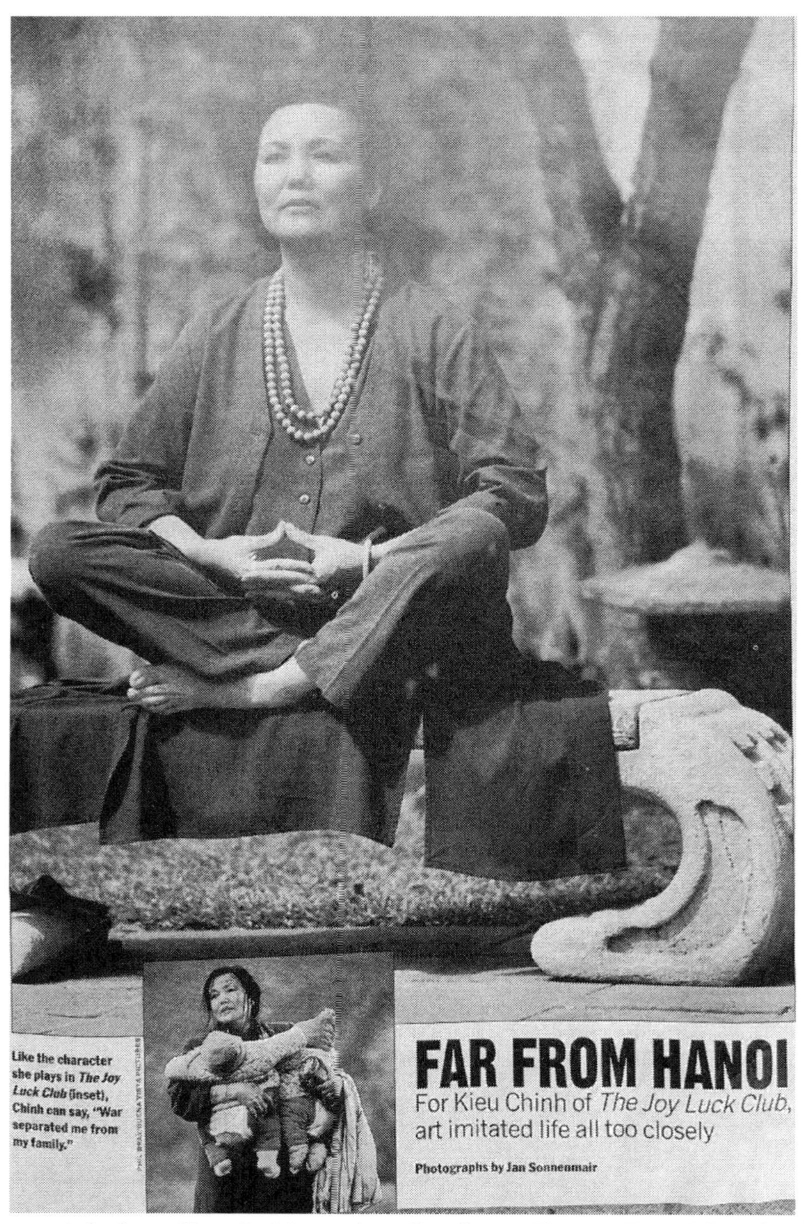

Like the character she plays in *The Joy Luck Club* (inset), Chinh can say, "War separated me from my family."

FAR FROM HANOI

For Kieu Chinh of *The Joy Luck Club*, art imitated life all too closely

Photographs by Jan Sonnenmair

An article from People Magazine: Far from Hanoi. For Kiều Chinh, The Joy Luck Club imitates life all too closely

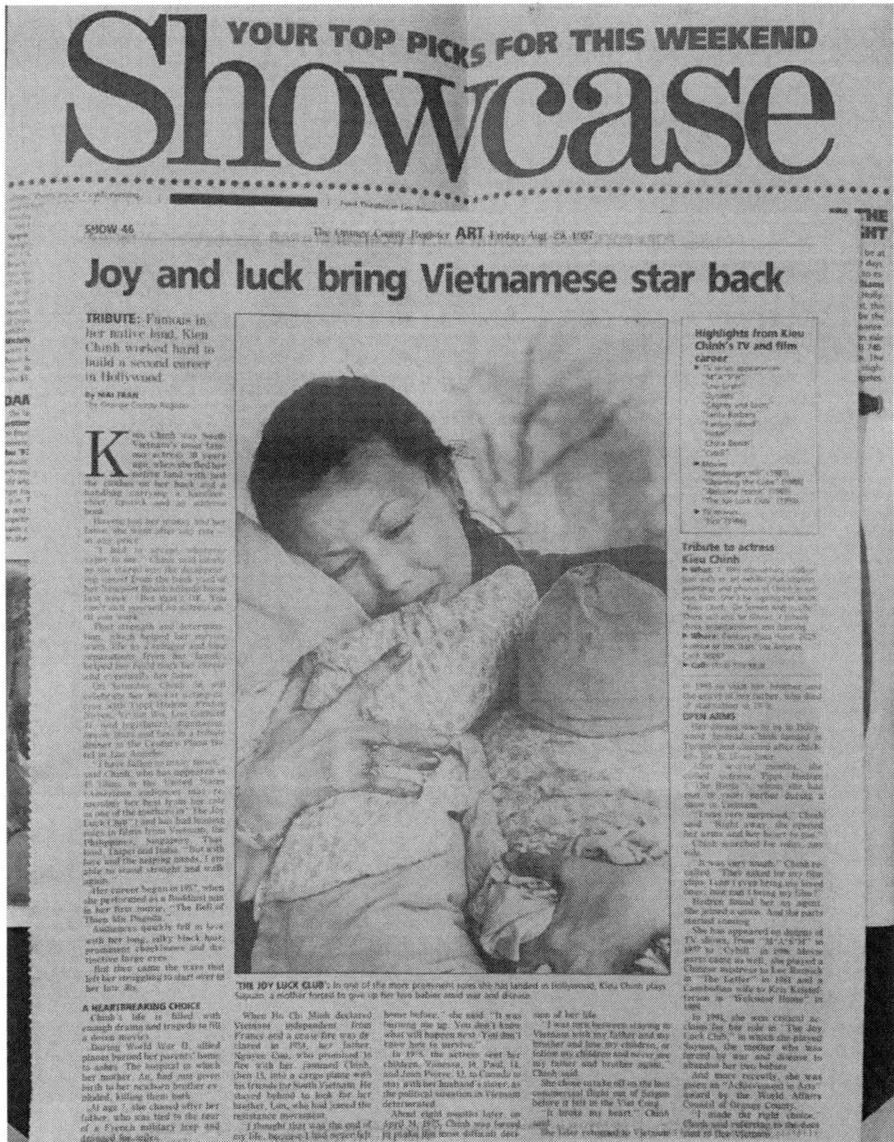

YOUR TOP PICKS FOR THIS WEEKEND

Showcase

SHOW 46 — ART

Joy and luck bring Vietnamese star back

TRIBUTE: Famous in her native land, Kieu Chinh worked hard to build a second career in Hollywood.

Highlights from Kieu Chinh's TV and film career

Tribute to actress Kieu Chinh

'THE JOY LUCK CLUB'

A HEARTBREAKING CHOICE

OPEN ARMS

The film "The Joy Luck Club" was noticed by many newspapers, such as NY Times, LA Times, etc...

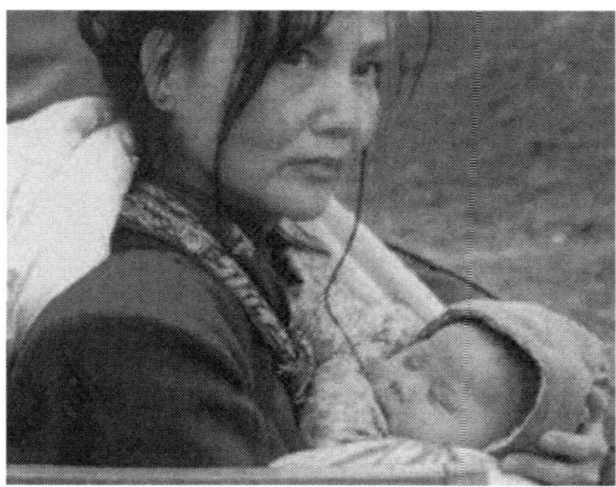

Kiều Chinh playing the role of Suyuan, a Chinese mother during the Second World War, who had to abandon her two children in flight.

22 The Joy Luck Club

Kieu Chinh, Ming-Na Wen (1993, Hollywood) The stories of four Chinese women and their difficult relationships with their daughters are explored in director Wayne Wang's relentlessly emotional adaptation of Amy Tan's novel. A chick flick through and through, the movie switches between the mothers' early lives in restrictive Chinese society—dealing with child marriage, domestic abuse, and infanticide—and the Asian-American daughters' present-day lives as they face loveless marriages, racist in-laws, and a major lack of connection with their moms. **KLEENEX MOMENT** The trophy of tears goes to the deceased Suyuan (Chinh), as a flashback shows how she had to abandon her twin baby girls by the road while fleeing the invasion of Kweilin.

Poster for the film "Vượt Sóng" by director Trần Hàm.

Kiều Chinh plays a grandmother with black teeth in the movie "Vượt Sóng" (Journey from the Fall).

Adrift on the immensity of the ocean in the film "Vượt Sóng".

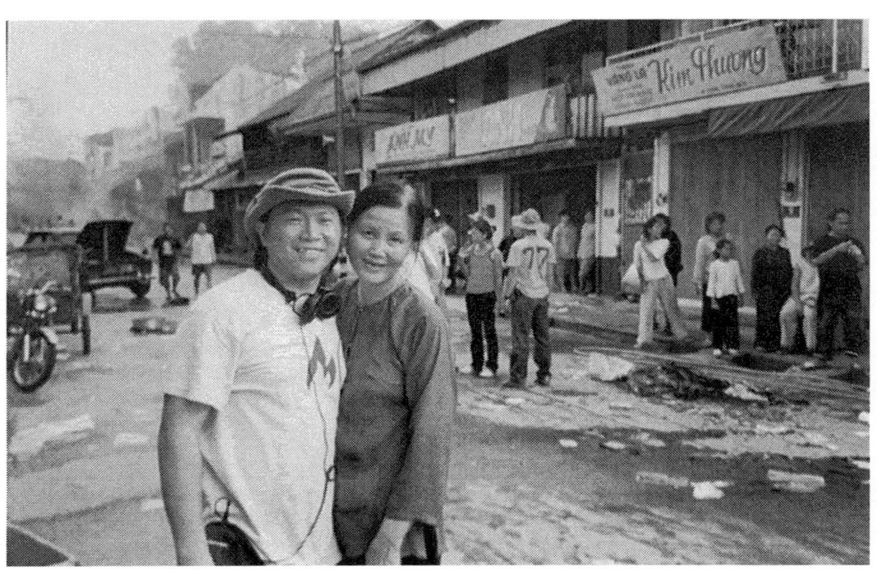

With director Trần Hàm on set in Thailand.

With actor Jason Momoa in the film Tempted, shot in Australia and directed by Maggie Greenwald

Poster for the film Tempted, aka "Returning Lily".

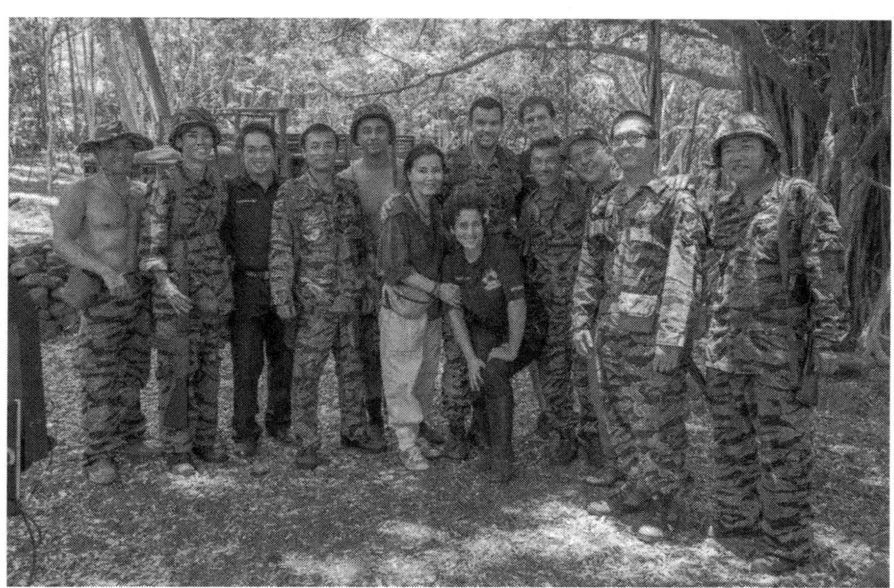

Kiều Chinh on the set in Hawaii with the director, producer and cast of "Ride The Thunder"

With Richard Bolkin, producer and author of the book "Ride The Thunder"

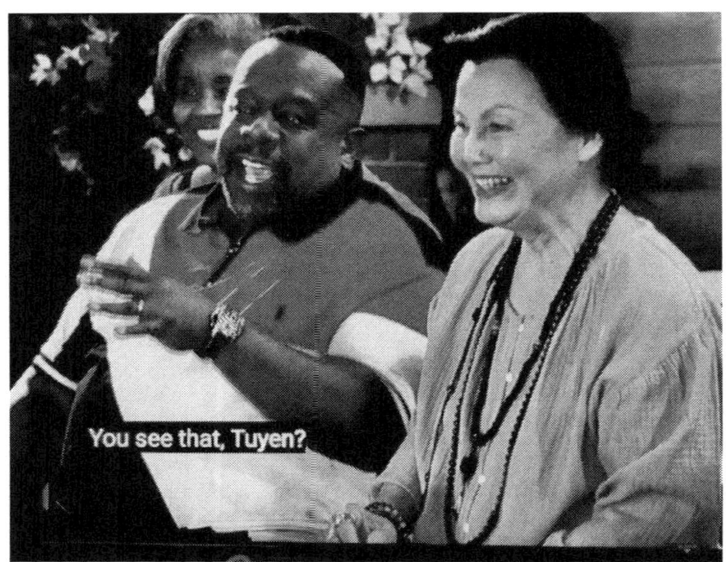

With Cedric The Entertainer in TV Show "The Neighborhood"

Kiều Chinh in the TV show NCIS LA with the two actors: Eric Christian Olsen & Daniela Ruah.

Kiều Chinh with director Andrzey Wajda. "It was an honor for me to be able to work with him on this Japanese opera", she says.

Kiều Chinh and actors play in the play Sansho The Bailif, directed by Andrzey Wajda.

Attending Toronto International Film Festival
(ảnh Getty Images)

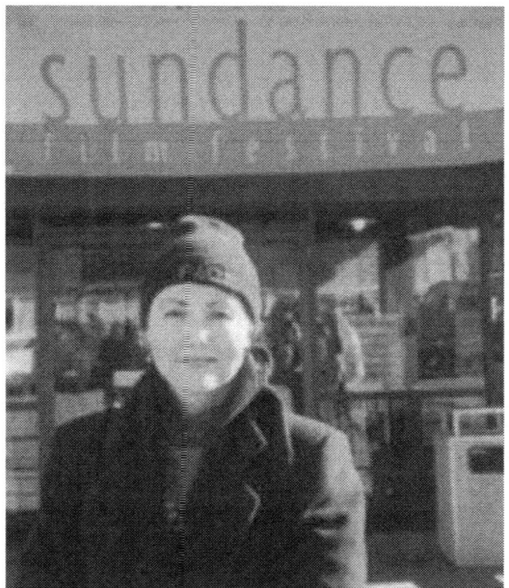

Kiều Chinh at Sundance Film Festival

Attending Asian World Film Festival
(ảnh Getty Images)

Poster for the film "Mission Overseas" shot in Thailand

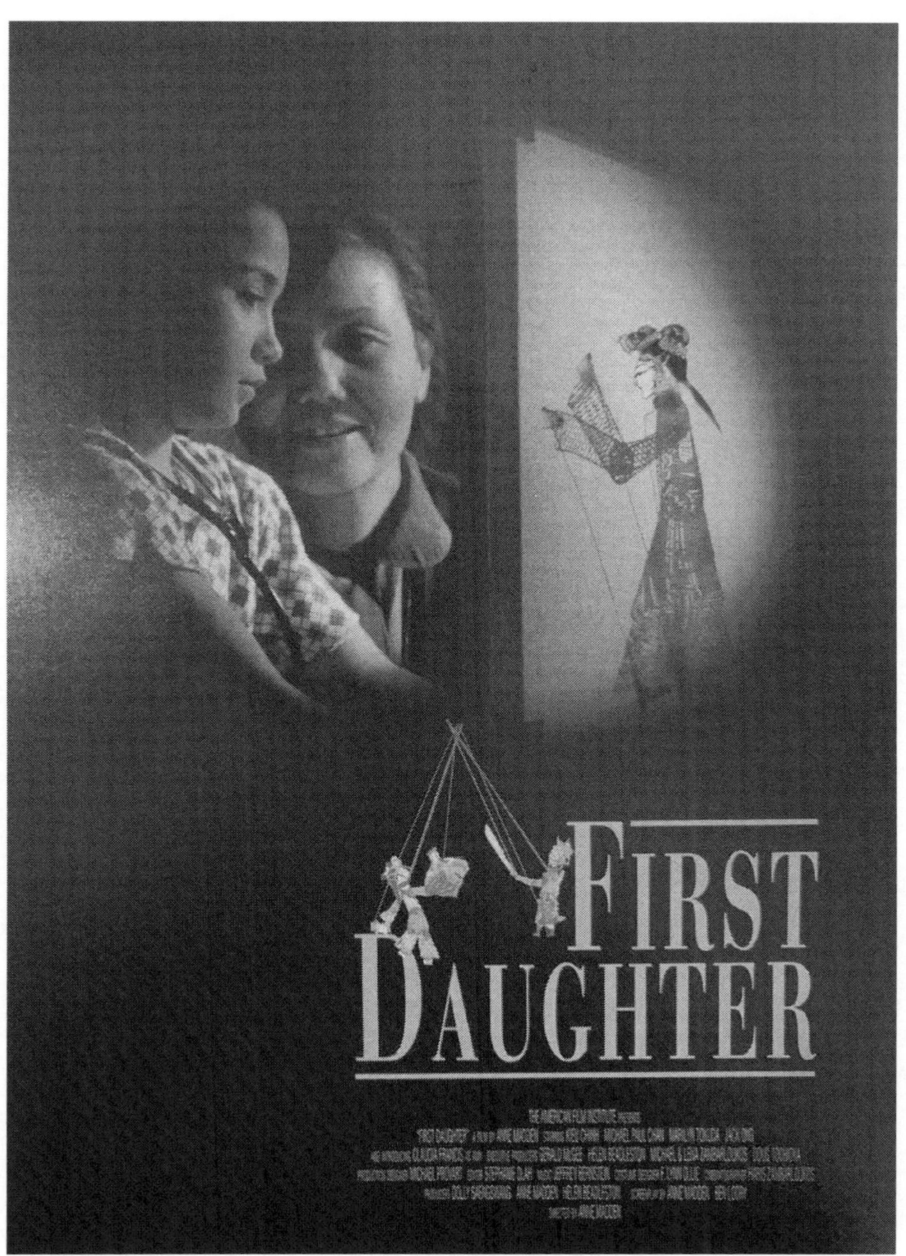

Poster for the film "First Daughter" directed by Anne Madden.

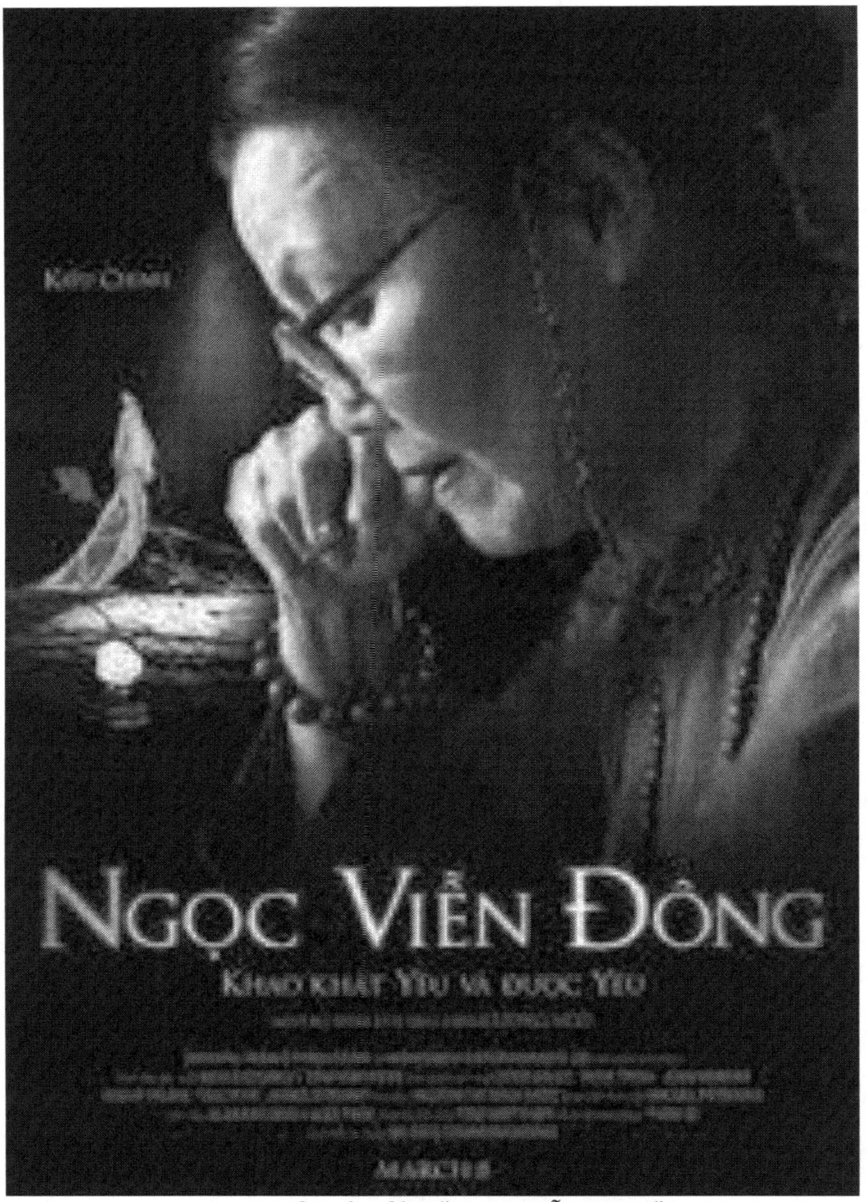

Poster for the film "Ngọc Viễn Đông"

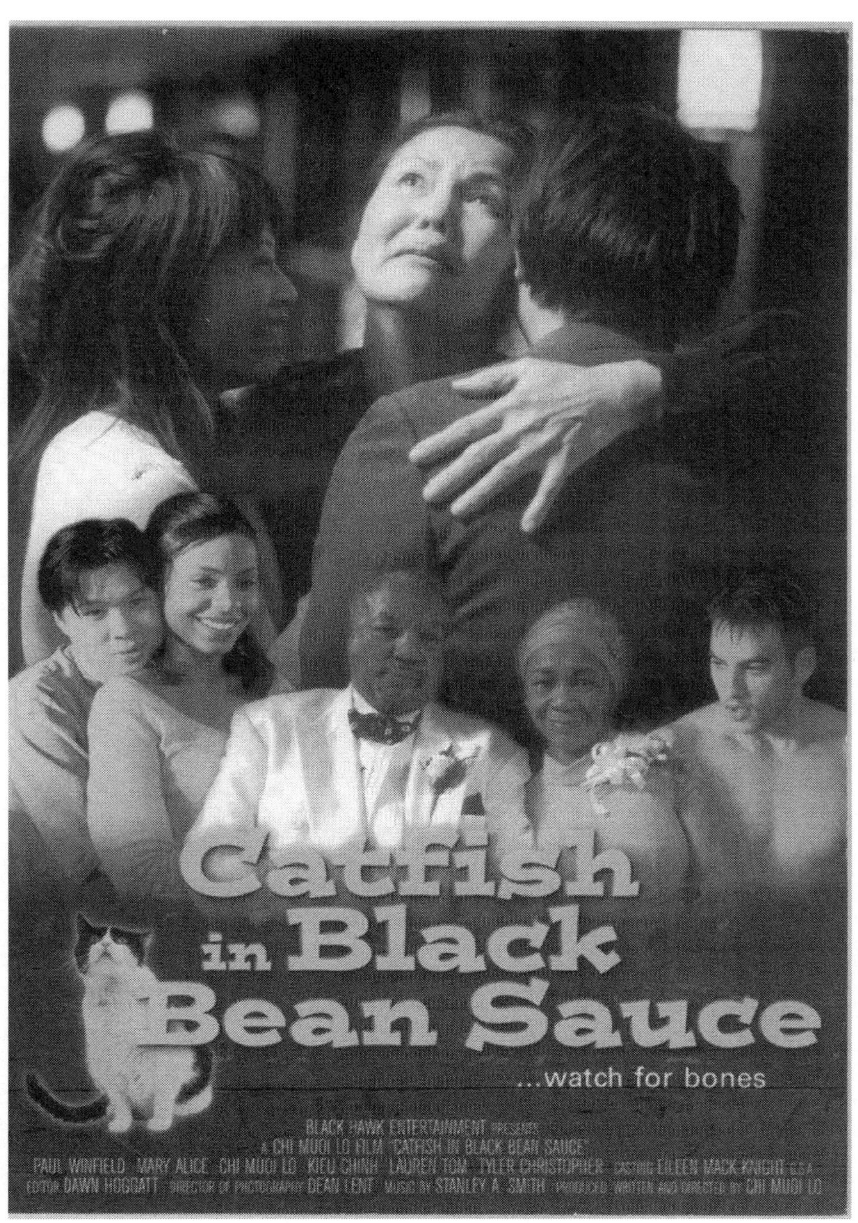

Poster for the film "Catfish in Black Bean Sauce" directed by Chí Mười Lô.

Poster for the film "Face" directed by Bertha Bay-Sa Pan

Winner of the Woman Warrior Award.

Delivering a speech when receiving the award for Refugee of The Year 1990, at The United States Congress, Washington DC .

Receiving the award for Refugee of The Year 1990, at The United States Congress, Washington DC .

Friends celebrate the Thirty years of Kiều Chinh's film career on the stage of the Performing Art Center, Costa Mesa, California.

Mr. Nguyễn Long-Cương, cctor in "We Want To Live" ("Chúng Tôi Muốn Sống"), one of the most successful films made by South Vietnam in the '50s, and now a well-known film editor in France, presents a plaque honoring "Kiều-Chinh's 25 Years in Film" in Paris.

With Patrick Perez,director of documentary film: "KIEU CHINH, A Journal Home"

MCI Telephone Company Congratulates Documentary Film Kieu Hinh: A Journey Home directed by Patrick Perez who won the Emmy Award

Director Patrick Perez and Kiều Chinh receive the Emmy award for the documentary film KIEU CHINH: A Journey Home direc- ted by Patrick Perez of Fox Tele- vision.

"Let us pray for the reunifica- tion of all the families divided by the wars of this world" KC

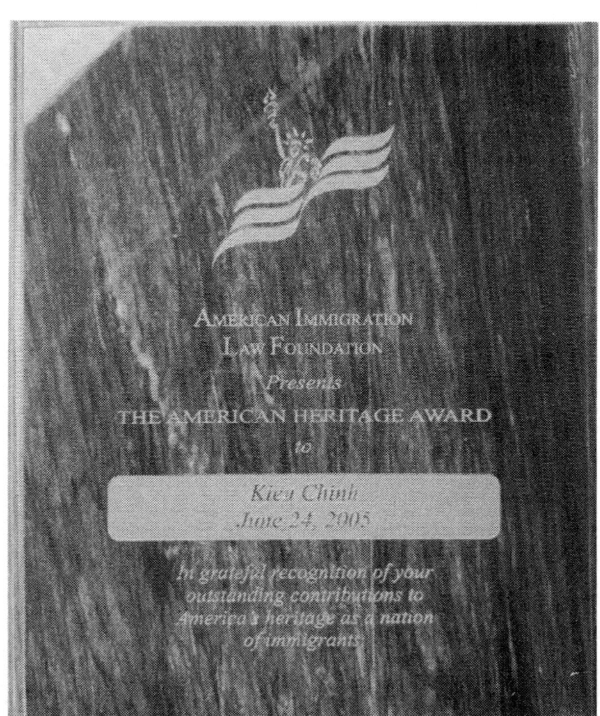

Winner of The American Heritage Award from the American Immigration Law Foundation, 2005.

Kiều Chinh is among the 5 international actors to receive the Special Prize of the Festival Internazionale Cinema Delle Donne, Italy.

At the San Diego Film Festival, Kiều Chinh receives the Lifetime Achievement Award. The film Vượt Sóng won the Best Film award. From left to right: actor Tuấn Cường, actress Kiều Chinh, producer Lâm Nguyễn, director Trần Hàm and producer Alan Vo Ford.

Senator Lou Correa honoring Kiều Chinh with a Congressional Record Award citation.

Receiving the Women of Color JTC Trailblazer Award.

Kiều Chinh among the 5 actors to receive the Lifetime Achievement Award. From left to right: Jackie Chan, Sonil Thapa, Kiều Chinh, Bappi Lahri, Martin Sheen.

With Mr. George Jojo Chamchoum, President of Asian World Film (AWFF) during the presentation of the Lifetime Achievement Award to Kiều Chinh.

PART IV

Pieces of My Life:

1. *Lecturer*
2. *The Media*
3. *Charity Work*

The Wall

Washington, D.C.

November 11, 1993, Veterans Day. I was invited by Jan Scruggs — ESQ, President and Founder of Vietnam Veterans Memorial Fund, to attend and give a speech at a memorial service for Americans who died in the Vietnam War.

The ceremony was solemn. All military branches were represented. The large crowd filled the entire area in front of the Vietnam Memorial Wall that listed the names of more than 58,000 service members. Special guests, including the president of the United States, each made a short statement and read some of the names on The Wall.

After my speech, many veterans came and gave me a hug. Some cried on the spot. I was so moved. I truly admired those who came in wheelchairs or on crutches with missing limbs; many were gray-haired men in uniform.

Afterwards, reporters asked me about my feelings and the tears I shed as I read the names. I told them:

"When I pronounced the Johnsons and Smiths, I couldn't help thinking about the Trần's, Lê's, Nguyễn's... More than two million Vietnamese also fell in the longest war the U.S. was engaged in. I wish that someday I will be able to do something for them, too, especially for the innocent children of war."

I was introduced to two people who later became instrumental in realizing my wish. The first was Lewis Puller Jr., a well-known Marine veteran. He'd lost both his legs, and his hands had several fingers missing. He was the son of Lt. General

Lewis B. Puller, the most decorated Marine in American history. He also was the author of the Pulitzer-winning autobiography *Fortunate Son*.

The second person was journalist Terry Anderson. He was taken hostage by the Islamic Jihad in Lebanon and held for six years, from 1985 to 1991. After his release, he wrote the best-selling memoir *Den of Lions*. I asked to meet both of them later *to present my desire to do something to honor the two million Vietnamese dead.*

Below is the short speech I gave at the Vietnam Memorial Wall on that day:

Being a Vietnamese-American, who has taken refuge twice, who has lost parents and siblings and almost everything because of the war, who has fidgeted with countless questions and contradicting thoughts, please let me share with you some reflections upon the Vietnam War – looking back from the Wall.

When joining the 10th Anniversary of the Wall, reciting names of the dead, I recognized that while standing there, at this place, and commemorating in front of the huge Wall inscribed with names of over 58,000 American casualties in the Vietnam War, all reasons for the war were faded and gone.

I looked at the Wall and saw the whole humanity and globe appear as one body. This common body of humanity, just like a person growing up step by step, is sometimes healthy, wise, and sometimes sick, unwise, self-inflicted.

One of the self-inflicted wounds of humanity is called the Vietnam War.

This wound is not small. Just look at the two sides of the Pacific Ocean. On one side, a country of just 320,000 kilometers square was ravaged, a people split. And on the other side, numerous American generations were divided. Over 58,000 American soldiers fell, and over two million people – soldiers, civilians, the aged and the young – died in the unfortunate land chosen by history to be the battlefield. This wound is still painful for millions, decades after the silence prevailed over the guns.

Vietnam veterans, returning from the battlefield with physical or spiritual wounds, continue their battles, not for inflicting more but for healing them when taking part with American civilians to build the Wall of the Vietnam Veterans Memorial.

Within a decade, over twenty five million people have come to it. And certainly millions more will come to it.

Vietnam Veterans Memorial has never been a monument of the war, but a hope for healing. It is a place where the dead remind the living of their hopes for a more peaceful world.

History shows that all the walls erected to separate and damage humanity have collapsed. But the Wall that has brought people together for healing, in the meaning of the Vietnam Veterans Memorial, will stand forever because it's made not only of stone but also of spirit, not only to stay on earth but also to live in human hearts.

The earth, our common home, is still increasingly intimidated by the destruction of more horrible weapons.

May the message from the Wall on the Vietnam War remind future generations to learn how to keep the earth safe for humanity growing up in a body intact, healthy, and peaceful.

Vietnam Children's Fund

The question was, *how can we honor the two million Vietnamese who died in the war?* To find the answer, the first person I reached out to was Lewis Puller, Jr.

One cold winter evening, I paid Lewis a visit at his home in Fairfax, Virginia. The house sat on a large piece of land with many tall trees. Dead leaves covered the pathway to his house.

A woman opened the door and invited me in. Lewis was sitting in a wheelchair in the middle of the wood-floored living room with very few pieces of furniture. He rolled toward me and introduced his sister, who had come over to help and bring him some food. On a small table in front of the fireplace was a bottle of wine, some cheese and grapes. There was only one guest chair.

Before leaving, Lewis' sister asked if he needed anything else. He asked her to open the bottle, bring him two glasses and a copy of *Fortunate Son* so he could autograph it for me. I also asked her to take a picture for us.

After she left, Lewis and I sat by the fireplace and talked. Once the initial pleasantries were dispensed with, our conversation dove right into Vietnam where Lewis had left two legs and several fingers. Apparently the toll from his physical wounds was nowhere nearly as heavy as that from the psychological one which radically changed Lewis' life.

At one point, we found ourselves talking about our fathers. Lewis' dad was, of course, a famous Marine general who was buried with full honors. Mine, on the other hand, was an unfortunate son of circumstances who was imprisoned by communists and had to die hungry in obscurity.

Lewis rolled his wheelchair toward the back door. A few minutes later he came back with some more firewood. I knelt down to take the wood from his arms. We fed the fire as we talked. Firelight shone on the disabled veteran revealing a handsome face. An intellectual. The hair hung a bit long, with sad eyes looking out from behind a pair of glasses. Suddenly I said, without thinking:

"My father was handsome, too."

Lewis looked at me but didn't respond. We both fell into a long silence, pursuing our own thoughts about our fathers — about the cruelty of war, obviously, but also about the pride we had as we strived to carry on their legacies.

I mentioned the day we met at the Vietnam Memorial Wall and said to Lewis: "I wish I could do something to honor the two million of Vietnamese who died in the war..."

Lewis immediately put the hand that had only two fingers on mine and said: "Such a noble thought. Count me in."

A few days later, I learned that Terry Anderson was giving a presentation in Las Vegas, so I flew in to meet him and his wife,

Madeleine Bassil. I told Terry about the burning desire I had been harboring. He agreed right away.

Terry was able to use his name recognition and vast network to set up several press conferences at the National Press Club in Washington, D.C. This caught the attention of many important people and news organizations in the country.

For my part, I was able to invite Jack Wheeler, past chairman of the Vietnam Memorial Fund responsible for building The Wall. Jack was an attorney with deep experience and broad knowledge, someone whom I thought would be indispensable for the organization we planned to launch — Vietnam Children's Fund.

Jack was then able to ask Marcia Landau to join us. During the Reagan administration, she was director of communications for the Vietnam Veterans Leadership Program.

Not to be outdone, Terry brought in The Honorable Edward Timperlake who once flew F-4 Phantoms in Vietnam. He later served as Assistant Secretary in the Department of Veterans Affairs in the George H. W. Bush administration.

We were also able to enlist many other prominent individuals such as Joy Carol, Patricia Derian, William B. Richards, Tom Kennedy, Anthony Acamando... All enthusiastically supported our mission and became the earliest VCF members. After several rounds of meeting and voting, the first VCF Board of Directors comprised:

- Lewis Puller, Jr.; Kieu Chinh; Terry Anderson: Co-Founders, Co-Chairs.
- Jack Wheeler: President.
- Marcia Landau: Secretary and Media Director.

Since our members were all well-known individuals and dignitaries, through their hard work and networking capabilities VCF received a lot of good press from major newspapers like the *Washington Post, USA Today.*

The majority of VCF members lived in the New York - D.C. area. I was the only Viet-American, and was based in California. In Vietnam, we also had Sam Russell who served as country director. Sam was the one who drew up blueprints for VCF school buildings and supervised their construction with the help of his very capable assistant Ms. Lan Viên.

Second Trip Home

In January 2000, I went back to Hà-Nội. Accompanying me were a reporter for the *Orange County Register*, John Gittelson, and his photographer Daniel A. Anderson. My purpose was to open the seventh VCF school in Nhân-Chính Village.

Sam Russell, our Vietnam VCF director, and his engineer assistant, Lan Viên, were instrumental in getting the project approved and finished on time. Without them, VCF would not have been able to accomplish our goals. Their contributions were absolutely vital to our success.

It wasn't until I got there that I learned Nhân-Chính was the new name of Mọc Village in Cự-Lộc, Hà-Đông — my paternal grandfather's home village. A large crowd attended the opening day, many were schoolchildren and village elders.

As we drank tea in a small temple nearby, an old gentleman told me that the land on which the school was built once belonged to Judge Phan, a great benefactor of the village. Not long after the judge died, the French occupied the town and razed his home to the ground, and built an army camp on top of the ruins.

I was flabbergasted. So this was my grandfather's land! The house that was destroyed by the French was where my siblings and I once lived after my mother and newborn brother were killed.

The man said he also knew the Judge's son, Nguyễn Cửu, because his house was right behind my grandfather's house and he was only a few years younger than Cửu. By now I could no longer contain my emotions:

"Oh my God! Thank you, sir. Nguyễn Cửu was my father!"

The old gentleman gave me an incredulous look, not believing what he had just heard. But when he realized it was really true, he hugged me and cried:

"Oh my Lord, so this is the descendant of the Judge. Thank you, ma'am for following in your ancestor's footsteps to build this school. All the villagers here are very grateful to the Judge. He erected our village gate and many other structures. Thank you, ma'am, for continuing the good work..."

I started to tear up. Memories of Dad and Grandfather came rushing back. For the rest of the day, I hung around the old man and listened to his stories. His voice blended in beautifully with the laughter of the children playing in the schoolyard. At one point I had to request that he stop calling me "Ma'am."

The school itself is a two-story building with eight classrooms, plus two rooms for the administrators and teachers. It also has two toilets and a playground with tall shade trees. Old men in traditional dresses joined the uniformed children to greet our delegation. At the end of my speech, I wished the children well and hoped that the school would contribute to their future success in life.

Since it was during Tết, I also brought along some presents for the students which my children and I had put together before I left. My oldest daughter, Mỹ-Vân, contributed 200 red envelopes containing two dollars each. My oldest son, Hùng, gave 200 plastic ponchos. Cường prepared 200 plastic bags with pens, pencils, erasers and rulers. I rounded out the package with 200 backpacks.

The students probably had never had a happier day than the opening day of that school. They sang songs to wish me health and longevity. My heart was filled with contentment seeing them so full of joy. At the end of the day, I was invited by the parents and village elders to a traditional Tết meal. Before I left, I went to the village temple to light some incense for my grandfather and father.

As Mọc got smaller and smaller in the rearview mirror, I knew that the longing for my beloved village would only get stronger in direct proportion to its physical distance away from me.

Apart from official VCF business at Nhân-Chính, I made plans to spend some time with family in Hà-Nội. I got together with my brother Lân again. His older daughter, Loan, and her husband, Tuyền, made all the preparations to take us to Sơn-Tây to visit our parents' graves.

Perhaps most emotional was the trip to visit my maternal grandparents' families in Gia-Lâm, Gia-Quất, on the other side of Long Biên bridge. I paid respects at the worship house for my grandfather. I also visited my mother's younger brother, Nguyễn văn Thành. The last time I saw him was the night the Japanese came looking for him. He was hiding in our house at the time because he was very close to his brother-in-law — my father. As the Japanese closed in, Uncle Thành grabbed his sword and, before jumping over the back wall, turned to Dad and said: "You take a different way, brother!" He looked just like a superhero.

Uncle Thành later became a well-known surgeon. During the battle of Điện-Biên-Phủ he spent most of his time in the underground makeshift hospital treating wounded soldiers. He was probably the only surgeon on that battlefield on his side. The worst part was that the constant bombardment caused him to lose his hearing.

At Uncle Thành's house, I also met the poetess Ngân-Giang, who once upon a time was a lady friend of my father. She told me many heartbreaking stories, especially of the day the country was divided. She and my father frantically looked for each other in the ravaged city but never found the other. She recited to me the poem she left for my father, but I was too emotional to remember it all:

You looked for me, I wasn't there
I looked for you, you weren't near
Oh friend, oh dearest friend
Please tell me where you are...

My tears started flowing as I pictured my father in those moments of total madness — lost and alone, with no one around for comfort. By the way, it was Uncle Nghị, my mother's oldest brother, who told me how this lady became Uncle Thành's wife. When Uncle Nghị was in California attending a conference at UCLA, he revealed that it was my Daddy Cửu who recommended that his poet friend Ngân-Giang should marry Uncle Thành.

Another brother of my mother's whom I also was able to see was Uncle Quang. A diplomat, he was Vietnam's first ambassador to the Soviet Union. He later spent time in many other countries in the world. He could speak both Russian and French fluently, as well as several other languages. When I arrived, Uncle Quang was already in a suit and waiting. The first thing we did was to light some incense at the family altar.

I also saw my mother's cousin, Nguyễn văn Tụng. After he came back from Hong Kong, Uncle Tụng spent some time in Sài-Gòn partnering with the scholarly brothers Lê Bá-Kông and Lê Bá-Khanh, teaching English at the Dziên-Hồng Institute. He later went back North and did propaganda broadcasts on the radio, enticing U.S. servicemen to turn against the war — like Tokyo Rose did for Japan in WWII. When he saw the two American journalists accompanying me, he switched into character and started talking like the old propagandist that he once was. It was hilarious!

I was staying at the Hà-Nội Hilton Opera right behind the Opera House. On my way back to the hotel one night, as I walked along Hoàn-Kiếm Lake, I was surprised to see that the area was swarming with people. It seemed everybody had come outside to say goodbye to the old year and welcome the new one. The cafés and shops were blaring music full blast. It was exceedingly noisy. I thought I had just landed on a different planet. I'd never seen Hà-Nội like this before.

Then firecrackers started going off. The crowd began to cheer. It was midnight, the new year had arrived. The sound of firecrackers became more deafening and intense. Next came the fireworks. The sky exploded with colors, their reflections on the lake looking like a million stars dancing to a cacophony of sounds.

Suddenly I saw a man chasing after a little girl, screaming: "Hold my hand! Hold my hand or you'll be lost!" I looked up to the sky, whispering: "Daddy, oh Daddy! How long have we lost each other? Has it been years, or forever?"

James V. Kimsey

One of the big name supporters of our VCF program was Fred Smith, former fighter pilot who later became CEO of FedEx. When I returned to Việt-Nam for the fifth time in 2016, it was to cut the ribbon for the 51st VCF school in Quảng-Nam, donated by FedEx.

But among our earliest and most ardent financial supporters was James V. Kimsey, Founder and CEO of American Online. James was a Vietnam War veteran. He donated money for the very first VCF school, which was built in Đông Hà, near the 17th parallel in the former DMZ.

I can never forget one trip to Việt-Nam with James Kimsey and his friend, retired General Jack Nicholson. They flew in his private plane from Washington, D.C., to Los Angeles to pick me up. There were only three of us on the plane, plus a small crew.

After dinner, we all had a nice sleep in the beds immaculately prepared by the attendants. I was awakened hours later by the pilot's announcement over the intercom:

"We are about to land in Russia to refuel. You won't need to leave the plane. After about twenty minutes we will head straight for Hà-Nội."

As the plane flew lower, I pulled up the shade to look outside. It was spectacular. The entire forested landscape was covered with snow. I immediately thought of the movie *Doctor Zhivago* and the scene in which Omar Sharif rode his horse through the snow looking for Lara. I took out my camera and started snapping pictures, running from one side of the plane to the other like a little kid. Close up shots. Zoom out shots...

After the plane landed, there were bright spotlights shining on both sides of our plane. The door burst open. Four armed men entered and trained their guns on us. A fifth man, unarmed, asked: "Who took pictures?" I raised my hand: "Me." All three of us stood up as the men pointed their weapons in our direction. The unarmed man ordered us to bring our passports and my camera and follow him. General Nicholson explained that we were U.S. citizens, that we only stopped for fuel and had no intention to leave the plane or step on Russian soil. Our pilot came over and showed them our paperwork.

The man asked me why I took photos. I said because the view was too beautiful, it reminded of *Doctor Zhivago*, and because I was an artist who loved to take pictures for souvenirs. In response, he took my camera and passport. After about 10 minutes he returned, handed me back my passport and camera but without the roll of film. I later learned that hidden behind those lovely snow-filled trees were rocket launchers!

There were other amusing memories with James Kimsey as well, albeit not as exciting or intense. Every time I flew into Washington, D.C., James would send someone to pick me up at the airport. The first time I came, he said:

"I'll have Kissinger pick you up."

"What?!" I asked. "Are you kidding me?

"Not at all. His name is Kissinger. He's my chauffeur, not the secretary of state."

Turns out "Kissinger the chauffeur" was a short, dark-skinned Laotian ex-captain. I was told he used to be a top marksman and could really throw a knife. Apparently, Kissinger was both chauffeur and bodyguard. He wore a pair of boots that had a knife strapped on the left and a pistol on the right. The Rolls Royce he drove was immaculately clean.

James had a gentle and polite way of talking that did not lack humor. One time he invited me to lunch and said he'd send someone over to "pick me up" around noon. I asked if that would be too late since it would take a long time to get from my hotel to his office on Pennsylvania Avenue during that time of day. He said it would be no problem at all; all I had to do was go to the hotel rooftop and wait for his helicopter. "Five minutes, max!" He assured me.

His office was on the top floor of a building that looked across a rectangular courtyard straight toward the White House. He had a lunch spread already prepared. Knowing I didn't eat meat, it only included lobster salad and a bottle of white wine.

I also remember a dinner at his home. The large estate which he had built from scratch sat on the bank of the Potomac River in McLean, an exclusive area in Virginia. Besides the main house, he also bought the house already on the property that was designed by Frank Lloyd Wright. One entire side of that house was a glass wall looking down at the Potomac River beneath which water was rushing through at a terrific speed. James used it as a guest house; I had stayed there overnight once.

One night, James invited me to a performance at the Kennedy Center, followed by dinner at the Terrace Restaurant on the same campus. As we walked down the hall toward the restaurant, I saw his name carved into the wall. James explained that he had donated $10 million during the construction of this complex. We also passed a very artistically decorated place named KC Café, James jokingly said: "This café is supposed to be yours!"

The next day we had lunch with John McCain, who was announcing his presidential bid. James was a strong supporter of the senator from Arizona.

The night before I left, we had dinner in the guesthouse. The only other guests were General Jack Nicholson and his wife. It was a warm and intimate meal by the fireplace. James' personal secretary brought out a rare bottle of wine. We wished each other good health and hoped to see everyone again soon. Unfortunately, that was our last time together.

On March 5, 2016, I returned to Washington, D.C. to attend James Kimsey's funeral, held at St. Matthew's Cathedral. Many people came from all over the world. After the funeral Mass there was a private "farewell party" at James' house. Each person was invited to say a few words. Some spoke about his many accomplishments or the many beautiful and famous women he knew, like Queen Nor and Bo Derek. When my turn came, I recounted:

"Yes, I know James met some very beautiful women in some very spectacular settings. But I had the opportunity to witness a very beautiful encounter as well. It was during our first trip back to Vietnam in 1995. After we were done with the opening ceremony for VCF's first school, built near the DMZ and financed by James, he asked me to accompany him to Danang to be his interpreter for a meeting with a woman that he already had his people search out ahead of time.

It was a hot April day in Central Vietnam. The heat was unbearable. Our driver dropped us off near the entrance to a commune. We waited by a rice field. After a short while, on a tiny dirt path that ran between the rice paddies a small figure appeared. James quickly ran toward the woman, picked her up and lifted her off the ground. She was an old Catholic nun, very small in stature. They started talking to each other like schoolchildren, I had to translate nonstop.

James asked her about some boy named "Bảy" and some girl named "Mai." He asked how the orphanage was doing. She told him they both had grown up and left. The two orphanages that James helped build when he was a service member in this area had fallen into disrepair and were in very bad shape. Meanwhile, the number of orphans was getting so large that there wasn't enough room for them to sleep.

Before we left, James gave the nun a big hug and stuffed into her pocket three thousand dollars. He promised that when he got back to the U.S. he would send her another $15,000 so she could build more rooms. She cried as they parted. James held her hand as if he was a child having to leave his mother again after a brief reunion.

The room was completely silent as I recounted the story. James' youngest son, Ray, gave me a hug and thanked me. He then led me over to a corner of the room where a small Buddha sat looking out at the Potomac river below: "This is the present you once gave to my father. He used to sit at this spot every day."

I said goodbye to General Jack Nicholson, to Kissinger the chauff-eur, and to that won-derful house which I'd probably never see a-gain. Farewell, James.

My dear friend, Rest In Peace.

Northridge Earthquake

I returned to Los Angeles from Paris via Rio. By the time I got back to my house it was already 1:30 a.m. The Chopin statuette that I nursed in my arms throughout the flight was immediately placed on the piano. I flipped on the lights. It looked perfect!

I brought my luggage into the bedroom but didn't feel like unpacking. After such a long, tiring flight, all I wanted to do was sleep. And soundly I did, until I was suddenly wakened by a powerful and thunderous jolt. I was violently thrown off the bed and onto the floor. All the lights went off. I was terrified. Thinking I was still in the Ritz Hotel in Paris, I started yelling:

"Au secours! Au secours!' (Help! Help!)

I flailed my arms about; touching my luggage reminded me that I was back home in California. But still I couldn't understand why it was pitch black, both outside and inside the house. The earth was rumbling beneath my feet. Then came a violent tremor and a thunderous crash.

It's an earthquake! Oh my God! An earthquake!

It was too dark to see anything, but I was able to make my way to the bedroom door out of reflexive familiarity. But then, there was something blocking my path. It was the piano! It must have traveled here all the way from the music room. I started calling for help.

The house stopped shaking. Someone was knocking on the door and shining a flashlight into the house. I climbed over all the furniture and got to the front door. It was Jeff, my younger neighbor from across the street. I held on to Jeff like a drowning person. He told me to come over to his house and stay with his wife and kids so I would feel more safe. He took my hand and pulled me along. All the street lights were out. Our whole street was completely dark, like a scene from sone horror flick.

In my mind, I just thought about my children, wondering if they were OK. I could not call anyone because all phone lines were down. As dawn neared, I could begin to see some of the damage to my house. The tall red brick column by the fireplace had collapsed on top of my car, crushing it.

I thanked Jeff and his wife and walked back to my house. It looked like a war zone. Overturned furniture everywhere. Picture frames littered the floor. The cupboard containing dozens of my antique teapots had dumped out all its content. In the kitchen, bowls and plates lay shattered. Cabinet doors were open; bottles and jars were thrown out. The Chopin statuette I bought at Le Louvre didn't stand a chance.

I found an old battery-operated radio that still worked and turned it on. The news said there was a magnitude 6.7 earthquake in Northridge.

Paranoia followed me around for weeks afterwards; I was afraid to go to sleep. Like a crazy bag lady, I'd wear all kinds of alarm devices on my body — whistle, flashlight, long-sleeved shirts, tennis shoes, etc. and go to my son Hùng's house to sleep over.

The large framed picture above my bed fell onto the mattress and shattered. I shuddered, thinking what could have happened to me had I not been thrown off my bed. The Northridge Earthquake occurred at 4:30 a.m. on January 1, 1994, and lasted for a mere 20 seconds, causing 72 deaths and injuring thousands.

Toronto International Film Festival

by Tôn Thất Hùng

The year 2018 marked the 25th anniversary of "The Joy Luck Club." The film received a special recognition at the Toronto International Film Festival. The following are excepts from a report by Tôn Thất Hùng, a long-time event organizer in the city's Vietnamese community.

The Toronto International Film Festival (TIFF) is the largest film festival in North America, and the second largest in the world after Cannes. This year, TIFF held a special event to celebrate the 25th anniversary of *The Joy Luck Club.*

The red carpet at the magnificent Elgin Theater was rolled out. Dozens of media crews were at the ready. About 1,500 people were in attendance. Most were part of a younger generation who laughed at the jokes and cried with Kiều-Chinh as she portrayed how families were separated by war. All the cameras immediately turned to Kiều-Chinh the moment she appeared.

Kiều-Chinh has been in the movie industry for 61 continuous years. She has worked in studios from Sài-Gòn to Hollywood and throughout Asia, including Hong Kong, Taiwan, Thailand, Singapore, and the Philippines.

She came to Toronto for the first time on April 30, 1975 — the day Sài-Gòn fell, and became the first Vietnamese refugee in Canada. In the ensuing forty-three years, Kiều-Chinh and the city of Toronto have remained connected. She has often come back to the city to work on a film, to speak, to attend film festivals and so on. This year, however, Kiều-Chinh has returned in full glory — as a major star in undoubtedly the biggest Asian-based Hollywood movie to date.

TIFF takes place over ten days and screens more than 340 films from all over the world, or an average of 34 films a day.

However, on this day, September 13, 2018, all eyes were on the *The Joy Luck Club* team — director Wayne Wang, actors Tsai Chin, Tamlyn Tomila, Kiều-Chinh. They took up much of the Canadian media's attention.

Thirty minutes after the conclusion of the Q&A session, people still lingered about, not wanting to leave. I asked to meet Kiều-Chinh but was told she had already left through a side door. I ran outside and tried to make my way around the building, fighting through a crowd, asking the other reporters to let me through because I was "a compatriot" of hers.

Everybody was trying to get a picture taken with our beautiful star. I only had a few seconds to get a photo with her myself. Afterwards the big body guards quickly ushered her and the others into a row of waiting limousines (each star had their own limo). Kiều-Chinh appeared reluctant to leave. She rolled down her window; fans ran toward her to snap more photos.

Two young African girls cried as they ran after the car. I asked them why? They told me Kiều-Chinh's Suyuan reminded them of their home country which also was mired in war and family separation.

Mainstream media and TIFF attendants have been talking up a sequel to *The Joy Luck Club*. We can only hope, and wait.

Fifteen Years As Lecturer

After coming to America, I also gained a new skill as a professional public speaker. I even have an agent — Greater Talent Network (GTN), based in New York.

Since 1993, GTN had sent me to speak at many universities in the U.S. — Cornell, Central Michigan, UCLA, USC, etc. I was also invited to speak at major corporations like Pfizer, Kellogg and so on, as well as at local events like the West Virginia Book Fair.

Perhaps most memorable was the speech at the Women's Day of America celebration held in Sacramento, CA, just one day after the 9/11 terrorist attacks. I opened the event and spoke in front of about 3,500 people, mainly women professionals and executives considered influencers in their industries.

Whenever I was booked for an engagement, I typically prepared my remarks well in advance. But the 9/11 attacks, which happened the day before, changed all that. Instead of talking about the many outstanding accomplishments of women as I had planned, I spoke directly from the heart with emotions that still were very raw. After my speech the audience rose up and gave me a standing ovation.

The last person to speak that day was Mme Benazir Bhutto, former prime minister of Pakistan. Both the first and last speeches of the day were on the subject of terrorism. Not long after our meeting, I received the horrible news that Mme Bhutto was assassinated by terrorists in Pakistan.

Speaking engagements typically are booked at least a year in advance. That gives the speaker enough time to prepare the speech. Sometimes I had to spend months at the library doing research. Like the time I was asked to speak at the West Virginia Book Fair in November of 2007.

The fair was held at the Olde Town in Martinsburg, known for its revolutionary role during the Civil War. I had to speak in front of many well-known writers even though I wasn't a writer myself. Among the forty or so bestselling authors appearing at the fair that year were: Loraine Despres, writer for the popular TV series *Dallas*; Bob O'Connor, winner of the Best Book Award in 2006; Doro Bush Koch, author of "*My Father, My President*."

I was the first to speak that day, while the last speaker was Doro Bush, daughter of the 41st president of the United States. Some international writers came to the fair as well, such as Korky Paul who wrote "*The Fish Who Could Wish*." Paul was also a renowned animated filmmaker in England.

My job at the fair, besides delivering the opening remarks, was to attend various discussion panels with other authors, screenplay writers, filmmakers, journalists and so on. It was also in this historic town that I was the keynote speaker at the West Virginia Theater Conference Mountain Masquerade.

I spoke to an audience made up mostly of students and professors of Film and Theatre. After that event, I was invited to be the keynote speaker for The Theatre Conference Organization in March, 2008, before an audience of about 1,500 professional stage and film professionals in America.

In the fifteen years spent on the lecturing circuit, I had the chance to speak in hundreds of events at universities, government agencies as well as private companies. But my fondest memories were at The Wall in 1992, the West Virginia Book Fair in 2007, and most poignantly Women's Day on 9/12/2001.

9/11

Like all Americans, I was shocked and stunned by the events on 9/11. Shortly after the attacks, a Vietnamese businessman I knew in New York named Trần Đình-Trường donated $2 million to the American Red Cross to help with the recovery. I called him and came up to visit.

Joining me from Washington was cameraman Phạm Bội-Hoàn who worked at the White House. Together we made several video reports from Ground Zero which were later broadcast by Little Sài-Gòn TV.

Mr. Trường owned several hotels in New York City, one of which was used as a rest stop and free lodging for first responders, rescuers, firefighters... He also provided them with food and drove a cart around Ground Zero passing out drinks and snacks. His wife explained that this was their way of thanking America for opening its doors to immigrants like their family.

After New York, we went to visit Washington, D.C. On that day there happened to be a funeral for a Viet-American engineer named Nguyễn Ngọc-Khang who was killed in the Pentagon attack. I met and comforted his widow. His toddler son was running around the coffin as he played with an older boy. At one point he called out for help, "Daddy, daddy, he's picking on me!" Apparently the little boy had not realized what death was. It broke my heart.

A few years later, I was in Washington, D.C., to attend the Vietnamese-American Heritage Exhibit at the Smithsonian. A woman brought her son to my book signing. She came up and asked me, "Ms. Kiều Chinh, do you remember me?" Then, without waiting for my answer she introduced herself, "I am Anh-Tú, the wife of Nguyễn Ngọc-Khang, and this is our son Nguyễn Ngọc-An." She was still wearing a mourning patch for her deceased husband.

Many more years later, after the 9/11 Memorial was completed, I went to Ground Zero to pay my respects. It was raining slightly on that day. I thought I was caught between the tears from Heaven and manmade tears as the waterfalls rushed into a bottomless well of silence.

The names etched on the black granite made me think of the more than 58,000 names on the Vietnam Wall and the two million Vietnamese killed by war. But that was the result of a fifteen-year long struggle. This memorial, on the other hand, was a giant tomb for three thousand souls murdered in a split instant out of pure evil and hate. I was overwhelmed.

Smithsonian

The road sign "Little Sài-Gòn, Next Right" usually seen in Orange County has been added, not to a highway but a museum — in front of the S. Dillon Ripley Center of the Smithsonian in Washington, D.C. Follow the sign and you'll be taken to an exhibit called "30 years of Vietnamese-Americans in the U.S."

The exhibit began on January 20, 2007. As guests entered, they would see photos on the walls depicting the story of Vietnamese in America. The most outstanding of them was that of a young Viet woman wearing a yellow *áo dài* carrying an American flag in a 4th of July parade. Dr. Phạm Hồng-Vũ, executive director for the Vietnamese-American Heritage Project at the Smithsonian Institute, said the photo represented the essence of the exhibit. It showed how successfully the 1.5 million strong Viet-American diaspora has integrated into society after having been through a tragic past.

The photos told the story of their journey that began in April 1975: helicopters pick up evacuees; the first refugees on Guam, Camp Pendleton, Indian Town Gap... In the opposite corner artifacts depicting life in a refugee camp: a canvas cot, clothes hung on a line... mimicking a scene from an actual photo.

After evacuation came the escape scenes: images of boat people in the ocean, some were dead on their boats. Pictures of Amerasians, sponsors, reunions... Finally, community gatherings as refugees became settled and began to form associations.

"This exhibit," said Dr. Vũ Phạm, "lets Americans and future generations see how Viet-Americans helped change the face of America. Each year, about 25 million people visit the 19 museums in the Smithsonian."

The exhibit was part of a larger program called the Asia-Pacific American Heritage Project headed by Dr. Franklin Odo, a Japanese-American historian at the Institute. The day before the exhibit opened, there was a formal reception with about 400 guests, American and Vietnamese.

In attendance were Senator Jim Webb (VA) and his Vietnamese wife, Hong Le Webb, with their newborn baby. James Webb is also an author and a Marine veteran who fought in Vietnam. He can speak and write Vietnamese fluently.

Other Vietnam vets included James Kimsey, Founder and CEO of American Online, and Jan C. Scruggs, Chairman of Vietnam Veterans Memorial Fund which built The Wall.

Senator Michael Honda (CA), of Japanese descent, said he really enjoyed the exhibit about Viet-Americans. In the '90s, another prominent Japanese-American, Norman Mineta, was instrumental in creating the Asia-Pacific American Program which has organized many events at the Smithsonian highlighting the contributions of Asia-Pacific Americans to our country. This exhibit was one of those. It was a survey of the rich cultural traditions and experiences that Vietnamese have brought with them to enhance the social fabric of America.

A curriculum was being developed to teach middle school students about the history of Viet-Americans within the larger context of U.S. history. After thirty years in the U.S., a successful new generation of Viet-Americans have emerged. The exhibit displayed some of their achievements. Of the thirteen individuals highlighted for their outstanding accomplishments, one was an actress. Her newly published collection of photographs, "Kieu Chinh, Vietnamese American" was introduced at the reception, followed by a book signing. The book also became part of the exhibit.

The Wounds of War

My work with the Vietnam Children's Fund unexpectedly led to a dark, unfortunate event.

Early in 2000, when Senator John McCain from Arizona was launching his presidential bid, I had a chance to meet him in Washington, D.C. at a dinner where VCF's honorary member James Kimsey was invited. James in turn asked me to join him. We sat together at John McCain's table. When James introduced me to the others around the table, the senator's campaign manager suggested that I introduce Mr. McCain to the Vietnamese community when he visits Little Sài-Gòn the following month. He also warned me that in an interview not long before John McCain used the derogatory word "gooks" to describe his North Vietnamese prison guards. Somehow, it became misconstrued that he was calling all Vietnamese that name. John McCain wanted to clear up that misunderstanding, and he wanted to do it in the capital of the Vietnamese diaspora.

I was asked to give a simple opening introduction: "Welcome, Mr. McCain, war hero from the Hà-Nội Hilton." As I mentioned earlier, 'Hà-Nội Hilton' was also where my father and brother were incarcerated for many months.

One March afternoon, Senator McCain came to Westminster, California. A stage was set up in front of the Phước-Lộc-Thọ shopping center on Bolsa Avenue — the Main Street of Little Sài-Gòn. The road was blocked off to all through traffic between Brookhurst and Magnolia streets. Thousands gathered to greet John McCain. A tall media tower had been erected for radio, TV, newspapers and so on.

I got there early and was taken to an area behind the stage to wait. When John McCain arrived, I was instructed to go on stage and make the introduction as previously rehearsed. Dozens of media organizations — American, Vietnamese, Chinese, Japanese, Korean, Latinos — trained their lights and cameras on me. It was so bright that I couldn't see what was below, but I could hear a lot of commotion from the crowd. At first I thought people were hollering to welcome me, so I took a quick bow. The voices kept getting louder, however. As I walked toward the microphone at the center of the stage and before I could say anything, someone angrily shouted:

"Get off! Communist! Kiều Chinh communist! Get off!"

More hollering followed, then I heard loud sounds of things crashing against each other. Before I knew what was happening, two tall Americans in blue shirts — I had been told earlier that the men in blue shirts were special agents, perhaps FBI, who were in charge of security for John McCain — came up on stage. They grabbed my arms and said: "Let's get out of here!"

They guided me through a crowd of angry people who were yelling things like: "Down with communist Kiều Chinh!"

My whole body shook, I could barely walk. Phạm Minh, a young friend, ran toward me and took my arm to lead me away from the mob. Suddenly a woman charged toward me and punched me in the chest, screaming: "Communist! Go the hell back there and live with your communists!"

A policeman came over and cleared a path for me. Andrew Hall, Chief of Police for the city of Westminster sent one of his men to drive me to my house in Newport Beach. That night, as I listened to the Vietnamese radio channel "Living in America," I was shocked to hear my name vilified with the most profane and vulgar language I had ever heard in my life. They even let callers call in to curse me out. One person compared me to the character 'Kiều' — from poet Nguyễn Du's epic 19th century masterpiece 'Kim Vân Kiều' — saying Nguyễn Du's Kiều sold herself to save her father, whereas I sold myself to the communist devils.

The next morning the director of Little Sài-Gòn Radio, Vũ Quang Ninh, came to see me and tried to cheer me up. To me, Ninh was like an older brother, like author Mai Thảo or composer Phạm Đình Chương. He told me there was a late night radio program that had recently been denouncing me publicly, using extremely ugly language, especially since my trip back to Vietnam with the two journalists from the *OC Register*. They whipped up anti-communist sentiment so that listeners would call in to publicly denounce me. I told Ninh:

"I wouldn't know. I don't ever listen to those stations, and certainly never in the middle of the night. I only heard it for the first time last night because I couldn't sleep."

He tried to console me:

"Don't be sad. Our community is quite large, not everyone thinks like that."

I didn't say anything. Ninh suggested (actually it sounded more like an order):

"Don't listen to that channel anymore! Where's the radio? Give it to me."

"But I've just bought it!"

"However much you paid for it, I will buy it from you for twice that."

I tried to make a feeble joke to hide the immeasurable sadness that was eating me up:

"You should go home. Mai Thảo and Hoài Bắc have already bought the radio."

At first, I thought my abuse by extremists was only known within our small community. But somehow Channel 9 got wind of it and sent their reporter David Jackson to my home to do a story. David asked me how I felt facing opposition from my own people like that. What did I think? Do I blame anyone? I answered:

"As a sensitive woman with not very thick skin, I was very hurt by what happened. As an artist, I stay out of politics. Of course I place blame, but not on any individual in our diaspora community. I blame war. I think the war has left too many wounds. Some can be cured with medicine. Others heal on their own with the passage of time. But there are also wounds that neither medications nor time can stem the bleeding."

In response to a different question, I said:

"As humans we all have a homeland and our people. Most people wish to be able to do something good for our country and our countrymen. Some choose to look at the past. Others engage the present. Still others do it for the future. I belong to the third category, with special focus on education. I'm the only person of Vietnamese descent in Vietnam Children's Fund. The rest are American, most are veterans who fought in Vietnam. We have only one goal: build schools in places that were destroyed by war to help children have a place to learn so they may have a brighter future."

In the days that followed, two Vietnamese in old military uniforms appeared every day in front of the always crowded Phước Lộc Thọ shopping center on Bolsa Avenue. They held up enormous signs bigger than a mattress that read: "Emphatically oppose KIỀU CHINH for supporting Vietnamese Communist Party." A van with similar messages written on it was also driven around Little Sài-Gòn to drive the message home. They even called local businesses I was affiliated with for advertising to request that they stop working with me because I was "communist," and they threatened to boycott any business that was associated with me.

Even though many of the businesses did not want to quit working with me, out of financial concerns they had to cancel their contracts, usually with a perfunctory letter of apology.

Meanwhile, the extremists kept cranking the volume and accused VCF of building schools for children of communist cadres.

I had to call a meeting with our VCF Board to explain the situation and offered to resign so that the organization's work could continue without being affected by this. But Terry, the former hostage, adamantly refused to accept my resignation: "We are former Marines. Our motto is to leave no one behind." James Kimsey, who fought in Vietnam and was CEO of American Online at the time and honorary member of VCF, said there was no need for me to resign. He emphasized that whatever I needed to do to protect my name and honor he would stand behind me all the way.

Thank you all, my good friends. I really didn't need to do anything at all. I just kept silent. I didn't want to call on anyone — even my family and friends, for help. I thought it best to leave them out of it.

And so for nearly two years I was out of work. All the existing advertising contracts were cancelled, and no new ones were signed.

At the time, I was living in a lovely little house on a hilltop in Newport Beach where the last sun rays at dusk were always a brilliant display of colors. In the distance, the ocean and the mountain were like an ever changing canvas upon which mother nature painted her secrets.

The upper balcony that ran along one side of the house was where I relaxed each evening, soaking in the peaceful scenery. I took many sunset pictures from that spot. There were no noises from bustling city streets; I was allowed to completely merge my mind and soul with the serenity and beauty of nature. Sometimes, when the clouds were lowered to my line of sight, I might even feel an extraordinary sensation of floating away with the wind.

I loved that house. I spent countless hours decorating and fixing it up, turning it into my own little world. I always thought it would be my last stop on earth. Unfortunately, as the extremists' boycott wore on, I eventually had to sell that house and move to a different area.

During that period, I rarely went out. I wanted to avoid the unfriendly stares people gave; they made me uncomfortable.

One day, the writer-poet couple Nhã Ca and Trần Dạ Từ invited me to lunch at Viễn Đông (Far East) restaurant, owned by the first Viet-American who entered mainstream politics, Tony Lâm Quang. There were two men near our table who kept looking at me. At first I thought it was nothing. But as we finished, they also stood up and followed us. Nhã Ca said: "Uh oh, looks like we'll have to escort Ms. Chinh to her car!"

Sure enough, the men walked over to my car and struck up a conversation. But contrary to what we were expecting, they politely apologized and said:

"Excuse us, ma'am. We are brothers from the Trần family. We're so thrilled to have met you here by chance. We didn't want to bother you while you were eating. My name is Trần Quang-Thuận, and this is my brother Trần Quang-Hải. We really admire your work building schools for children in Việt Nam. Although we're living in the U.S., we've been wanting to build a school for our home village. We hope you can help us. We will come up with all the funds required, we just need the expertise of your organization. We hope to see you again to discuss in detail."

Their straightforward explanation and sincere manners put me at ease. I was both surprised and happy. We met again, and I was introduced to several other prominent members of their Trần clan: doctors Trần Quốc-Lễ and Trần Quốc Nhu, whom we also helped later with a different project.

On one occasion, I was invited to a familial celebration at Hải's house where I met many more in the Trần clan. A year later, VCF inaugurated the Trần's school in Văn Ấp commune, Bồ-Đề village near Hà-Nội.

A few years later, I had the chance to visit this school during a trip back to Việt-Nam. The Trần's welcomed me like a member of their family. It was heartening to see the handsome little school we built and the strong bond among members of the clan in spite of geographical distance. After Dr. Nhu passed away, his wife also asked VCF to build a school in Pleiku in the Central Highlands where her husband used to serve as an Army doctor and became friends with many families there.

It's safe to say that I'm like a Trần now. Every Tết, Dr. Thuận would invite me to their home for a celebration dinner, with delicious traditional Tết foods prepared by his lovely wife. Whenever they invited me to a party, his youngest brother, Dr. Lễ, would offer to be my chauffeur.

These unexpected rewards helped me regain my faith in humanity. My friend Nguyễn Quang-Ninh once said that what I did might annoy a minority for whatever reasons, but it was definitely supported by a silent majority who were totally behind it and willing to chip in. After receiving such terrible criticism from within my community, I could take comfort knowing that there were so many more who understood and agreed with my work.

Tippi Hedren, My Sponsor

Mother of Nails

Tippi Hedren was involved since the earliest days of the first wave of Vietnamese refugees in America. More than 500 families were staying at Hope Village in Sacramento, waiting for sponsors to help them resettle. Most of them spoke very little English. All were anxious and worried about the future.

From talking to the women in the camp, Tippi quickly understood their economic concerns. She came up with the idea of teaching them to do nails. She then organized the first classes, which were taught by one of her friends.

The inaugural class had twenty students. After finishing with the instructions, they learned how to take the exam and obtain a license. And thus the Vietnamese nails industry in America was born. From then on, all the women who graduated from

Hope Village's nails school (if you could call it that) easily found work once they got out of camp. Through word of mouth, the number of Vietnamese women who chose this profession kept getting larger. Pretty soon, most nails businesses, salons and supplies stores in North America were owned by Viet-Americans.

This miraculous development did not escape the attention of mainstream media. Everyone started calling Tippi Hedren the "Mother of the Vietnamese Nails Profession." Indeed, without Mother Tippi, it would have been impossible for Vietnamese in America to have such a dominant presence in the nail business.

On the 40th anniversary of the birth of this industry, the original class of students organized a reunion at the office of *Người Việt (Vietnamese)* newspaper. Many people from Hope Village showed up.

Then on September 23, 2015, the Beauty Changes Lives Foundation and Creative Nail Designs (CND) — a leading nail products company, held a celebration in Beverly Hills to honor Tippi Hedren. Hundreds of people came. Dr. Tam Nguyen, owner of Beauty College, and I were invited to speak.

In a highly emotional moment after our speeches, Jan Arnold, co-founder of CND, announced the creation of a scholarship named "The Tippi Hedren Nails Scholarship." The initial amount for the scholarships, donated by CND, was $184,000!

I'm always so proud anytime I'm asked to talk about Tippi, someone I consider not just as a benefactor and a friend, but also as a sister and the Mother of the Vietnamese nails industry.

Giver of Hope

In 1992, Congress designated October 31 as "Refugee Day." Statute 2569 recognizes contributions from refugees who help build this great nation.

Americans — in one sense or another, in one historical period or another — are immigrants. From the earliest boat people who came in their tattered sails to those still coming today. Once arrived and settled, they tried to bring over their extended families, to reunite with their people. The first refugees in this country also became themselves sponsors. One group of refugees would extend their hands to another, one generation of refugees would help the next. We transcend geographic and cultural boundaries until all become one big family — like Michael Jackson once sang: "We are the world!" It's that rich tradition that created the United States of America.

When I was invited to speak on Capitol Hill on the first "Refugee Day" in 1992, I had the chance to reflect on this idea. And it immediately made me think of Tippi Hedren, my sponsor.

In late 1964, the war in Vietnam started to escalate. American troops began arriving in larger numbers. Sài-Gòn at that time didn't yet have a TV station. Each evening, a large military plane would circle the city very slowly, broadcasting TV programs for American service members. One of them was *Combat*, I recall. This period also marked the birth of Vietnamese television.

In those days, I was the hostess of a TV show myself, and thus had the opportunity to welcome many American celebrities into our humble studio. They were members of the USO who came over to entertain the troops. It was here in 1965 that I first met famous Hollywood personalities such as: Johnny Grant, Joey Bishop, Danny Kay, Diane McBain and Tippi Hedren. All were well known in the industry, of course, but Tippi was getting a lot of attention at the time due to her most recent work with Alfred Hitchcock in *The Birds*.

Since we were both in the movie business, Tippi and I hit it off really well. We had a very friendly and warm interview. She especially liked the gifts I gave her before she left Việt-Nam: a red *áo dài* made from Hà-Đông silk and a pair of terra-cotta elephants from Biên-Hoà.

When I went to America in 1969 to attend the opening of *Doctor Zhivago,* I saw Tippi and also met her husband Noel Marshall, producer of the blockbuster *The Exorcist.* Our friendship was maintained in the years that followed through an occasional postcard with simple greetings. Little did we know that our correspondence would one day lead to a lifelong relationship after the Fall of Sài-Gòn, as I already described in an earlier chapter.

It was Tippi who obtained my visa into the U.S. by designating me as her guest at Hope Village. On our way from the airport, Tippi said:

"Give me a hand, Chinh. We'll do some volunteer work here for a few days before going back to my house."

By choosing the refugee camp as the place for us to meet and work together, Tippi gave me the opportunity to start my new life as a refugee by serving others who were in the same boat. My tasks were not very demanding: set up meals, distribute clothes, interpreting, help fill out forms, or simply listen to people's stories and sharing their feelings of fear and helplessness. But through these small endeavors I was able to regain my own strength and find the meaning of living for the rest of my time on earth.

And I will never forget the emotional flag ceremony when thousands of us rose up and sang the old national anthem before the yellow flag of South Vietnam. I cried. I'm sure many others did as well.

It was from Hope Village that thousands of Vietnamese became Californians. We were some of the first people to work in the nascent electronics industry in San Jose, which later grew to become Silicon Valley. It was also here that the first groups of Tippi's "nail graduates" fanned out to set up shops and eventually created the dominant industry that it is today.

Years later, more than once and at many different places, whenever I took an elderly person to the hospital, or drove around to pick up donated clothes for children during Christmas, or did charity work at a refugee camp in Southeast Asia, I'd catch myself whispering "Thank you, Tippi. Thank you so much."

The Humanitarian

I think Tippi Hedren began her charitable work very early, perhaps in the '60s while her film career was in full swing. She made many trips to third world countries to help victims of drought and hunger in Ethiopia, Bangladesh, Peru; volcano explosion victims in Managua; war victims in Vietnam and Nicaragua etc. Tippi even learned to pilot airplanes and was co-pilot of a DC-3 bringing aid to hungry children in Africa. And it was Tippi who was working on board the S.S. Akura in June, 1979, to help pick up Vietnamese boat people in Southeast Asian waters.

Alongside her humanitarian work, Tippi also helped protect endangered animals. Ever since making the film *Satan's Harvest* in Africa where she worked with lions and leopards, Tippi felt like she couldn't abandon those wild creatures. The result was that she and her family became foster parents to 95 animals that included elephants, tigers, leopards, lions and others.

Tippi Hedren excelled in every role she played — model, movie star, humanitarian, wildlife advocate. But to me she was first and foremost a friend, a sponsor, a sister who always lent me a hand when most needed — the person who opened the door for me to my second home and my second life.

After a few days working at Hope Village, Tippi took me to her house in Sherman Oaks near Los Angeles. "Melanie has gone away," Tippi said. "You can take her room." Melanie Griffith was Tippi's 16-year-old daughter who would later become a famous actress on her own in *Working Girl,* for which she won a Golden Globe Award for Best Actress.

The room was on the first floor, with a large glass door that opens to the swimming pool in the back. There was no bed, just a twin-size mattress on the floor. Pinned to the wall right above the mattress was a life-size photo of a handsome young man so realistic that at first I thought it was a real person standing there looking at me. It was a picture of Don Johnson, Melanie's boyfriend, who later would also become a famous actor in the

TV series *Miami Vice* and voted one of the sexiest men in Hollywood.

Even though I had been to the U.S. prior to 1975, I didn't know much about American culture. On the first night, I was puzzled as to why no one cooked anything when it was way past dinner time. When she found out I had not had anything to eat, Tippi laughed and took me into the kitchen. She toasted some bread, opened a can of Chicken-a-la-King and fixed me a sandwich. I quickly learned that in Tippi's house, except on weekends or special occasions, in the evening everyone just went to the fridge and made whatever meal they wanted.

After several days eating nothing but American food, I began to crave Vietnamese food like mad. Once I knew how to go shopping on my own, I went to a Chinese grocery store and bought some rice, fish sauce, vegetables, and chopsticks. That night, I showed off my culinary skills by making Vietnamese spring rolls for everyone. Tippi really loved the spring rolls, especially the dipping sauce.

Life in America for me already was strange and full of surprises. But living in a house like Tippi's was even stranger. One night I suddenly heard someone scream upstairs. I ran up and saw that everyone was midwifing Partner, the family dog. Tippi was petting the mother while Melanie directed Don Johnson to get a towel and warm water. As the puppies came out with their eyes shut, each was carefully handled like the most fragile thing in the world. I could not help thinking about my war-torn country where even children didn't get that kind of attention.

Another time, I was awakened in the middle of my sleep by a strange noise. I opened my eyes and was terrified to see a huge lion on the floor below my feet, snoring away like a dog. After getting my heart beating again, I gathered all the courage I had to quietly slip out of the room and close the door behind me. Then I started screaming at the top of my lungs, calling for help. Everyone panicked, but when Tippi learned what happened she smiled and assured me:

"Oh, don't be scared. Pharaoh is very fond of Melanie, he likes to go into her room sometimes."

Tippi talked about Pharaoh like he was a little kitten. Of course, Pharaoh wasn't Tippi's only wildlife friend. She had another 95 even wilder friends at a ranch named Shambala.

Shambala

Shambala was situated in the middle of the Acton desert, about a two-hour drive from Los Angeles. A unique ranch, it was where humans and animals lived harmoniously with each other. It was on this 40-acre stretch of mountainous desert that Tippi, with the help of her husband, Noel Marshall, and their children took care of 56 African lions, five Siberian tigers, six spotted leopards, five black panthers, two African elephants and hundreds of other smaller animals.

One hot afternoon, Tippi took me to Shambala. A large truck drove up, kicking up a thick cloud of dust as we were preparing lunch. Tippi warned: "Don't go outside. I have to take care of them first."

She opened the gate and let the truck in. It dumped a mountain of meat and bones in the middle of an open field. After the truck left, Tippi closed the outer gate and opened the inner gate. Loud roars immediately rose up. The ground began to tremble as dozens of lions and tigers and leopards rushed toward the mound, tearing at the meat, fighting with and growling at each other. Two animals gnarled at one another as they tried to rip apart a horse's hind leg. It was the most brutal lunch scene I'd ever witnessed.

In no time at all the mountain of flesh was reduced to a giant pool of blood. The indescribable smell of red meat mixed with blood and hot desert wind blew into the trailer when Tippi walked back in. "Now it's our turn," she said with a smile. I had to fight hard to suppress my shock at the raw and violent beauty of Shambala as we sat down before a lovely lunch spread prepared by my imperturbable hostess.

The evening presented a totally different setting that was no less impressive. Deep within Shambala, a two-story house monumentally rose up on a lake with two mountain ranges serving as backdrop. It was named African House. From its balcony one could look out and see the entire ranch. As I let my mind drift into the beautiful desert sunset, I was suddenly startled by a powerful series of roars coming from afar. The kings of the jungle were howling goodbye to the sun. I looked across the lake; silhouettes of Tippi's lions were pacing in a futile dance against the encroaching darkness.

The story of Shambala was made into a film called *Roar*. It involved all of Tippi's family. Written and directed by Noel Marshall, it starred the "Six super-loving people" as Tippi liked to call them: Noel, Tippi, and their children Melanie, Joe, John, Jerry. Also co-starring were the animals themselves.

Every animal citizen in the Shambala Kingdom was given a name by Tippi. Some lions were named after Noel and their sons. The African elephant was named Timbo. Tippi's most beloved were a pair of spotted leopards that Noel gave her as presents; she named them Rhett Butler and Scarlett O'Hara, characters from *Gone With The Wind.* Looking at the fearsome leopard, I couldn't help smiling as I compared him to the dashing Clark Gable.

The love Tippi's family had for the animals was quite incredible. One day, I was astonished to see in the *Los Angeles Times* a photo of Tippi being hung upside down by the trunk of Timbo. The news article noted that her leg was sprained by the incident and she had to be taken to the hospital. Another time, I heard it was Noel's turn to be hospitalized. I immediately came to visit the *Roar* director. He was lying in bed with one leg hung up in a cast. He had been bitten by a lion when trying to dissuade it from a starting a fight with another lion. Noel told me: "Don't be angry at the lion. It doesn't know that it hurt me."

The Acton desert would sometimes be flooded by sudden bursts of downpour. Whenever that happened, Tippi and her family had to use every means possible to evacuate their animals to safety. One time two lions — Melanie and Mary, were washed away from the camp and shot dead by someone. The two were born in Shambala, and Tippi was their midwife; she was the one who bottle-fed them from day one. The image of a forlorn Tippi Hedren mourning her lion babies made me wonder if humans were the only species whose females could be the mother for all creatures?

After the film *Roar*, the story of Tippi Hedren and her beloved animals were written into a book — "The Cats of Shambala" (1985). Whether in a film, a book or real life, Tippi Hedren was undeniable proof that it is possible to achieve understanding and harmony between humans and wild animals.

The Sponsor

Tippi didn't just familiarize me with wild lions and tigers, she helped me with myriads of mundane tasks as well. She drove me around to the various government agencies to get my paperwork in order. She helped me get settled in the U.S. by asking a friend of hers — French actress Michelle Mercier (lead role in the series *Angelique*), to let me stay with her temporarily in Beverly Hills while she looked for a suitable apartment for me and my family.

It was through Tippi's tireless efforts that I was able to bring my family to the U.S. from Canada where my three children had been going to school since before 1975. And, of course, I'll never forget that when I first moved to the U.S. I had nothing more than a plastic bag containing some personal belongings, and a nightgown which Tippi gave me along with a $20 bill.

On my first Christmas in the U.S., while I was home alone feeling lonely and sad, Tippi appeared at the door:

"Merry Christmas!" She cheerfully said. "I thought you might like to see some souvenirs from Vietnam. I think it's time these elephants came back to their owner!"

They were the pair of terra-cotta elephants from Biên-Hoà that I gave Tippi in Sài-Gòn in 1965, except that each now also had a red ribbon tied to their neck. Not only that, Tippi also brought a thick piece of glass to serve as a tabletop, with the two elephants acting as legs!

Even after I was able to buy a house, I still saw signs of Tippi and her mother everywhere. When I made coffee in the morning, I was always reminded that the cup and spoon I was holding came from Tippi's mother and her lady friends.

In the small house that I live in today, objects reminiscent of Tippi are everywhere. The pair of terra-cotta elephants still tirelessly hold up a pot of candles, reminders of our decades long friendship that started in a tiny TV studio in Sài-Gòn. I haven't seen Johnny Grant for awhile. But in a small picture frame hung on the wall are photos of Diane McBain and Tippi Hedren; both attended the celebration of "Kieu Chinh: 35 Years in Film" in 1991.

Just one week before the event, Tippi had an accident. But still she came, albeit with one arm in a sling, wearing the red Hà-Đông silk *áo dài* I gave her in Việt-Nam. That evening Tippi stood on stage and tearfully listened to Diane recall how the three of us met in Sài-Gòn so many long years ago.

When *Hello*, a British publication, wrote about Tippi in 1990, they also mentioned the long and special friendship between two artists — one American, one Vietnamese. I read with some embarrassment that Tippi called me the most courageous woman she had ever known. In reality, Tippi knew very well that her friend had more than once shown her clumsiness and vulnerability.

Even though we live fairly far apart and sometimes don't see each other for six months or more, we both know one could wake the other up in the middle night to ask for advice about anything, especially if it's serious or important.

"Stay put, Chinh," Tippi has more than once told me over the phone. "I'll be right over!"

It's in times of trouble like that which has strengthened and deepened our friendship. Like in 1982 when she went through perhaps the hardest period in her life as her 17-year marriage with Noel collapsed. That Christmas, knowing she was alone at Shambala, I brought Tippi her favorite Vietnamese spring rolls with the dipping sauce made just the way my friend liked it.

And so it was on that Christmas Eve, when all the creatures in her kingdom were asleep, Tippi and I sat by a single lamp in the middle of the desert and talked. After a few hours and more than a few glasses of red wine, I had to say goodbye. Before I could leave, however, Tippi insisted that I take the swinging chair in her trailer back with me.

In the middle of a cold desert night, the stars in heaven were privileged to witness two tipsy women struggle to get a chair out of Tippi's place and into my car. That chair is now comfortably situated in my private room, where I like to sit and look out to my backyard and reminisce about the past.

Tippi has been given many awards for her professional as well as humanitarian work. I can say with pride that I was able to attend many of those occasions to help celebrate my dear friend. In 1993, to reaffirm the greatness of Hitchcock's masterpiece *The Birds,* Hollywood made *The Birds Two*, with Tippi having the honorary role of overseeing the next generation of actors playing her iconic character. Unfortunately, I was not able to attend that occasion as I was in China filming *The Joy Luck Club*. But that just goes to show how precious time is when you're living in the fast lane in America, especially if you work in Hollywood. And yet somehow Tippi could always find time for me.

On a Saturday evening in August, 1993, actress Annette Benning hosted a special screening of *The Joy Luck Club* at the Crest Theatre in Westwood, reserved for artists and close friends. It was followed by a reception at the Armand Hammer Museum. Once again I had my friend Tippi by my side on this joyous occasion.

Also attending that night was Alison Leslie Gold, author of "Anne Frank Remembered" (1987) which has been translated into sixteen languages and made into a film. Alison also has written about the friendship between Tippi and me. That night, on our ride home in a car provided by the studio, Alison looked at Tippi's beaming smile then turned to look at me. Perhaps she was remembering what she wrote about the day Tippi brought me to Sacramento in 1975.

All through the years, Tippi has never stopped giving me the warmest friendship in a most unassuming manner. Her way of giving is so natural and easy that the recipients never feel they are obligated or owe her anything. To me, it's like her saying: "No one can possibly repay everything we receive from others and from life itself. So don't bother repaying. Just keep on giving. One person gives to another. Then that one gives to the next. Then on and on for ever our giving goes..."

From that first flag ceremony in 1975 with 500 refugee families in Sacramento, more than a million Vietnamese have resettled in the U.S., not to mention many millions more who came from other countries. How many of those have been silently contributing their time and effort so that America could continue to take in new citizens? I'd say a lot.

There have been countless inspiring stories about refugees and their sponsors. I have had the opportunity to look up at the Statue of Liberty on Liberty Island and whispered Emma Lazarus' immortal words:

> *Give me your tired, your poor*
> *Your wretched masses yearning to breathe free...*

Lady Liberty is the ultimate symbol of America: A sponsor. Like so many sponsors who came before her and many more who have come since.

Like Tippi Hedren, my *sponsor*.

And, as we ourselves are — or at least as we ought to be.

The Houses in "My World"

My financial situation improved greatly in 1995 after *The Joy Luck Club*. I was able to sign advertising contracts with MCI and many other companies in Hong Kong and Taiwan. I decided to sell my small house in Studio City and buy a larger one in Newport Beach to be closer to the Vietnamese community.

Mai Thảo used to jokingly tell me to move to Orange County because Studio City was too far for him to visit. Sadly, by the time I did it he had already moved on — to another world.

It was a four-bedroom, four-bath house with a pool near the ocean. I really liked this house because it sat high on a hill in a quiet neighborhood. The upper balcony in the back ran along the entire length of the house. The view to the right was the city and Disneyland. Every Fourth of July the whole family would get together for a feast then go out on the balcony to watch fireworks.

The view to the left was the Pacific Ocean. I loved watching the sunsets from this spot, each one was beautiful in its unique way; I took many photos of the colorful clouds. Sometimes, when the clouds were near eye level, I even had the sensation of floating among them.

By this time all my children were settled with their own families and had given me four lovely grandchildren: Stephen Dao, son of daughter Mỹ-Vân; Jean-Paul and Aimee, son and daughter of Hùng and Trang; Nguyễn Lê Nam, son of Tuấn-Cường and Ý-Lan. As a bonus, Hùng was also able to buy a house within walking distance to mine; we visited each other often.

We had many parties at this house for all sorts of reasons, from holidays to birthdays to just about any kind of day we could think of. Many good friends had been here, too: actor Lê Quỳnh; Tế (father of my children); poet/writer couple Trần Dạ Từ - Nhã Ca and their children; composer Cung Tiến and his wife Josephine...

One beautiful morning painter Nguyễn Trung, who was visiting from Việt-Nam, painted a portrait of me on that balcony.

My sister Tĩnh and her children — Lysa, Christian, David, also stayed here when they came from France. We had a terrific reunion, with lots of singing and music through the night.

I thought I'd live in that house for the rest of my life, but as I recounted previously, I was "publicly denounced" by extremists as a communist sympathizer. I was boycotted by the Vietnamese business community and lost virtually all my advertising contracts. As a result, I had to sell that house and bought a smaller one in Garden Grove.

Garden Grove

Thanks to the silent majority who knew and understood me, the brouhaha finally faded away. I picked myself back up and went back to being an activist again. This time I was even busier than before. Luckily, my agency was able to book for me many speaking engagements — from university lectures to community or literary events all over the country. This became my main source of income for quite some time.

With that money, I decided to build a new "My World" in a Hà-Nội style. The place took two years to construct and fully decorate in and out. It was spacious and displayed antiques from Việt-Nam. The concept was to create a mini-museum of my own which I could later bequeath to my children and grandchildren.

There were bronze-age and tribal musical instruments like horns, gongs, bronze drums, bronze bells, flutes etc. Traditional stage and musical traditions from North Vietnam were also represented. There were books about Vietnamese history, culture, cuisine, war... There were photos and films as well. On the walls were hung paintings by artist friends like Choé, Nguyễn Trung, Đinh Cường, Trịnh Công Sơn...

A large bronze bell was hung from the 19-foot high ceiling, reflecting sunlight by day and moonlight on some nights. There was a separate room containing a collection of *antique áo dài* dresses, given to me by Trịnh Bách, and a two-piece sindora wooden table-bed. I also designed a tea bar that reached the top of the ceiling to house my collection of about 70 teapots and various kinds of tea.

In the large backyard I built a mini-temple with Buddha statues in varying sizes, a tea house, and two ponds — one for Koi fish, the other had a miniature waterfall and lotuses. I planted trees that are native to Southeast Asia like boddhi, willow, four varieties of bamboo (black, yellow, green, short), pomegranate, grapefruit, three varieties of pine... I had three different types of rocks: mountain, forest, ocean. I also built a traditional Five-Fortune gate, and a foot-path all around to practice zen walking.

I truly loved this house which I had spent so much time and effort to build. It wasn't palatial or extravagant or anything like that. Contrariwise, I think it was quite rustic and pastoral. The first time Cung Tiến came to visit, he walked around the place with his hands behind his back and inspected every little corner. The composer of some of the most timeless Vietnamese music then boldly declared:

"This house has two flaws!"

"...??"

"No telephone. And no computer!!"

When artist Đằng Giao came from Sài-Gòn to visit, he and Trần Dạ Từ spent hours hanging paintings for me. Buddhist monk Thích Mẫn Giác, on the other hand, helped in a more metaphysical way. He blessed my mini-temple and chose for me a religious name. I asked him to give me something simple since I considered myself nothing more than a grain of sand. He obliged and gave me the beautifully simple name Chân-Sa, which means "true sand."

It was also at this house that we had the party celebrating the success of *Journey From The Fall (Vượt Sóng)*. Director Trần

Hàm, producers Lâm Nguyễn and Alan Vo Ford, and the entire crew and cast were there. We all had a blast!

On the tenth death anniversary of writer Mai Thảo, we held a ceremony in front the little worship house in the backyard. Dozens of our friends attended; some came from as far away as Washington, D.C. and Houston.

My grandson Đào Đức-Minh even came to live with Grandma for a while in this big house. We had some very happy days together under its roof. The city of Garden Grove suggested that I turned my mini-museum into an "Open House" so they could add it to their tour of beautiful homes in the city. I politely declined.

I thought that this house would be the last station on my route through life, that it would become a family museum to be passed on from one generation to the next. But once again calamity struck — this time not just for me but for millions of Americans as well. It was the Great Recession of 2007-2010.

Millions of people lost their jobs, their homes. I had no income for two years. I tried to hang on by selling my collection piece by piece. I had an Open House and held auctions. A lot of people came. Some to buy things while others just to peek inside the house.

In a repeat of the estate sale at 10 Lê Trực in Hà-Nội, I could only watch as people carried off valuables I had spent years collecting. The pair of Đông-Sơn bronze drums. The antique *áo dài.* Paintings... Even my beloved teapot and teacup collection. But even so, I could only hold out for one year. The economy continued to tank, and I had no choice but to sell the house.

Yet that was only half of the problem. It was a buyer's market at the time. I could only sell my $2M museum for half price.

The Orange County Register even had an article about my home sale. It said I cried over "losing a million dollars." I don't think the reporter understood anything about what I had lived through all my life. I don't think he knew that I had lost many things that were much, much more valuable than a piece of property. Moreover, at the time I was but one among millions of

Americans who lost their homes, and many were in much worse shape. There was absolutely nothing for me to cry about.

Sad and disappointed? Yes.

But tears? No.

Huntington Beach

Not long after, I was able to find a house in Huntington Beach where I still live today. It's my fifth home in the U.S., and hopefully the last.

It's a small house on a piece of land that's not very big. It doesn't have enough space for me to put all the things I could bring from Garden Grove, and I can't display them the way I want, either. But that's OK. As long as I have a place called my own. I like to remind myself that when I first came to this country I had nothing.

Even though it's small, the house is still full of love. On my in-laws' side, the oldest brother, Nguyễn Giáp-Tý, has visited and stayed here. So has his sister, Mão, and her family from Toronto. Even my ex-husband Tế and his wife, and the youngest brother Hiếu and his wife have visited. The house is so small, sometimes people had to sleep on the floor. And that was fine, too, as long as we had each other.

In due time, a bamboo bush sprang up. The weeping willow grew a bit taller beside the large stone. Nature slowly takes its course. I can hear birds chirping in the morning and see them fly home in the evening. I've put up the sign "My World" once again. It still has the names once given to it by friends who are now gone. Mai Thảo, Phạm Đình-Chương...

I want to thank God for having given me a house and a life so that I can continue in "My World" as an artist in exile.

The Passage of Time

2014

I used to think that once retired I would have more time — to visit friends, to work in the garden, to read books, to watch movies. But no. I only became busier, from family matters to community events — even though I consider being invited to those events an honor — a book launch, a charity music show, ribbon cutting for a business...

It seems like there's always something on my calendar every weekend. Especially funerals. A church here. A pagoda there. And that all-too-familiar cemetery. When we first came to the U.S., our get-togethers were mostly weddings for children of our friends. Then came birthday parties for their children. Now it's to say goodbye to old friends.

In 2014, besides a few minor acting gigs, I spent much time behind the camera in *Ride The Thunder*. The film was based on a book of the same name written by Richard Botkin who also was executive producer. The story is about two officers — one American, the other Vietnamese, who fought together in a major battle in Đông-Hà, Quảng-Trị (which, incidentally, is where VCF's first school was built in 1995) and their disagreements due to politics. It was directed by Fred Costa on a shoestring budget raised entirely by Richard Botkin. It was filmed in Hawaii, starring Eric Saint John and Joseph Hiếu.

After the making of this film, I gained a new friend in Richard, someone who cares very deeply about Vietnam. So much so that he spent his entire savings to make this film, and even lost his job because he spent too much time on the project.

2018

The year of 2018 was a busy year due to all the traveling. I can't remember how many hours were spent in airports and among the clouds. Beyond destinations in the U.S. — from Texas to Washington, D.C., were several places in Europe.

Most memorable of all was the surprise meeting with my sister Tĩnh in France and attending her 83rd birthday. The reunion was not planned, which made her tears all the more special. I also visited Uncle Nghị's home where I first met him in 1968. Uncle Nghị had died, but I was taken to his vacation home on the Côte d'Azur by his four children: Patrick, Christine, Johan and Luc. I was able to spend a few days there, strolling the beach with loved ones, reminiscing about the past.

I also visited Lake Como in Italy. When I was a young girl studying piano in Hà-Nội, I used to love a piece called "Lac de Côme" by Giselle Gamos, but never knew what the place was like. Floating down the lake while hearing the melody in my head, I came to appreciate and love that song even more.

After spending time with my family, I had the chance to reconnect with many of my artist friends in France. Literary critic Thuỵ Khuê, writers Vũ Thư Hiên and Từ Thức, composer Lê Thành Đông,
director Trần Anh Hùng and his wife, actress Yên Khê. And, of course, photographer Nicolas Võ Doãn Đạt who took some superb pictures for us!

And thank you, Christine Nguyễn, who drove me all the way to Normandy so I could visit the site of the invasion that inspired the movie *The Longest Day*, which I have seen at least three times.

In October of 2018, I flew to London and then Italy with my daughter Mỹ-Vân and grandson Stephen Đào. Stephen and I have a rather interesting bond since we have travelled to many places and attended many events together. In London, I visited BBC News and was interviewed by Giang Nguyễn, Director of BBC Vietnamese, for a TV special. He also wrote an article titled "Kiều Chinh, a Vietnamese Woman in the Ups and Downs of Her Homeland."

Also in October of 2018, I had the great honor to meet many Viet-Americans in uniform. It was at an event organized by the

Vietnamese-American Uniformed Services Association (VAUSA), held in the nation's capital. I felt so proud seeing so many of the younger generation, children of refugees, serve in all branches of the military. At last count there are more than 3,000 of them. Some are fairly well known in our community such as Major General Luong Xuan Viet, Major General LapThe Chau Flora and Rear Admiral (Lower Half) Nguyen Tu Huan. Then there is retired Lieutenant Colonel Ross Cao Nguyen Nguyen, Lieutenant Commander (now Commander) Christopher Phan, Lieutenant (separated) Huey NguyenHuu, Colonel Tam Dinh, CAPTAIN Mimi Phan. There are many more than I can name. What I was most impressed with was the presence of so many women.

Birthday & Surprise Present

James Kimsey and I had been friends since 1993. He died in 2016, making ours a 23-year-long friendship. When James was still alive, I would receive something from him always exactly one day before my birthday — cards, flowers, presents... But this year there was nothing. I couldn't not think about James, a loyal and dedicated friend not just to me but also to Vietnam.

We miss you, James.

On the other hand, this year I was given a very meaningful gift from the talented sculptor Nguyễn Tuấn, author of the monumental work "Two Soldiers, American and Vietnamese" displayed at the Vietnam Memorial in Westminster, California. His many works can be found at locations all over the world.

For my birthday, Tuấn made me a 3-foot tall black bronze statue of a sitting woman wearing *áo dài* titled: "Kieu Chinh Vietnam." Thank you so much, Nguyễn Tuấn, I am very honored.

Another fabulous birthday present came from my family, organized by none other than my impish grandson, Stephen Dao: a three-day wine-tasting escapade in Napa Valley with everyone in the family. Needless to say, there was much love and laughter all around. Thank you, children — and grandchildren!

The year of 2018 also marked the 25th anniversary of *The Joy Luck Club*, the first successful Hollywood movie about Asian culture and starring Asian actors. The elaborate silver anniversary celebration was held at the Academy Theater in Beverly Hills with more than a thousand participants.

Producer Oliver Stone, author Amy Tan, screenplay writer Ron Bass, director Wayne Wang, and the entire cast came to what we lovingly called "Reunion of The Joy Luck Club." It was apparent that twenty-five years had not diminished our enduring friendship and camaraderie one tiny bit.

To round off an extremely busy but exciting year, I was invited by the Toronto International Film Festival to a special 25th anniversary screening of *The Joy Luck Club* at a beautiful theater in Toronto, Canada. I was greeted by more than 1,500 fans and walked the red carpet in the city where forty-three years earlier I had come as the first refugee from Việt-Nam, and where I took my first job as a chicken farm cleaner.

From the bottom of my heart I would like to thank everyone who helped me live a year filled with beautiful memories. Heartfelt thanks also go to all those who gave me the opportunity to be in the movies for over six decades.

I have travelled many miles. I have been to gardens with ambrosial flowers and exotic plants. I have walked through brambles and thorns. I've been greeted by dawns filled with birdsong and said goodbye to twilights full of sorrow and fear. I have lived through violent storms — and darkest nights flooded by tears.

I have but a few miles left to go. I don't know if the rest of the road will be smooth or rocky, but it matters not — after it sets the sun rises again, blue is the sky after a rain. I just hope there will be peace. Just peace. Like the last words from my Daddy Cửu:

"Be brave, my dearest Chinh!"

Dharamsala Diary

When I heard from my friend Đỗ Minh that the Dalai Lama was having a special retreat and lecture session at Dharamsala on April 30, 2014, I knew right away I had to go. I needed to be there.

The year of 2014 marked sixty years since I left Hà-Nội. April 30, 2014 would mark almost forty years since I left Sài-Gòn. I wanted to have a different April 30 experience. Besides, Dharamsala was a place I had always wanted to see.

I left California for New York at 10 a.m. to catch the flight to New Delhi. After a six-hour flight from L.A., I had only 15 minutes to make the connection in New York. I ran like crazy from gate 52 all the way to gate C121, only to find out when I got there that the New Delhi flight had been delayed for one hour. So I sat down and take a deep breath. I closed my eyes and thought I was back in April, 1975, hopping from airport to airport looking for a country to apply for asylum.

The announcement overhead brought me back to reality. It is April 26, 2014. The United flight to New Delhi flight is now boarding.

April 27, 2014

After fifteen hours flying non-stop, we touched down in New Delhi at 9 p.m. Forty-two years ago, I also landed at this airport. I had come to India to make *The Evil Within*. I was greeted at the arrival gate by Director Rolf Bayer and several folks from the film crew. Local media were also there, waiting to take pictures. Someone put a garland of flowers on my neck. Flash bulbs went off.

Now Rolf had moved on to another world. There was no welcoming party, no flowers. Just me and my carry-on suitcase.

Someone called. I turned around. The person asked in Vietnamese: “Are you going to Dharamsala, too? We’ve just come in from Australia. We’re waiting for a flight from

Bangkok; Mr. N and Ms. H will be our guides. There will be a group from Việt-Nam also."

More people arrived. They came from all over the world — Germany, Canada, the U.S. We went to a hotel near the airport to spend the night. Tomorrow we would be driven to Dharamsala.

April 28, 2014

Dharamsala is 514 km from New Delhi, 1800m above sea level. A mountainous region in the Himalayas. The capital of exiled Tibetan Buddhists is a small town up high, with the mountain at its back and looking down on a valley.

The rough drive up took almost 10 hours on small twisty roads. The driver drove so fast I got quite dizzy. It was dark by the time we arrived. The main Hotel Tibet was full. Since I had not reserved a room, I was sent to the much smaller Chonor House instead which, as it turns out, was only about 100 meters from Namgyal monastery where the Dalai Lama stayed.

Chonor House is considered typical "Little Lhasa" architecture. It was designed by an Englishman with an eye toward harmony with the natural surroundings. Even though it has only 11 rooms, each room was uniquely decorated with murals on the walls and ceilings done by painters from the Norbulinka Art Institute. Every time he came to Dharamsala, actor Richard Gere always stayed at Chonor House.

The building clings to the side of a cliff so you can't drive up to it, but must walk along a winding path. I stayed in Room No. 2, a really beautiful unit. Its murals of Tibetan art and history took my breath away. Even the bedsheets and pillow cases were art work. It was incredible.

That night, I slept well, feeling so secure in such a peaceful place. However, I was jolted awake before dawn by a deep and droning sound coming from the valley below. Tibetan chants! I opened the window and looked outside. It was pitch dark. The chants seemed to be rising from deep within the earth and bouncing off the mountain walls.

Dawn came. Mountain ridges appeared as silhouettes against the gradually brightening sky. Finally the sun peeked out from behind a mountaintop. Morning light broke through the tall pines. It was like watching a canvas being painted with music added. I wrapped a scarf around my neck and quickly stepped outside.

The wind sang through the trees. My scarf suddenly blew off, I looked in its direction and saw a monk taking pictures of the sunrise. My scarf was caught on a branch by the slope. The monk gently took it off and handed it to me. He spoke beautiful English. As we walked together down the mountain path, I learned that his name was T. and he was a teacher. He was taking advantage of the beautiful morning to take some photos for a book he was writing about Dharamsala.

The chants abruptly stopped. We could only hear birdsong. I felt I had gone too far. I asked T. if there was a shortcut back to Chonor House. He said there was, and that he would also have to go that way to get back to his place. We followed a trail to the left and came up against an old woman carrying an insulated bag containing a pot. In her other hand was a smaller bag with a few ceramic cups. T. said she was a tea vendor, her customers were hikers like us.

He put some money in her well-worn bamboo tube and took a couple of cups from her bag, placing one in my hands. The old woman bowed slightly then poured tea into my cup. We sat down on a large rock on the side of the trail. The air was chilly. I cupped the hot tea with both hands and took one small sip at a time. Its warmth slowly spread throughout my body; its scent was subtle yet filled me with a simple joy.

On the way back I told T. the reason for my pilgrimage, and that in the next two days our group would meet and hear the Dalai Lama speak. The rest of the time we were free to explore Dharamsala on our own. Before we said goodbye, T. said he was certain we would see each other again and that he would be glad to serve as my tour guide.

April 30, 2014 – The First Day

Cars pre-arranged by Inova picked our group up at 8:30 a.m. and took us to the Main Hall of the Gyuto Monastery, home of His Holiness the 17th Karmapa, Ogyen Trinley Dorje. There we attended a Fire Puja ceremony performed by the head monk to cleanse one's soul of negative energies.

I spent the afternoon visiting the town. I walked the long but narrow main street where most commerce in Dharamsala was concentrated. It was crowded with people walking everywhere, even in the middle of the road. Cars could barely get through. Little shops line both sides of the street, selling everything imaginable — Buddha statuettes, prayer beads, bracelets, necklaces, stone tablets carved with Tantric verses, clothes, sandals, luggage, souvenirs of all kinds...

The entire street is no longer than two miles, yet was full of colors from all over the world — black, brown, white... speaking a myriad of languages. Many were young backpackers in torn jeans with sleeping bags slung on their backs ready to crash anywhere, or so it seemed.

Locals tend to have a dark complexion, square-jawed faces and clear bright eyes that exude inner strength. Though quite colorful in attire, they were unostentatious in manners. The merchants were a real joy to shop from. I bought a few Buddhist necklaces, bracelets and silk scarves which I planned to have the Dalai Lama bless to give to friends and loved ones back home.

It was raining lightly when I walked up the slope back to Chonor House. I felt light and at peace.

According to schedule, starting tomorrow, April 30, the Dalai Lama would have two sessions for our group of pilgrims. Each person could write his or her own prayer to give to him after the session to have it blessed. I spent a whole night at Chonor House thinking about what I wanted to write. After several aborted attempts, I put down:

Your Holiness,

The Mekong, a major river in Asia, starts in the Tibetan highlands and ends in Vietnam as it merges into the Pacific Ocean.

Please help us pray for peace for Tibet and Vietnam. Please pray for all the peoples who live along this waterway that they be spared of calamities, whether natural or man-made.

April 30, 2014

We arrived at Namgyal Monastery at 7:30 a.m. to go through security checks. From 8 to 12 we would attend a lecture by the Dalai Lama. Afterwards we would have lunch there.

The hall was packed; there weren't enough seats. There were Vietnamese from all over the globe. I could hear French and Chinese, too. Finally, the 14th Dalai Lama appeared. He waved his hand and beamed a friendly smile. I was seated on the front row directly facing him; we were no more than two feet apart.

He spoke for more than three hours, in an easy manner and at a deliberate speed. The topics he touched upon were deep — the meaning of living, the paths to happiness... Yet he had a masterful way of simplifying things: *Happiness is not something pre-made; it comes from our own actions.*

Every so often he looked straight into my eyes and smiled slightly as he spoke, as though to emphasize something just for me. I would lightly bow my head in response.

After the talk and before the Dalai Lama left the room, I and others gave his secretary envelopes containing our prayers which were put inside a basket. At 9 p.m. that night, I was surprised to receive a text message from his secretary telling me His Holiness would like to meet me individually at 7 a.m. the next day, during his morning tea.

I could not sleep that night. Lying in bed, I gave thanks to the holy spirits that had led me to this place. The paintings on the walls and ceiling seemed to dance to the sound of the winds as I experienced an April 30 so different from any other. Different not because it helped me forget the events that happened but actually remember them more. With more understanding. Or as the Dalai Lama said — with more love and compassion.

May 1, 2014

I got up early to get ready. Although I was too excited to sleep last night, I didn't feel sluggish at all. In fact, both my mind and body felt great.

Pre-dawn chants could be heard coming from afar. The sun began to come out, the sky glowed a gentle pink. I quietly closed the door behind me and walked out of Chonor House alone. It was a bit chilly, the dew was still on the grass as I walked up the hill toward Namgyal.

An assistant took me to the Dalai Lama's office which was higher up beyond the entrance. He asked me to wait at the door. There was a small flower garden in front. In the soft early sunlight, it looked like a miniature garden of Eden. While admiring the spectacular mountain scenes all around, I suddenly thought of Dad, of my children and grandchildren. I wished they could have been here with me at this moment...

The door opened. I turned around and saw a group of security guards walk out. The Dalai Lama appeared in a robe as fiery as the red sun. I put my hands together and bowed. He came over and placed a hand on my head. Then he took my hand. I looked up. His photographer ran up and took a picture. He squeezed my hand and pulled me a little closer, looked into my eyes and smiled. The photographer took the second picture.

"His Holiness..." I began.

Without letting me finish, he smiled and said; "Yes, blessings, blessings..."

His warm, comforting tone gave me such a sense of peace, of compassion coming from a spiritual teacher. I remembered what he said in his lecture the day before:

"I'm just a simple monk. My religion is very simple. It is kindness."

An assistant brought hot tea. He invited me to sit down. We shared a lovely morning tea conversation.

After the second day's lecture on how to apply Buddhist teachings in our everyday activities to keep our lives balanced, our group left Namgyal to visit the Tibetan's Children Village. It was started and run by the Dalai Lama's sister, Tsering Dolma Takla, until she passed away in 1964. Her sister Jetsum Pema took over since then.

The small village sits on a large plateau fairly high up. When we arrived, a group of children was picking up dry leaves in the yard. They stopped what they were doing and ran over to greet us. I then joined them in picking up leaves. There was so much laughter.

That evening I attended a Tibetan musical performance called Opera Prince Norsang. I was especially impressed by a dance titled "Promoting Peace Through Arts" by a large group of masked dancers in bizarre costumes, accompanied by a traditional Tibetan band. Just as the performance was coming to a climax, the stage went dark and the music stopped. When the lights came back on, all the performers had removed their masks and costumes to show themselves as elderly monks in their earth tone habits, stomping their bare feet on the stage while reciting a prayer. I was blown away.

May 2, 2014

Our day trip began at 7 a.m. It was still cold outside as our van started climbing up the mountain. In the valley below, tall pine trees glistened in the morning sunlight. About halfway up, the van stopped at a small clearing. The driver said he couldn't go any farther, but we could get out and wander around. He told everyone to meet back here in exactly one hour.

I separated myself from the group and started walking along a small dirt trail. The path started to climb. Monkeys sunbathed by the side of the road; they didn't seem bothered by humans.

The trail gradually got steeper; my breathing became harder. Suddenly a yellow scarf came out of nowhere and flew into my face.

As I lifted it off, I saw an old monk walking toward me. Not far behind him was a small cabin. I bowed slightly and with both hands gave him back the scarf. He took the scarf and turned to walk away without saying a word. I decided to run after him and asked while gasping for air: "May I have some water, please?"

He gave me a look and, seeing that I was just an old woman who was running out of breath, signaled to me to follow him.

The cabin was just one simple room. On the right side was an altar with a photo of the Dalai Lama and stacks of books. On the ground to the left was a mattress, at one end stood a table with a kerosene lamp and a book of sutras.

The monk prostrated before the altar to pray. I also bowed and prayed. He then handed me a bowl of water.

What serendipity it was. In clear and precise English the monk began to answer my curiosity. He was a hermit monk practicing a form of Buddhist yoga called Vajrasattva whose adherents refrain from all interaction with others. Only those who had passed certain tests would be allowed to leave the monastery and live alone up here like this. From the moment they wake up to the time they go to sleep, all their thoughts are focused on attaining Buddhahood and self-actualization.

About twenty monks lived scattered across this mountainside, each in his own little cabin. There is neither electricity nor running water up here. If someone had an emergency, he'd write a note, wrap it around a rock and throw it to another monk's cabin. Others have used plastic guns to shoot their messages. But some monks wouldn't even care to do that. They would just stay in their cabin and die; by the time they were discovered their bodies would be "dry as a dead bird," he smiled wryly.

The first three months were the hardest, he said, because of the extreme isolation and lack of activities. Some monks gave up and went back to the monastery. Once you choose to come up here, you must accept putting yourself through severe hardship, mostly psychological rather than physical. You must renounce all former relationships, even with your parents or family members lest your mind be distracted. Summers are hot here, but winters are even harder to bear due to the isolation.

I asked him what was the reason and purpose for this. He smiled and said:

"It is about giving yourself up completely in order to help save others. It usually takes thirty years to comprehend this."

It was time for me to leave. The monk prostrated before the altar again and prayed. I did the same. After that we said goodbye.

As I walked back to the van, I tried to not trip over rocks while reminding myself to inhale and exhale in rhythm with my steps.

May 3, 2014

Last day in Dharamsala. T. visited me in the afternoon. We sat in the garden of Chonor House and had tea. Below us, the Kangra Valley appeared in layers of colors. Far in the distance were the snow-capped Himalayas shining brightly against the clear blue sky.

In 1959, when the Chinese army overran Tibet and drowned Lhasa in blood, the Dalai Lama had to cross those mountains with his people and came to India as exiles. There were only about 8,000 of them, with nothing more than the clothes on their backs. This desolate mountainside is where they chose to build their new home. It was here that the Dalai Lama wrote his first book "My Land, My People," which helped raise awareness about the plight of Tibetans.

Now the whole world knows about "Little Lhasa." T. told me that his brother was among the more than 130 Tibetans who recently immolated themselves to protest the Chinese occupation

Sunlight began to fade. T. took from his pocket a Buddhist necklace and gave it to me as a parting gift. I tried to remember the teaching of the Dalai Lama about seeking spiritual peace.

May 4, 2014

I put on the rosary necklace that T. gave me, pull up my suitcase and walk out of Room No. 2. The pre-dawn chants from the valley below pursue my steps. Their echoes rise from deep within the earth, bounce off the mountain walls and reverberate inside my head.

Farewell, Dharamsala. I will miss you.

PICTURES
PART IV

Pieces of My Life:

4. Lecturer

5. The Media

6. Charity Work

With:
His Holiness the Dalai Lama
Pop John Paul II
King Bảo Đại

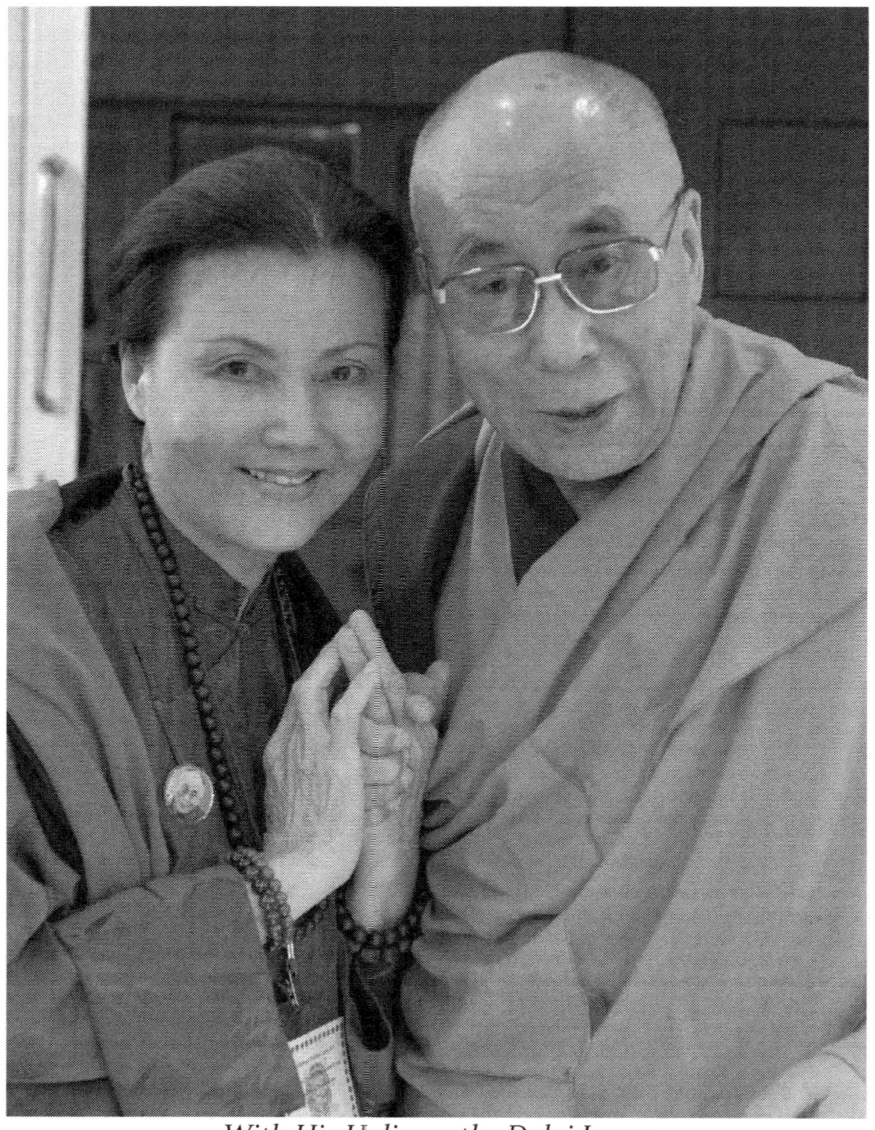

With His Holiness the Dalai Lama

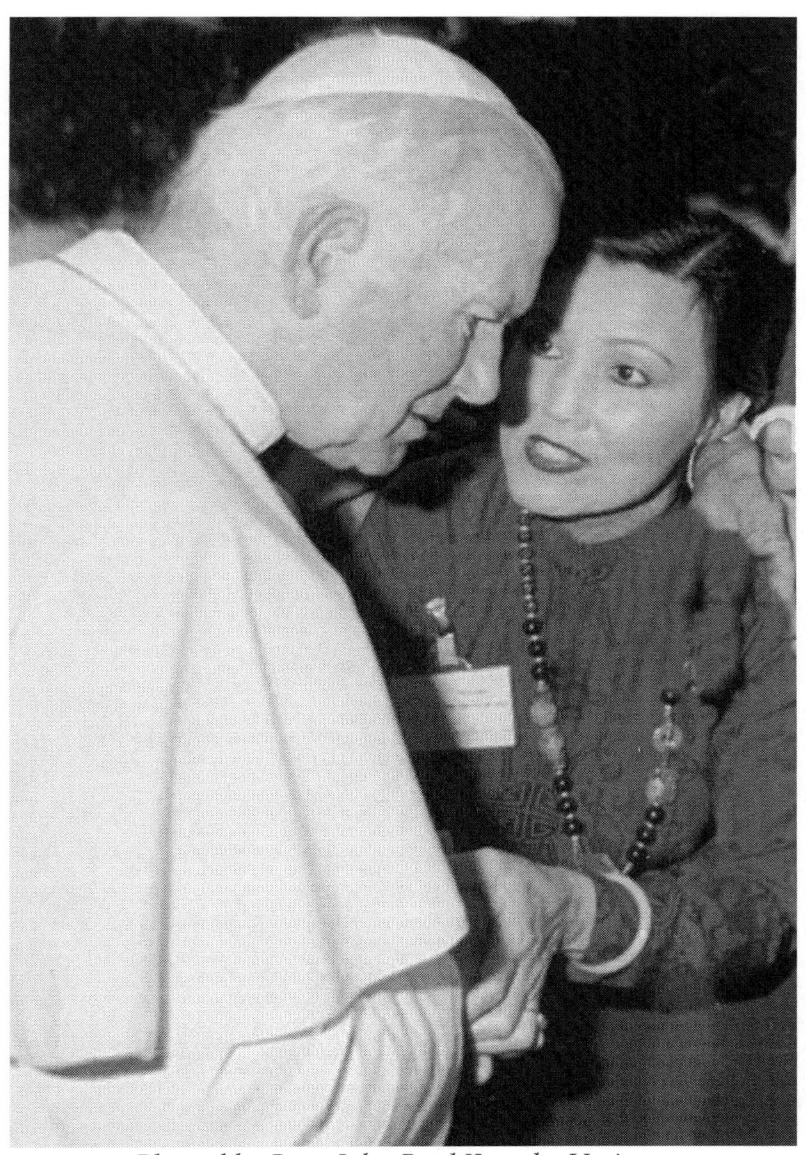

Blessed by Pope John Paul II at the Vatican.

With the Sisters ɔf Saint Mary in Assissi, Italy

With former emperor Bao Dai, the last emperor of Vietnam.

Fifteen Years As Lecturer

Kiều Chinh delivers remarks at the Vietnam Memorial in Washington, DC. Seated just behind her is Jan Scruggs - wearing dark glasses - President of the Vietnam Memorial Fund (promoting the construction of the Memorial)

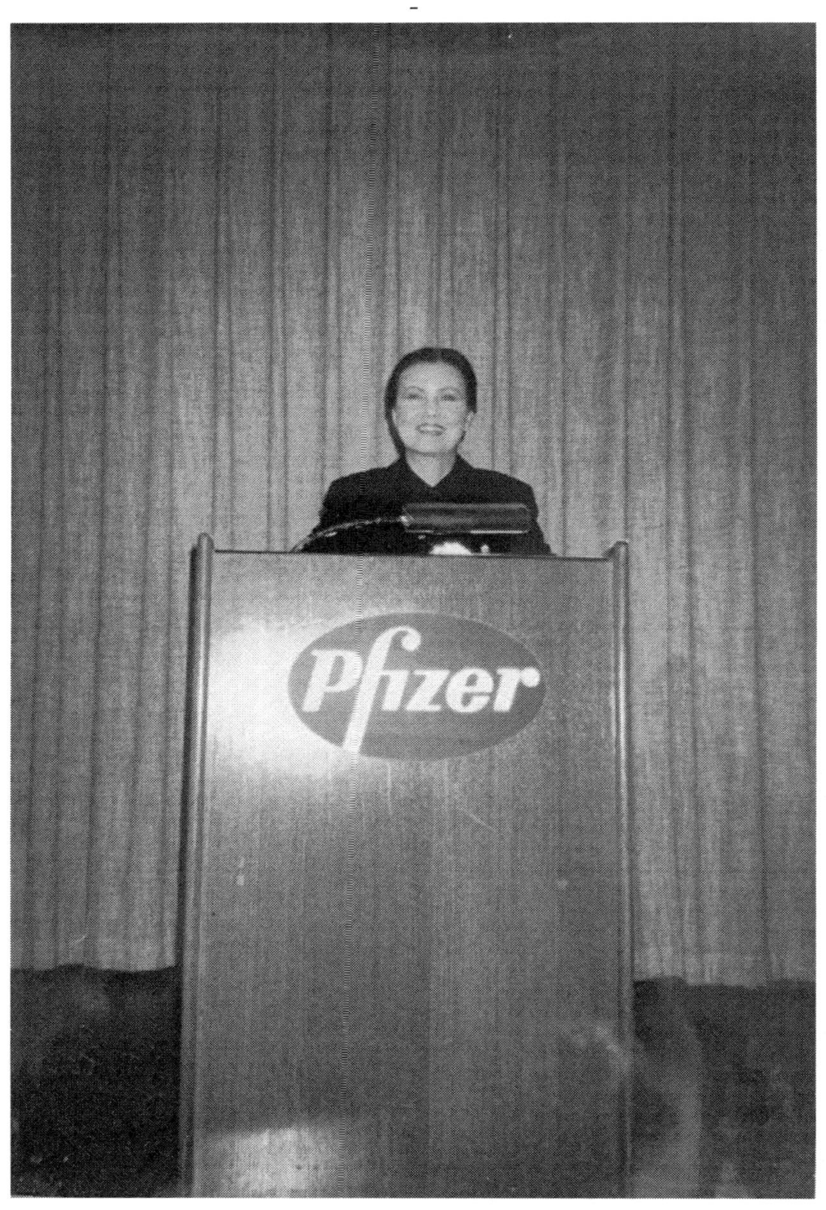

Speaking at the headquarters of the Pfizer Pharmaceutical Corporation..

Speaking at the headquarters of the Kellogg Foods Company

Visiting Cornell University on a speaking engagement

Speaking at Combodian Town Festival

Speaking at US Press, Washington D.C.

Kiều Chinh opens the National Congress of Women of America

With Ms. Benazir Bhutto, Prime Minister of Pakistan who clɔsed the National Congress of Women of America.

The Media

Mr. Lê Văn of Voice of America, Washington, D.C interviewing Kiều Chinh.

Mr. Nguyễn Giang, Director of the Vietnamese Section of the BBC, interviewing Kiều Chinh.

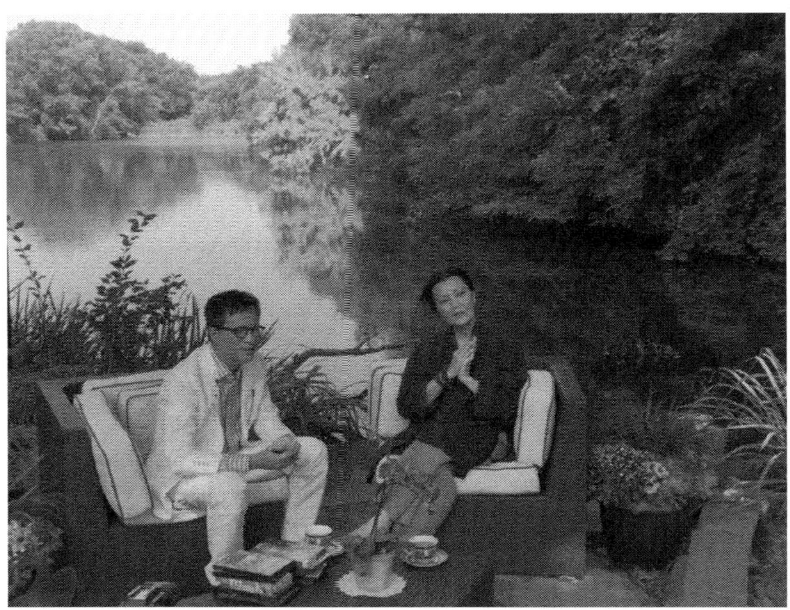

Tôn Thất Hùng interviewi:g Kiều Chinh on the occasion of the Intertional Film Festiv:l of Toronto (TIFF) in Canada.

Jimmy Nhật Hạ – The Jimmy Show - interviewing Kieu Chinh at her ho:se in Huntington Beach.

Journalist Lê Hồng Lâm interviewing Kiều Chinh.

Broadcaster Leyna Nguyen, an Emmy Award winner, interviewing Kieu Chinh for CBS-TV.

TV Channel 7 Los Angeles announcer David Uno interviewing Kieu Chinh

Kieu Chinh gives an interview to broadcaster Sam Ruben of TV Channel 5 Los Angeles.

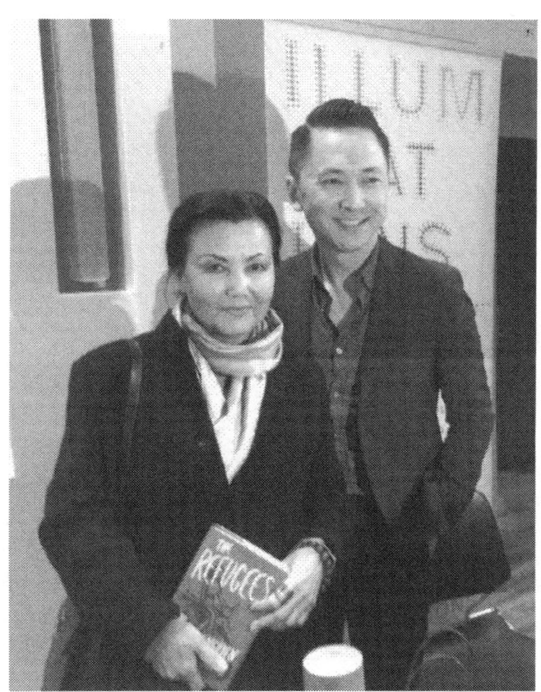

With Viet Thanh Nguyen, the author of "The Sympathizer", won the Pulitzer Prize

Frank Snep, journalist, writer, author of "Decent Interval"

Kieu Chinh and Lawyer Dinh Viet, Chief Legal and Policy Officer of Fox Corp.; Former Assistant Attorney General of The United States under President George W. Bush

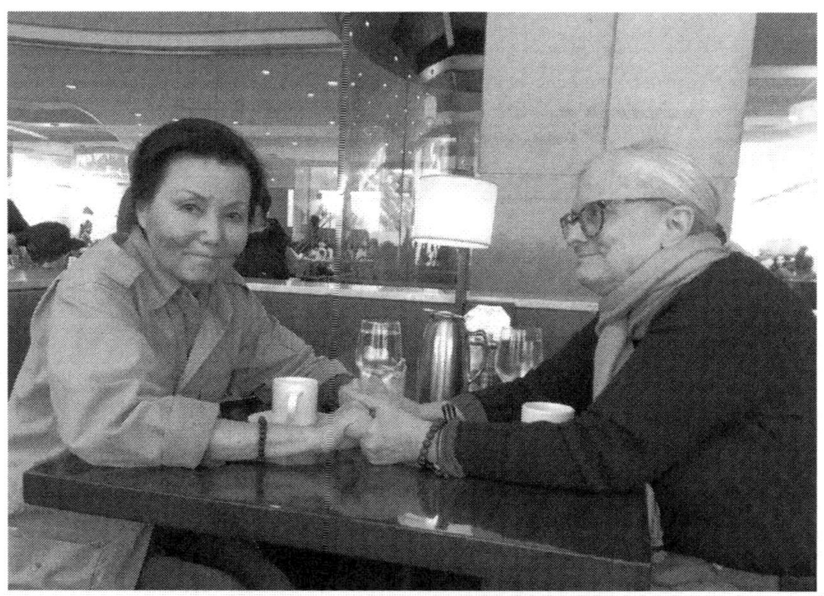

With close friend, writer Allison Leslie Gold, author of the famous novel "Anne Frank Remembered"

With longtime friends, which we meet every year. From left to right: Peter Arnet, Nick Ut, Kieu Chinh, David Kennerly. All three have been awarded Pulitzer Prizes in American journalism.

With 3 friends, from left: Linda Deutsh, Journalist AP, Dodi Fromson and Valerie Komor, AP New York

With Robert Kovacik, President LA Press Club. He is also a TV reporter and broadcaster for NBC-TV, a Pulitzer Prize laureate.

From left to right: Tippi Hedren, Kiều Chinh, and Kareem Abdul Jabbar, famous basketball player of LA Lakers

At the home of actress Tippi Hedren. She is famous for her horror movie "The Bird", directed by Alfred Hitchcock.

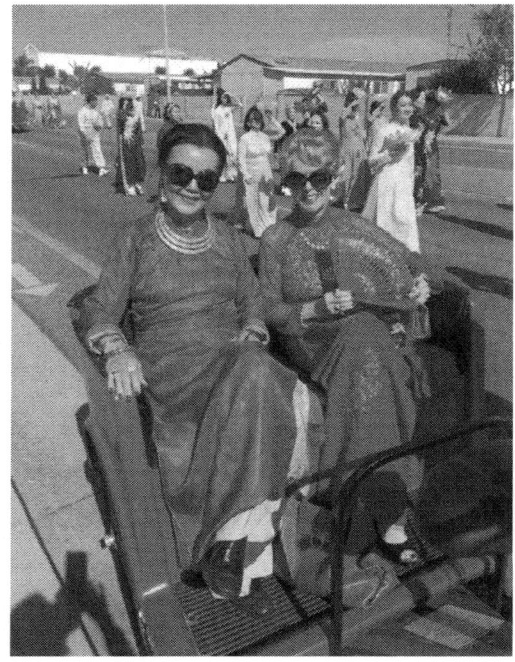

Kieu Chinh & Tippi Hedren attend the Vietnam New Year fair in Orange County.

Melanie Griffith, the famous actor in the movie "Working Girl", the daughter of Tippi Hedren is introducing Kieu Chinh, her mother's best friend, during the star ceremony for her on Hollywood Boulevard.

Melanie Griffith with her mother, Tippi Hedren and Kieu Chinh at the BEL-AIR Film Festival

With Tippi Hedren and Johnny Grant, Honorary Mayor of the Walk of Fame.

With her patron, actress Tippi Hedren and the tiger in her Shambala camp.

Charity Work

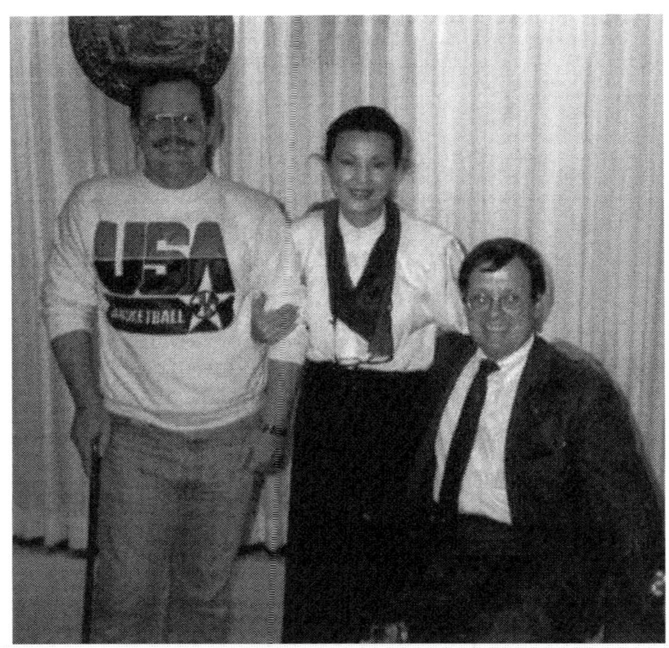

From left to right: Terry Anderson, Kieu Chinh, Lewis B. Puller, Jr., co-founders of Vietnam Children's Fund.

Kieu Chinh spoke at a meeting of the VCF association. Seated at the front table: Lewis Puller, Jr., Jack Wheeler and Ed Timberlake.

Kieu Chinh and Lewis B. Puller, Jr., Vietnam veterans, amputee, lost many fingers, in wheelchair. Pulitzer Prize Winner for Fortunate Son. Co-Founder of Vietnam Children's Fund (Vietnam Children Fund). Photo taken at his home.

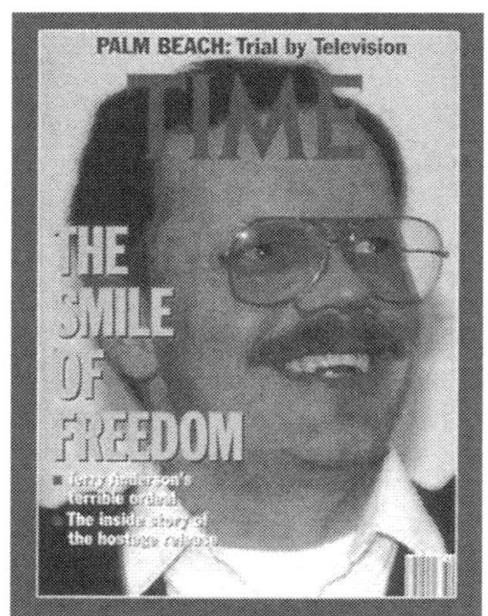

Journalist Terry Anderson, who was held hostage for over 6 years in the Middle East, and co-founder of the Foundation Sponsoring Vietnamese Children (VCF). Time magazine cover image.

VCF Board of Directors. Thumbnail above: three schools in Ha Nam, Thua Thien and Kontum provinces among more than 50 schools scattered throughout the North, Central and South regions, built by the Fundraising Association.

From left to right: Journalist Terry Anderson, Kieu Chinh and Mr. James V. Kimsey on the first trip to Vietnam, 1955.

Kieu Chinh and James V. Kimsey, founders of AOL company on their way back to Vietnam by James' private plane, cut the ribbon to inaugurate the school sponsored by James.

With Fred Smith, founder of FedEx,
who sponsored the VCF association to build 4 schools in Vietnam

US Ambassador Pete Peterson, Kieu Chinh and journalist Terry Anderson cut the ribbon to inaugurate a VCF school, built in Dong Ha, where the 17th parallel, once divided the country.

Sam Russell and Kieu Chinh cut the ribbon to inaugurate VCF's 51st school in Quang Ngai province. Standing next to Sam Russell was his assistant, Ms. Lan Vien.

Nhân Chính primary school (former Dong Ha province) was built by VCF.

Journalists Terry Anderson and Kieu Chinh with students in a classroom at a school sponsored by VCF.

Students of VCF school surrounded Kieu Chinh.

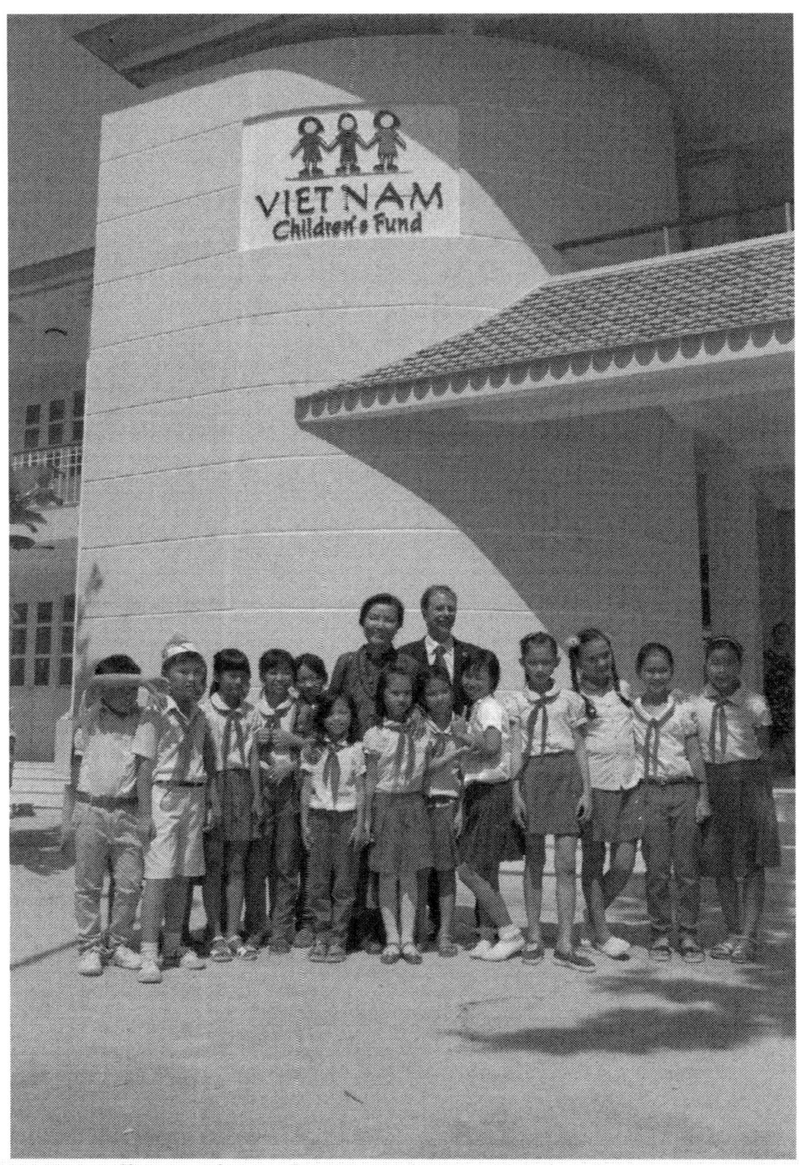

Sam Russell, president of VCF, and Kieu Chinh take souvenir photos with the students in front of the school gate.

Returning to Vietnam in 2000 with two journalists John Gittelsohn and Daniel A. Anderson of the Orange County Register newspaper

Banners protesting against Kieu Chinh supporting the Communist Party of Vietnam on Bolsa Street in Little Saigon, California.

Kieu Chinh and the First Lcdy of the Philippines, Amanda Marcos, visit Bataan refugee camp

With the First Lady of the Philippines, Amanda Marcos, visit Bataan refugee camp.

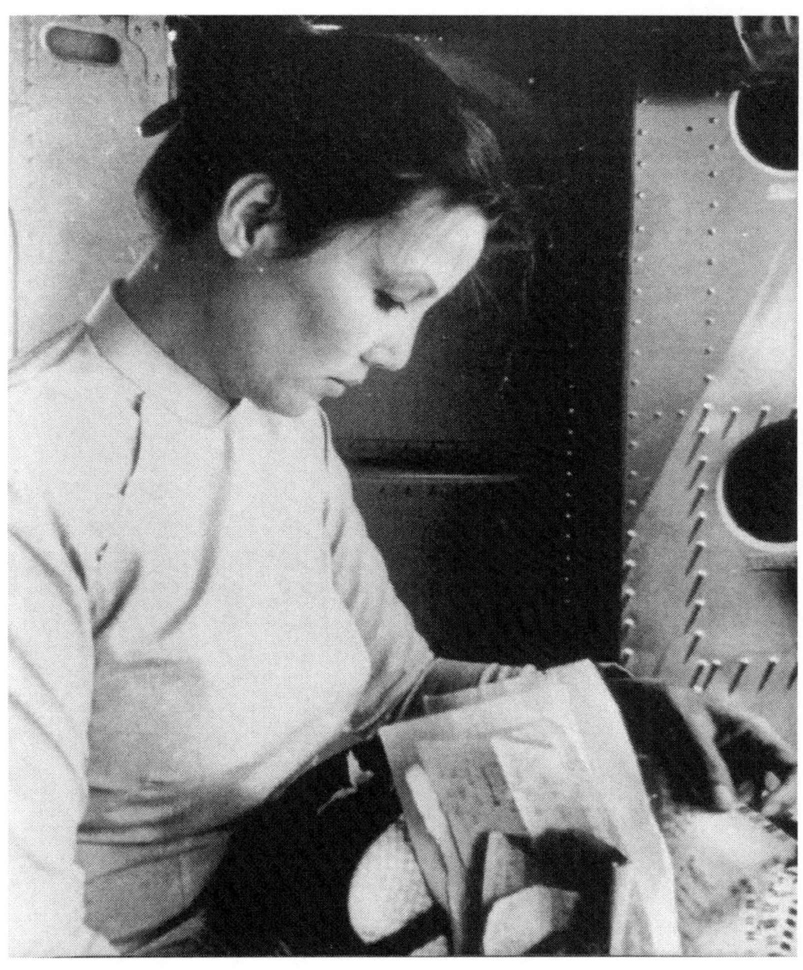

On the way home, Kieu Chinh brought letters from the boat people at the refugee camp to send to their families everywhere.

Kieu Chinh talks with compatriots at the Thai refugee camp

Kieu Chinh at the US-Mexico border during a business trip as a member of the US immigration Advisory Board.

Kiều Chinh's Houses

Studio City

The first small house in Studio City

Kieu Chinh, on the piano keys in a small house in Studio City

Newport Beach

Newport Beach's house

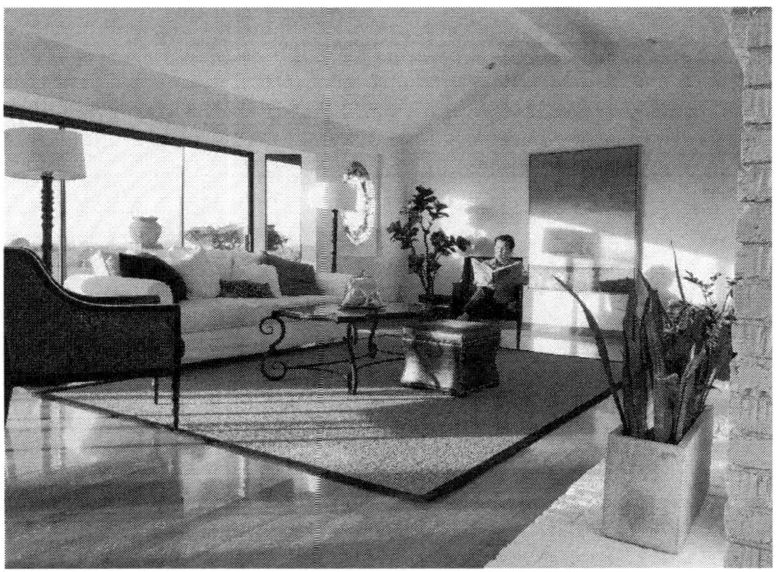

Inside the Newport Beach's house

Garden Grove

The mini-temple and tea house in the back garden of the Garden Grove's house

The Garden Grove's house

Buddha statue in the mini-temple at the Garden Grove's house.

Tea Bar inside the Garden Grove's house

Huntington Beach

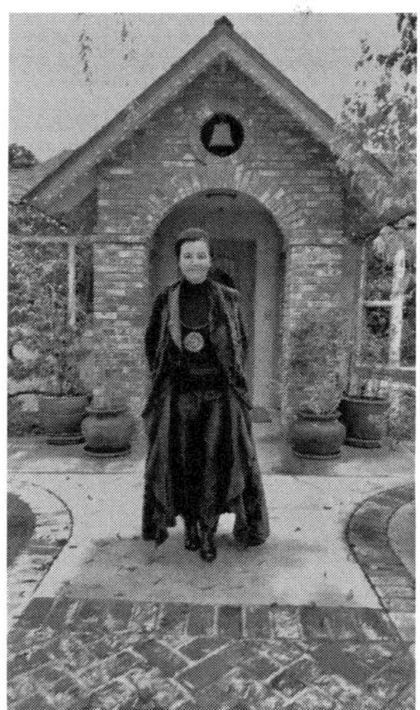

Kiều Chinh, in front of Huntington Beach's house

Office at Huntington Beach's house

PART V

1. Sculpture and Painting by talented artists

2. Friends

Kiều Chinh.
Hà-Nội. Sài-Gòn. Hollywood.

by Mai Thảo

Mai Thảo (1927-1998) was founder of the literary group Sáng Tạo (Creativity) in South Vietnam in 1956, around the same period that he first met Kiều Chinh in Sài-Gòn. This speech was given at the launch of Kiều Chinh's book "Hà-Nội - Sài-Gòn - Hollywood" in Little Sài-Gòn, Southern California.

The year was 1957. The war between the North and South was escalating. The movie industry in Vietnam was still young, and so was Kiều-Chinh. She was only 18.

But already she was becoming the leading actress and anchor for the nascent film world in Vietnam, thanks to her beauty, tenacity, and a limitless passion for the art form. She was the main actress in dozens of movies, some of which won major awards in Vietnam and at film festivals throughout Asia.

She regularly starred alongside renowned veterans. Not only that, she is also a remarkable Vietnamese woman in the best sense of the word — progressive and indefatigable in the face of a very trying time in our society. She is attuned to the issues of women.

She works tirelessly for social causes. From relief work to charity to humanitarian projects. She's also a champion for freedom and human rights not just within the context of the Vietnamese diaspora community but the world community at large as well. That is also Kiều-Chinh.

In that respect, she was a member of the Advisory Board for the U.S. Office of Immigration as well as the Advisory Board for Refugees for the State of California. Furthermore, she participated in many community activities sponsored by the Los Angeles City Council.

She has deservedly received many awards as a matter of course. I'll name just a few:

In 1980, Tom Bradley, mayor of Los Angeles, gave her the title "Today's Woman," which was voted on by Bullock's from a list of 36 American activists.

The year 1983 marked the 25th anniversary of Kiều Chinh's movie career. Vietnamese communities all over the world held many events to honor her achievements — from California to Texas to Washington, D.C., even in Europe.

In May 1985, Kiều Chinh was honored by the Asian Pacific Women's Network of Los Angeles alongside Cambodian Oscar-winning actor Haing S. Ngor.

The following year, she was named "Woman Warrior" of the year by the Asia-Pacific American Women Association, the largest Asian-American organization to date.

More recently, she was chosen to represent all refugee communities in the U.S. to speak before both houses of Congress on the first "National Refugees Day." The speech that she gave to open the session touched on issues that refugee families must face daily. It was given an ovation by lawmakers and others in the room.

And most recently, on April 19, 1991, the Los Angeles City Council and the Asian-American Association of Greater L.A. named Kiều-Chinh the most successful female activist of the year.

The above accolades are like stars in the sky that have shone upon the three decades of Kiều Chinh in the film world. Thirty years of non-stop participation. Thirty years of non-stop excellence. Not only that, but they are accompanied by an artistic and professional attitude that is simultaneously measured and charming. It has given her a reward which in my opinion is even more valuable than any awards or medals: sincere adoration and respect from audiences far and wide. It has been like that for thirty years. It has been like that from Hà-Nội to Sài-Gòn, and now to Hollywood.

This book, with almost 220 photos and articles, interviews and excerpts from 29 authors — six of whom are not Vietnamese, with three pieces in particular from Nhã Ca, Lê Văn, and Alison Leslie Gold (author of the best-selling "Ann Frank Remembered") is but a small sample of the love and adoration for Kiều Chinh by people from all walks of life as I have just described.

Shortly before his death in 1998, Mai Thảo published his first and only book of poetry. In it was a poem he wrote for Kiều-Chinh titled *Since Ancient Times Was Your Myth*:

Dead end is straight, says the road
Whose definition was: The way
That's full of turns and remote
Will lead to ten worlds away.

Away was your world since youth,
While mine by then had been aged.
What's age? The winds and the moon
Inside our souls have not eased.

Make your own clouds, your own sun.
Don't borrow them from nature,
So that when they all are gone
Moonlight we'll manufacture.

Since ancient times was your myth,
And I from God's bliss was blown.
We're both the same—two artists,
An angel each at her throne.

Don't cry, the rains are your tears;
Don't hurt, the rocks feel your pains.
Your Buddha heart is my heart
From which we'll light this incense.

(Translation by ianbui, 2021.09.16)

Em Đã Hoang Đường Từ Cổ Đại

Con đường thẳng tắp con đường cụt
Đã vậy từ xưa nghĩa cái đường
Phải triệu khúc quanh nghìn ngả rẽ
Mới là tâm-cảnh đến mười phương

Em đã mười phương từ tuổi nhỏ
Ngần ấy phương anh tới tuổi già
Tuổi ư? Hồn vẫn đầy trăng gió
Thổi suốt đêm ngày cõi biếc ta

Chế lấy mây và gây lấy nắng
Chế lấy, đừng vay mượn đất trời
Để khi nhật nguyệt đều xa vắng
Đầu thềm vẫn có ánh trăng rơi

Em đã hoang-đường từ cổ-đại
Anh cũng thần-tiên tự xuống đời
Đôi ta một lứa đôi tài-tử
Ngự mỗi thiên-thần ở mỗi ngôi

Đừng khóc dẫu mưa là nước mắt
Đừng đau dẫu đá cũng đau buồn
Tâm em là Bụt tâm anh Phật
Trên mỗi tâm ngời một nhánh hương

– Mai Thảo

A Bouquet for Kiều-Chinh

by Nguyên Sa

Nguyên Sa (1932-1998) was a poet and teacher of literature in South Vietnam before 1975. His poem "Hà-Đông Silk Dress" was put to music by Ngô Thụy-Miên and became an instant classic. This speech was given as Kiều-Chinh received a bouquet of flowers to kick off the event "Kiều-Chinh, 25 Years of Films" in Paris.

Rue Champollion runs parallel to Boulevard Saint Michel, but only for a little bit because Champollion is short whereas Saint Michel is very long. It's directly behind the row of nice-looking buildings facing the well-known boulevard.

When I returned to Paris in 1997, Champo was still there on the corner of Champollion. I joined the line, the wait was about an hour. That day Champo was showing Charlie Chaplin, but not the Charlot of the *Limelight* era but of the silent era. I had stood in line at Champo many, many times. There was Hitchcock Week and *The 39 Steps*; South America Week with *La Red* and *O Cangaceiro.* Then a week of immense greatness with someone named Cecil B. De Mille. The week of John Ford era movies and *La Bicyclette* opened the door to Italian films and stars like Ana Magnani, Sophia Loren, Mastroniani...

Every time I meet Kiều-Chinh I'm reminded of Champo. I don't meet her very often, true. But oddly enough, every time I see this famous movie star I think of Champo — the unique movie house which shows films that have left indelible imprints on the history of filmmaking. There's a different theme each week — a certain actor, director, or a poet such as J. Cocteau back in the days when he carried surrealism on his back and entered the movie world with flying motorcycles and a beautiful woman who walked out from a broken mirror just to have her image shattered like pieces of glass which started dancing as free as the language of surrealistic poetry.

If there ever was a Vietnamese shopping district — either here or anywhere in the world that had a Champo for movie buffs and connoisseurs, I surely would have my Kiều-Chinh Week. And I certainly would go see them all. Just off the top of my head:

Bells of Thiên-Mụ (1957) to kick things off. Then *Forest Rain* (1959). *Clouds Float Forever* (1962). *Year of the Tiger* (1963). *Her Eyes* (1963). *Last Message from Sài-Gòn* (1964). *Operation CIA* (1965). *Parting of the Heart* (1965). *From Sài-Gòn to Dien-Bien-Phu* (1966). *At The Frontier* (1966). *Waiting for Dawn* (1967). *Destination Vietnam* (1968). *The Faceless Lover* (1970).

Then there were four films in 1971: *The Evil Within, Love Storm, Yen Island, My Reason for Living.* Only one in 1972: *Late Summer*. Two in 1974: *Five Overseas Mission,* and *Don't Cry, My Darling* (I told Kiều-Chinh yesterday I really liked that title.) *Full House* (1975), which she told me was the last film she made, in Singapore, before the Fall of Sài-Gòn.

I still have that crazy idea. I think life, after all, is just a useless passion. What doesn't eventually fade away into nothingness? These days I have more than one crazy idea, I actually have three or four. But first I want to find a Champo somewhere to realize my Kiều-Chinh Week. Unfortunately, I can't talk about my other ideas here.

I reminded Kiều-Chinh that when she goes on stage on the first day to thank the audience, be sure to bring her hair from *The Faceless Lover*; to look at them with *Her Eyes*; to bring out emotions from *Bells of Thiên-Mụ*; to bring the courage of a woman who won the "Woman Warrior" award in 1986 from the Asian-American Women Association; to bring the image of a woman who has to contend with a life in exile while struggling to make a living, who has to race against herself while trying to better herself.

I also very thoughtfully reminded Kiều-Chinh to bring her exquisite elegance, her lovely hair that always tilts so gracefully under the spotlight. She is incredibly attractive. I recall Mai Thảo was there. So was General Nguyễn Cao Kỳ. And poet Du Tử Lê. And of course Kiều-Chinh brought her distinctively warm voice. She isolated the outside world, pushed into far off oceans other people and scenes. She made real the sound of miracles, the world of novels and the realm of imagination. Kiều-Chinh is, without question, an attraction that is absolute.

Since that day I discovered that the key to open up my shut and frozen soul, and make it vibrate, is essentially sound. When the hand of sound holds my hand and leads me, I simply go along without resisting. When Kiều-Chinh stopped reading, smiled, fixed her hair, and the applause echoed through the room, it took me a long while before I could get back to the meeting.

...

I can talk about a great many things. But I definitely will not talk about what I've been looking for: "It seems Kiều-Chinh harbors a deep sorrow." I know how to look into a woman's soul. Every time I meet Kiều-Chinh, her voice and her eyes always betray that sadness. I have not told anyone my discovery.

When I handed Kiều-Chinh the bouquet of flowers to kick off Kiều-Chinh Week this morning, I officially invited her to write her memoir. I hope to find in it what I'm looking for.

The House in Studio City

by Trần Dạ Từ

Poet Trần Dạ Từ (b. 1940) co-founded the literary magazine Gió Mới (New Wind) with Nguyên Sa in 1960. He and his wife Nhã Ca — author of the seminal "Mourning Band for Huế" about the Tet Offensive, are close friends of Kiều-Chinh. They are frequent visitors to her home.

In Studio City there is a little house. The willow in the front yard weeps silvery green in the spring and golden yellow in autumn. Trees and plants in the back yard include banana, persimmon, grapefruit, lime, hot pepper, basil, mint and other herbs. The side patio is fragrant with many flowers. Beneath the plum blossom by a small red-tiled courtyard hangs a hammock.

That house is what Kiều Chinh calls "My World." Inside that small and peaceful house, every now and then flames in the fireplace burn a little higher to greet dear friends from near and far.

When she chose to move into this house, only her youngest son, Tuấn-Cường, was living with his mother. The two older children had moved out and had their own families. But on weekends you can still hear children's laughter here. Đào Đức-Minh usually monopolizes grandma's back, and the fire feels warmer with hugs and kisses.

Yet the fire isn't always warm. One winter night in 1985, the car driven by Tuấn-Cường was hit and rolled down a mountain-side. It burst into flame. Cường was pulled out minutes before the car exploded. He was severely burned. It took him three years to fully recover. During that time his mother dropped everything she was doing to take care of him.

Through it all, the family altar is never neglected. Of blood relatives, only her mother's brother in France, Dr Van Nghi, had been to this house when he came to UCLA to lecture about acupuncture at a medical conference. She had met her sister only once in France; the two of them had not reunited with their older brother for thirty-seven years. Death anniversaries for her parents were subdued, simple affairs.

On the other hand, Tết or death anniversaries of her children's paternal grandparents were always full of people. Besides her ex-husband, Tế, and his wife were Tế's brother, Hiếu, and his wife. Kiều-Chinh and Hiếu had been close friends since they were teenagers. The two appear together in a Photo-stop picture taken on Rue Catinat in September 1954, not long after they migrated to Sài-Gòn.

When Richard Bernstein of *The New York Times* described the pair of terra-cotta elephants, the tea set, the small bamboo garden at the Studio City house, he remarked that *"It was as though she was still trying to hold on to pieces from a past life."* A Western writer with sharp attention to details like Mr. Bernstein surely must have been surprised to see this professional actor, someone who possessed every means possible to live the American-Hollywood lifestyle, had chosen instead to remain within the cultural confines of a poor, ancient country half way around the world.

Yet Richard Bernstein would have been even more surprised had he known that inside the space which housed this woman's soul was a traditional Northern daughter-in-law living side-by-side a world-famous movie star. A stereotypical Vietnamese mother sacrificing her own happiness within a beauty queen of the modern era. An intelligent being with a forward-looking aptitude inside a woman imprisoned by the shackles of history.

Yet they all have always existed together harmoniously. And no one ever hears a word about the price she has to pay for that strangely unique harmony.

The poet Du Tử Lê once said, "To me, Kiều-Chinh is the very image of a Vietnamese woman at the turn of the [20th] century." Writer Mai Thảo observed, "She spends in her own currency."

Under the weeping willow tree there are a couple of large rocks that lean against each other. When asked, she answered, "I carried them myself." And the willow tree? "I dug and planted it." What about the red-tiled court on the side of the house? "Oh, that was easy. One car trip at a time, ten pieces each. I didn't stop until I finished."

That's Kiều-Chinh. From the smallest task to the biggest job, she just does it. In her own way. Always controlled. Always with self-discipline. Hard on herself, yes, but always cheerful toward others — in her private life as well as in her professional one.

Alan Alda, lead actor in the TV series *M.A.S.H.*, once exclaimed, "She is so talented!" Yet that talent didn't just come naturally. After arriving in the U.S., while having to work to support her young children, the 36-year-old war refugee knew what she wanted and needed. She made her way to the John Robert Powers school for aspiring models and actresses. She scrimped, she saved, she fasted. She studied with Elia Karzan — director, actor and screenwriter extraordinaire whose pupils include names such as James Dean and Marlon Brando. Within three years she completed all the JRP courses while still taking care of the family.

In Studio City there's a little house. A Vietnamese woman used to live there in the last decades of the 20th century, the bloodiest century in the history of humankind. Like her countrymen and her country itself, she too experienced tragedies. Yet after every setback she always picked herself back up. Ever cheerful, ever stronger than before.

From a poor, war torn country she arrived in Hollywood, New York City, and even the United States Capitol — but not as a tourist. She came to represent not just the voice of Vietnamese refugees but of refugees from all nations, to tell perhaps the most powerful legislative body in the world about the plight of families languishing in refugee camps from Southeast Asia to the Middle East. And when the City of Los Angeles honored her with a service award in April, 1991, Kiều-Chinh said in her acceptance speech:

"I like to think that our common world is a one big family. Some members of our family are facing difficulties. I'm referring to the Kurdish refugees, the Boat People and others. In the spirit of a family gathering today, let us pray for the less fortunate members of our human family."

She has been to many places. From glittering parties in Beverly Hills to filthy prisons holding immigrants on the U.S.-Mexico border. From demonstrations for human rights on the streets of Los Angeles to protests against deportation at refugee camps in Southeast Asia.

But as Richard Bernstein correctly pointed out, although for the past sixteen years her daily work was in Hollywood, the world that occupied her the most was Việt-Nam. And the place she will continue to come and go more than any other is the Vietnamese community.

The house in Studio City is humble and small. But the heart and soul of its owner, with her extraordinary inner beauty and compassion, have long transcended all physical and racial boundaries. The woman who survived that tumultuous century is a citizen of the world yet at the same time very Vietnamese.

Her name is Kiều-Chinh.

That's Kiều-Chinh

by Nguyễn Long

Nguyễn Long (1934-2009) was a stage and film actor whose career began in 1955 in Sài-Gòn. He appeared in over 70 plays and films. He produced and directed at least a dozen movies in which he also acted.

On June 29, 1983, Channel 9 showed *A Yank in Vietnam*. The movie's original title was *Year of the Tiger*. It was made in Việt-Nam in June, 1962, and I had a part.

Most of the shooting was on location in Hóc-Môn, Hố-Nai and Bảo-Lộc. Inside scenes were shot at Alpha Films (on the corner of Hiền-Vương and Trương Minh-Giảng). Filming started on June 10 and finished on July 20. Afterwards we had to add a few more takes between Kiều-Chinh and Enrique Magalona.

... Kiều-Chinh was born Nguyễn thị Chinh, in Hà-Nội. In the period of 1953-1954 she used to participate in plays staged by university students at Hà-Nội Opera House to raise money for relief. In 1955 she worked at the MACV office on Trần Hưng-Đạo Avenue in Sài-Gòn.

In June, 1956, through the introduction of a mutual friend, [singer/comedian] Trần văn Trạch and I paid her a visit at her place of work and invited her to act in a play by Vũ Đức-Duy, but she declined. Toward the end of that year she did some work with Lê Quỳnh in *The Quiet American,* directed by Joseph Mankiewicz. I played the character who opened the film and introduced the main character.

Because she was careful about which script, director and producer she wanted to work with, Kiều-Chinh declined quite a few projects. *Year of the Tiger* was the first American movie that had a Vietnamese actress in the lead role. To this day, Kiều-Chinh still is the only actress from Việt-Nam with enough talent to co-star with some of the most famous and celebrated actors in the movie world.

After *Year of the Tiger,* in 1965, she starred alongside Burt Reynolds in *Operation CIA* by Peer Oppenheimer. In 1968, it was *Destination Vietnam,* directed by Rolf Bayer; filmed on location in Tây-Ninh and Premier studios in Quezon City, Manila. I also took part in that film.

She later founded her own movie studio called Giao-Chỉ Films. Its first production was *The Faceless Lover,* directed by Hoàng Vĩnh-Lộc. Next was *Late Summer,* directed by Đặng Trần Thức, in which her husband Nguyễn Năng-Tế also played a part.

She also acted films made by other studios like *Hòn Yến* by Thiên-Mã Films, and *Shadow on the Pavement* by Kinh-Đô Films.

Compared to other actors at the time, Kiều-Chinh did not appear in many movies. However, she had tremendous credibility and was universally respected by her peers. When the Vietnam Film Association was established in October, 1971, she was elected its first Chairperson. I was its Secretary.

In October, 1974, she travelled to Thailand, Indonesia and India to make a number of international films. She returned to Vietnam in early 1975, only to leave again soon after and became an exile.

I've known Kiều-Chinh a long time, but I've only had the chance to work with her in two movies. She's gentle but principled, charming yet resolute — both on and off the set. On the first day of filming *Year of the Tiger* there was a memorable incident. Management had devised two meal plans. One was for American and Filipino cast and crew (she and I somehow were included in this group), which was 20 VND, the other was for Vietnamese and others which was 10 VND. Kiều Chinh immediately stood up to protest and refused to eat. The next day management had to scrap their plan and provided everyone with the same 20 VND meals.

When we were shooting *Destination Vietnam* at a Philippine military base in Tây-Ninh, actor Đoàn Châu Mậu and I liked to shop at the PX on base because it was five to six times cheaper than outside. During the entire 40 days of our shoot, Kiều-Chinh never once set foot inside the PX. She would buy everything she needed, even just a towel or a bar of soap, at Tây-Ninh market.

In and out of work, she was always cheerful and helpful to everybody. She was our source of stability and sanity. She was counsellor to anyone who had personal problems. She arbitrated disputes and disagreements we had on the set with unflappable charm and gentle persuasion. We all love and admire her very much.

After former Hollywood actor Ronald Reagan became president of the United States, we liked to joke that if Kiều-Chinh were elected prime minister of our exile community, things could get very interesting, indeed!

PICTURES
PART V

1. *Sculpture and Painting by talented artists*
2. *Friends*

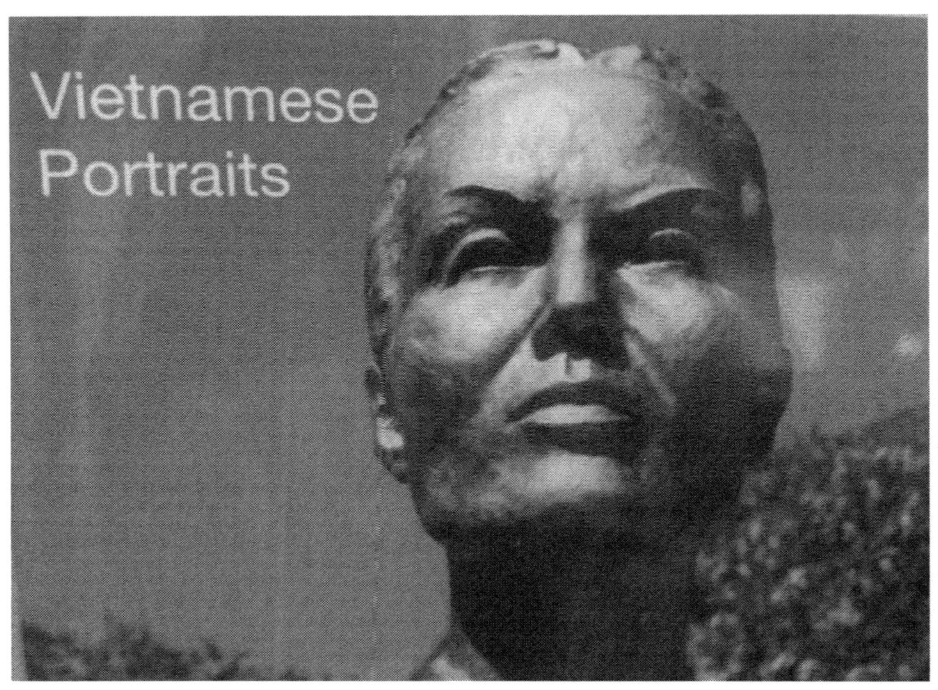

Statue of Kieu Chinh by sculptor Ưu Đàm

Sculptor Nguyễn Tuân and Kiều Chinh

"Kiều-Chinh Việt-Nam," a three-foot tall black bronze statue by sculptor Nguyễn Tuấn as a birthday present to Kiều-Chinh.

Portrait of Kiều Chinh by Choé/Nguyễn Hải Chí. A gift six months after meeting him in Sài-Gòn.

With artist Choé/ Nguyễn Hải Chí.

Kiều Chinh, by Nguyễn Trung

Kiều Chinh, by Đinh Cường

Kiều Chinh, by Nguyễn Quỳnh

Trịnh Công Sơn painted and wrote on the picture: "Looking at Kiều Chinh like that in 2000"

With composer Trịnh Công Sơn (A few months before he passed away)

Kiều Chinh and Thomas Đặng Vũ.

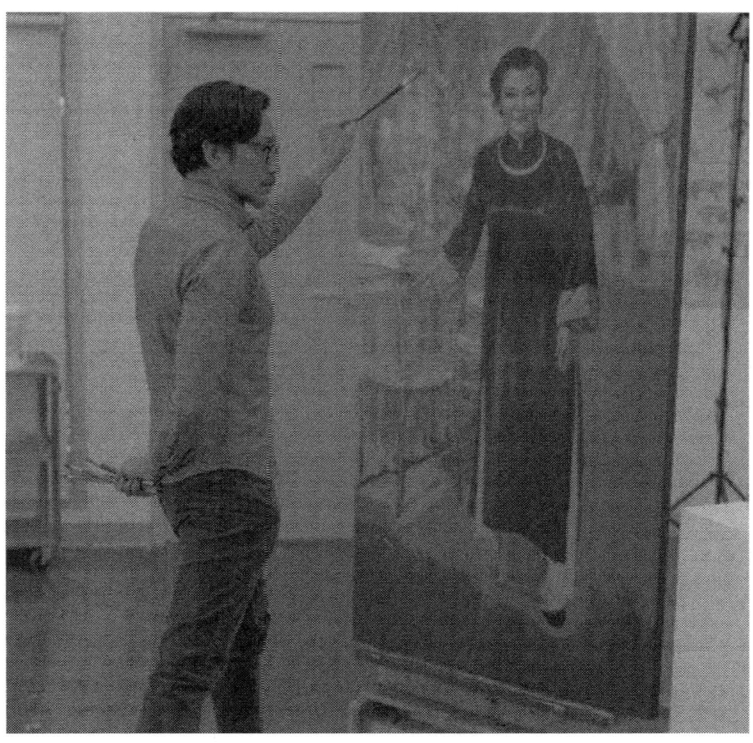

Art professor Thomas Đặng Vũ is finishing portrait of Kiều Chinh in "real people" size

Portrait of Kiều Chinh in "real people" size painted by Professor Thomas Đặng Vũ

Sir Daniel Winn and Kiều Chinh at the unveiling ceremony of the painting drawn by Sir Daniel Winn

Sir Daniel Winn and Kiều Chinh

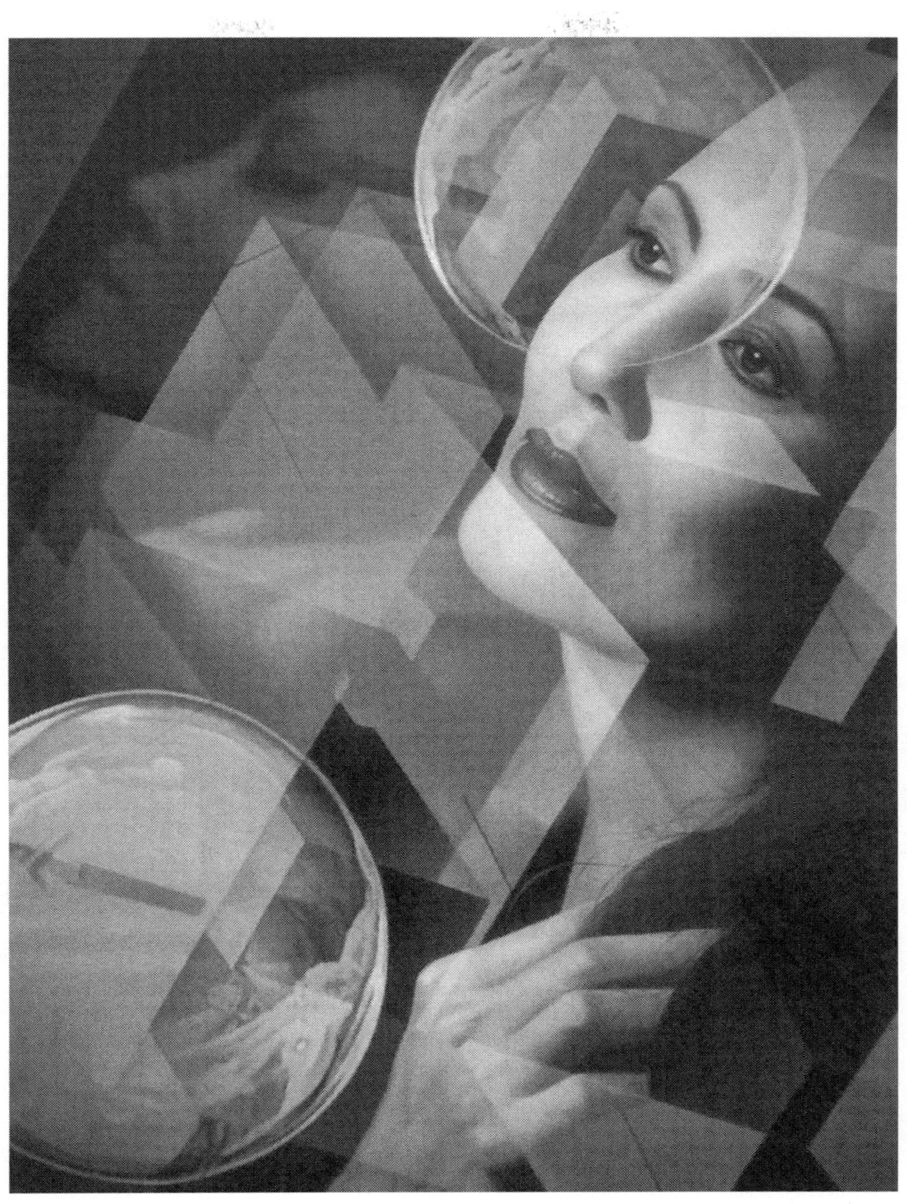

Portrait of Kiều Chinh painted by Sir Daniel Winn

With Mr. Bùi Diễm, former ambassador to the U.S. He also produced my first film, "Hồi Chuông Thiên-Mụ" in the '50s, which kicked off my movie career.

Toast with writer Mai Thảo

Kiều Chinh in a visit to the grave of writer Mai Thảo.

With poet-philosopher Phạm Công-Thiện (left) and writer Mai Thảo

With Nguyễn Chánh (left) and Lữ Liên as I sing traditional Northern style music called "ca trù" at the Maubert Hall in Paris.

Composer Phạm Đình-Chương accompanies on the piano as I sing his song "Nửa Hồn Thương Đau" at "Cõi Tôi" house in Studio City.

With the inimitable diva Thái Thanh on her last birthday

Composer Phạm Duy plays guitar
as Kiều Chinh and Lê Văn sing "Giọt Mưa Trên Lá"

Composer Hoàng Thi Thơ, Lê Quỳnh and Kiều Chinh
on the stage of Maubert Theater, Paris

With singer Kim Tước

Với ca sĩ Khánh Ly

With conductor Nghiêm Phú Phi in a music hall at "Cõi Tôi" in Studio City

With three Vietnamese writers living in exile (Paris).
From left: Từ Thức, Kiều Chinh, Trần Thanh Hiệp, Vũ Thư Hiên.

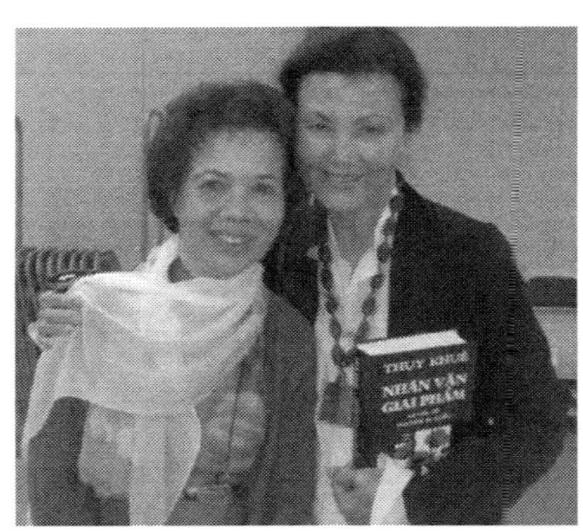

With Thụy Khuê, a scholar in Literature, in Paris.

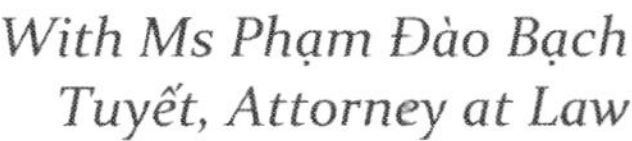

With Ms Phạm Đào Bạch Tuyết, Attorney at Law

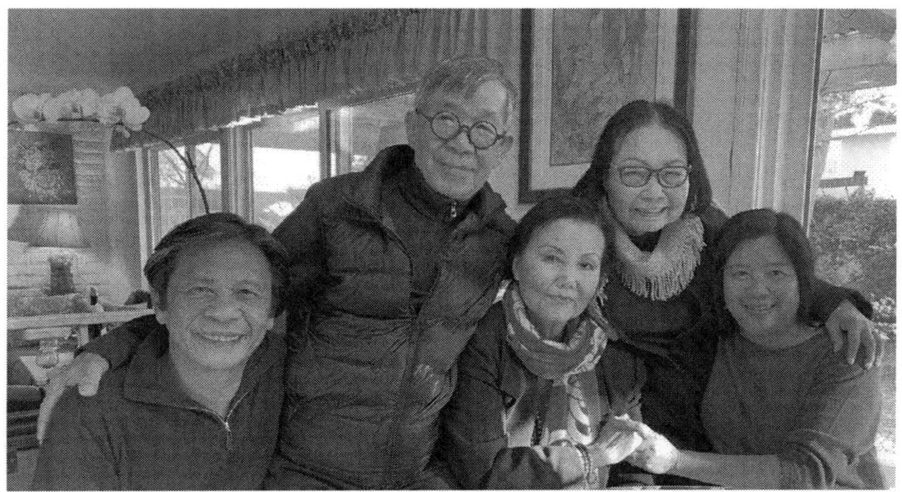

With husband and wife, poet Trần Dạ Từ - Nhã Ca, husband and wife Phạm Quyến & Dung

Friends from the younger generation, from left to right: Kevin Tran, Kiều Chinh, Hòa Bình, Thắng Đào, Sông Văn.

With the great family Việt Báo

Standing row: jounalist Đinh Quang Anh Thái, writer Đỗ Quí Toàn,
Sitting row: music composer Cung Tiến, Kiều Chinh
and poet Trần Dạ Từ

With grandson Stephen Đào at GLADD festival.

*Attending the GLAAD festival in New York. (GLADD stands for **G**ay & **L**esbian **A**lliance **A**gainst **D**efamation.)*

With photographer Nicolas Phạm

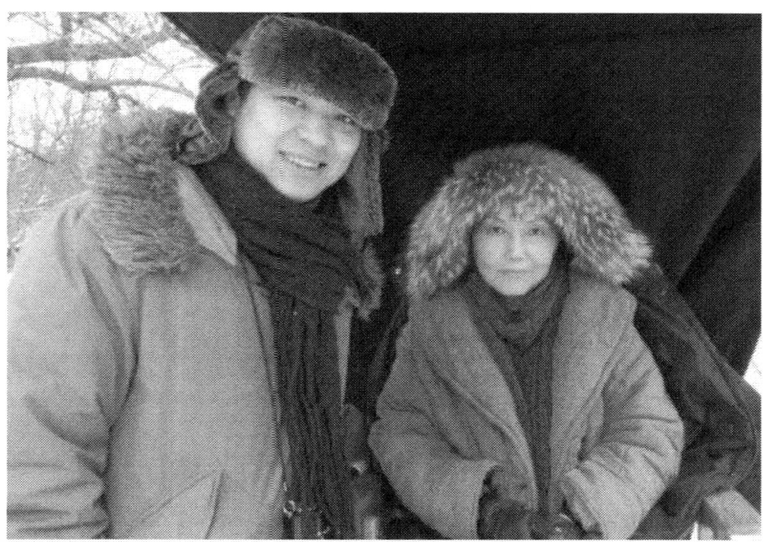

With director Cường Ngô on the filming site "Ngọc Viễn Đông" in Toronto, Canada. Temperature is very cold, 20 degrees minus!

With three directors, from left to right: Dustin Nguyễn, Trần Anh Hùng, Kiều Chinh, Victor Vũ.

On the filming ground of "Rồng Xanh" (Green Dragon) directed by Timothy Linh Bùi (on the right), and Tony Bùi (on the left)

With Ysa Lê and members of the Vietnamese International Film Festival (VIFF) at Kiều Chinh's office.

With Dustin Nguyễn at film festival VIFF

At the Smithsonian Exhibit, from left: Jan Scruggs, Kiều-Chinh, James Kimsey, Senator James Webb.

With female representative soldiers of different countries

A souvenir with: Navy Rear Admiral Huấn Nguyễn, Navy Commander Mimi Phan

From left: USAR BG Lapthe Chau Flora (now MG) and his wife, Thuy Flora; Kieu Chinh; USA LTC (Ret) Ross Nguyen and his wife, Dr. Emma Tearrah Cristiani-Nguyen.

With poet and writer Trịnh Y Thư,
Editor of this book: KIỀU CHINH - Exile

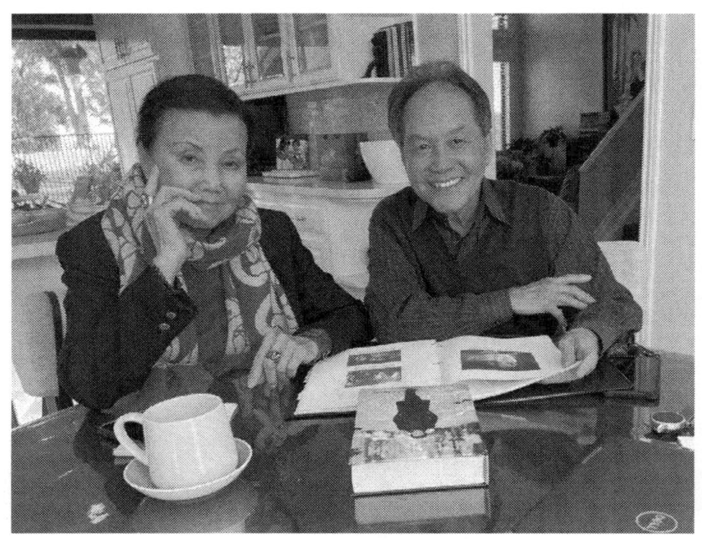

With poet Lê Hân
("Nhân Ảnh" publisher for 2023 edition of this Memoir)

Translator of this Memoir: Bùi Trọng-Nghĩa

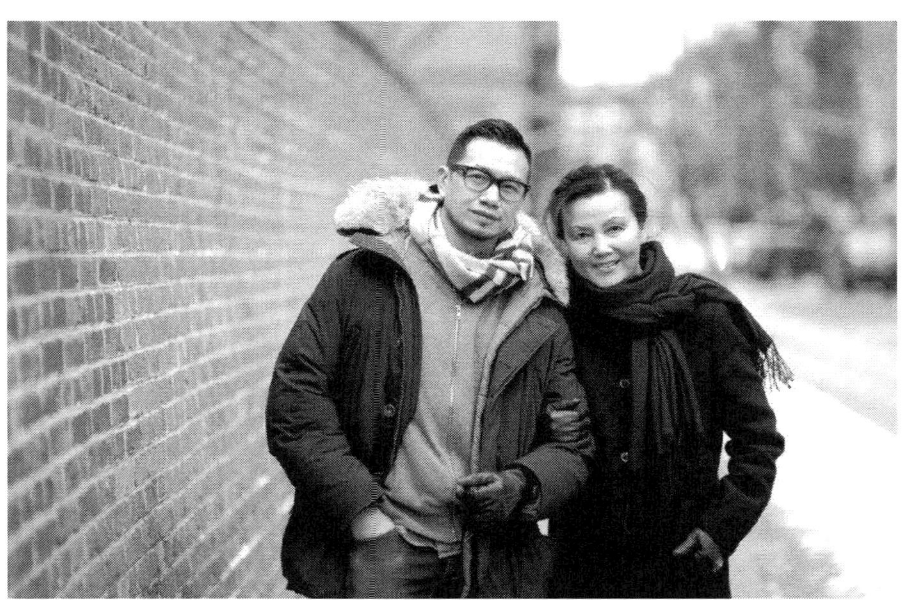

With Thomas Đặng Vũ, who took the photo on the cover of this Memoir.

EPILOGUE

Like millions of other family stories from my country, mine, too, is a story about a family torn apart by war. But more than that, it's also about the trials and tribulations of an artist in exile. I wrote it:

To thank my Creator.
To thank my parents.
To thank my family.
To thank my friends.
To thank the film world for the career I was given.
To thank the benefactors who helped me through hard times.
To thank all who have come and gone, all the people I've met on the road of life.

What a long road it has been. And a hard one, too. Many times I have tripped and fallen down. And just as many times I've picked myself back up, stood up straight and moved on.

Yes, I have travelled thousands of miles across several continents. I have witnessed as much joy and happiness as I have sorrow and despair — enough to know that my hardships are minuscule compared to many others.

The sufferings in the world around us are too enormous. We see them even more clearly during the global pandemic. And as I write this epilogue, scenes of panicked Afghans at the airport in Kabul triggered flashbacks in my mind of the last days at a Hà-Nội airport in 1954, and at Sài-Gòn Tân-Sơn-Nhứt in 1975.

Afghan families fleeing the Taliban will become the next wave of refugees in the U.S. just like Vietnamese families were forty-six years ago.

I pray that all families who get separated by war can reunite.
I pray that there will be less pain and suffering in the world.
I pray that all children of mother Earth can find peace.

As I look back on almost fifty years living in exile in this land of freedom, where I rebuilt my life from scratch, I can say that I've only made it this far because I kept pushing. Forward. Forward... And whenever I feel frustrated or exhausted, I remind myself that I'm not the only one.

Millions of Vietnamese have been scattered all over the globe. Each of us is a unique story; mine is but one which I've shared with you. My only regret is that I cannot show this book to my erudite friend Mai Thảo who, I'm sure, would have had a field day critiquing it. To which I would respond:

"I'm sorry, brother, that I waited too long. Had I had your help, this Memoir would have been much more literary and polished. However, I did take your advice. I wrote it *'as you normally tell a story — in 'language parlant'*"

– Kiều Chinh
Huntington Beach, California, May 2021.

Ảnh Kiều Chinh chụp tại phim trường Alpha Films.
(Lần đầu Mai Thảo nhìn thấy Kiều Chinh như vậy.)

Kiều Chinh at Alpha Films studio
(for the first time, writer Mai Thảo looked at Kiều Chinh like that)

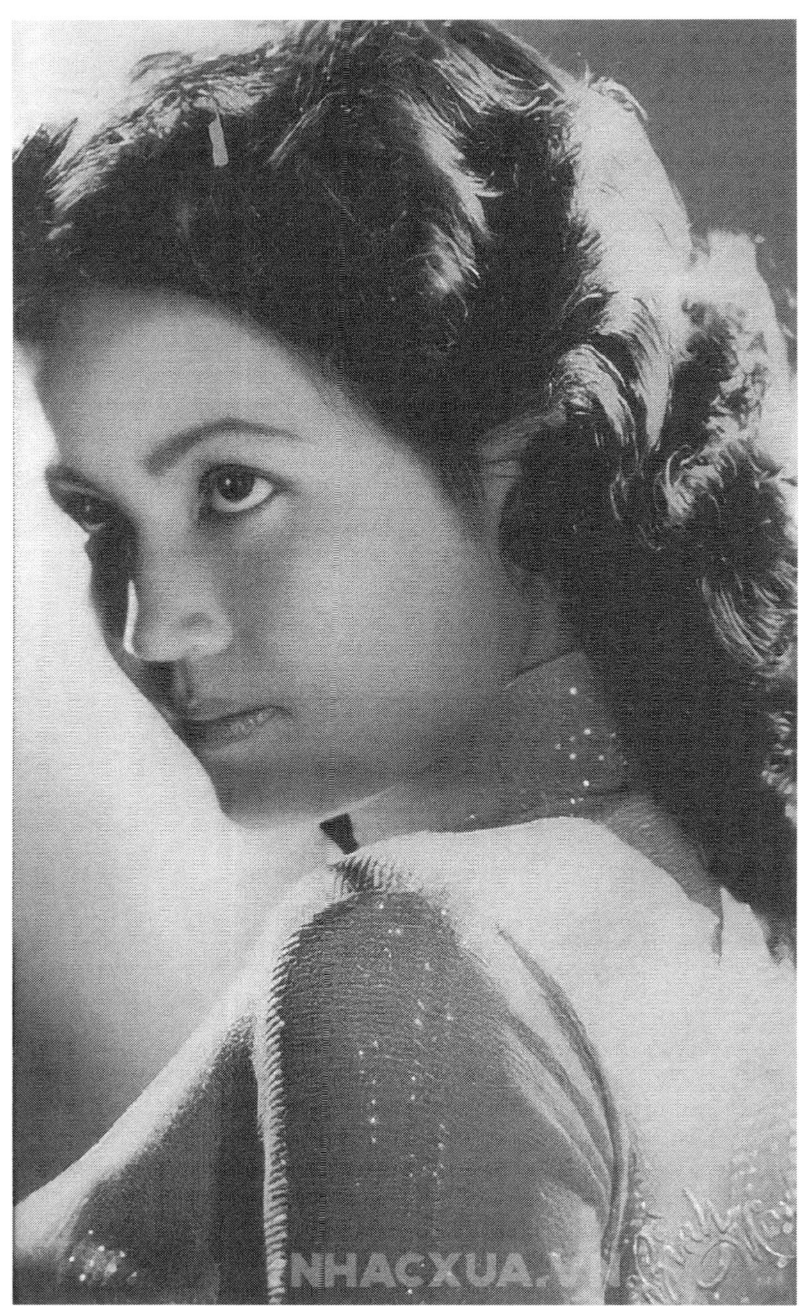

Kiều Chinh, in Sài Gòn before 1975

Kiều Chinh, in USA after 1975

On Côte d'Azur beach (photo by Pauline and Jean-Claude)

On Côte d'Azur beach (photo by Pauline and Jean-Claude)

On Côte d'Azur beach - first visit to France
(photo by Pauline and Jean-Claude)

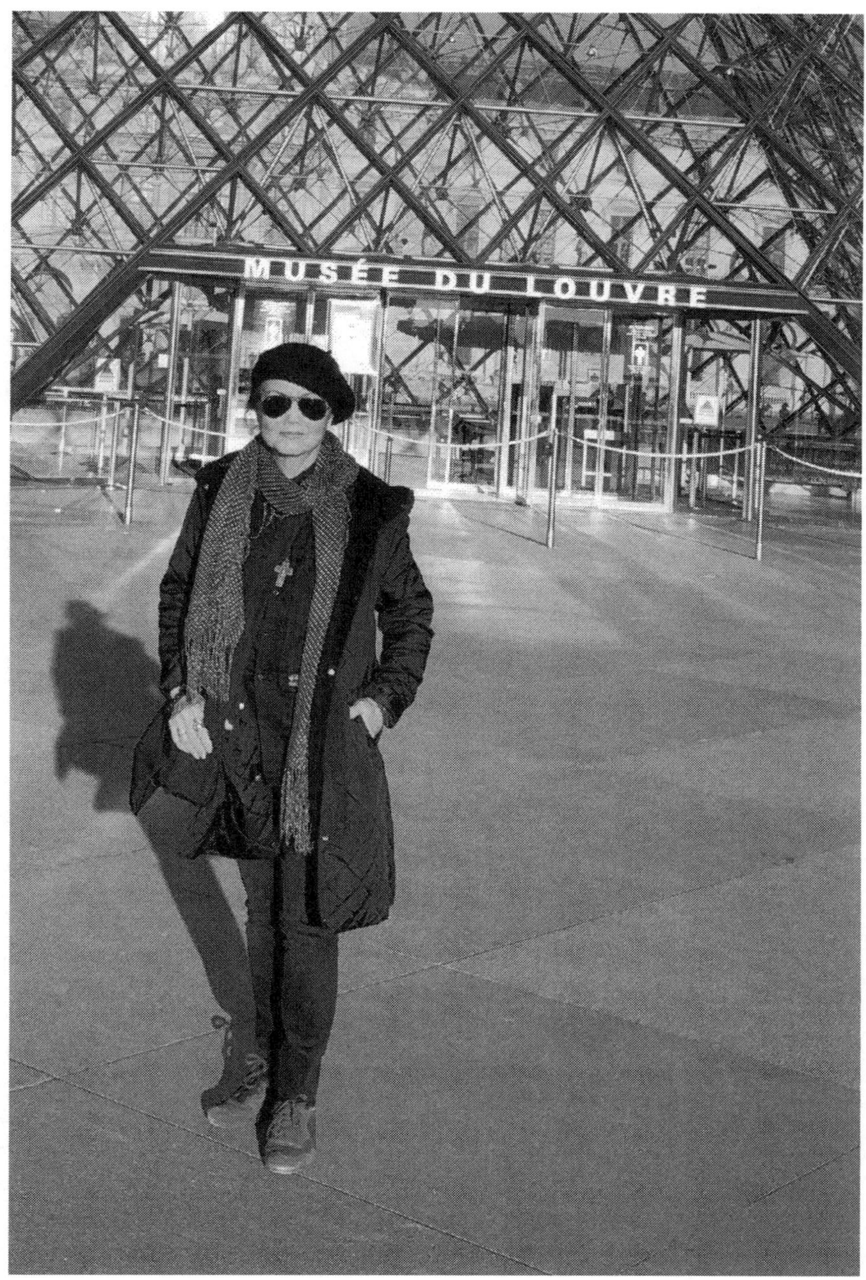

At Musée du Louvre, Paris. (photo by Từ Thức)

Arc de Triomphe, Paris.
("áo dài" designed by Thụy Cúc – photo by Nicolas Phạm)

On the red carpet at the San Francisco Film Festival
("áo dài" designed by Sỹ Hoàng)

Kiều Chinh won the Humanity Award of Asia World Film Festival
("áo dài" designed by Thái Nguyên)

Kiều Chinh, "áo dài trống đồng" designed by Thụy Cúc

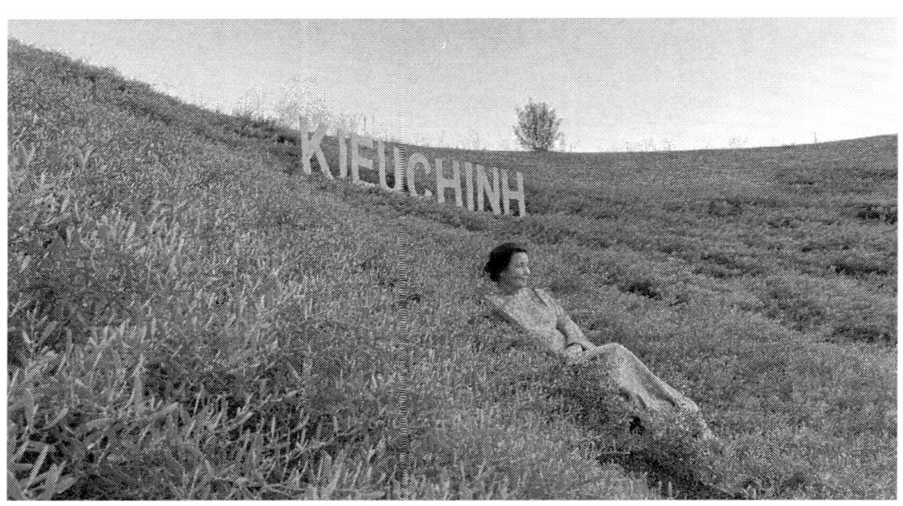

Thank you Hoa Binh and NTM team for implementing the word "KIEU CHINH" on the hill behind Linh & Roman Kochan's house

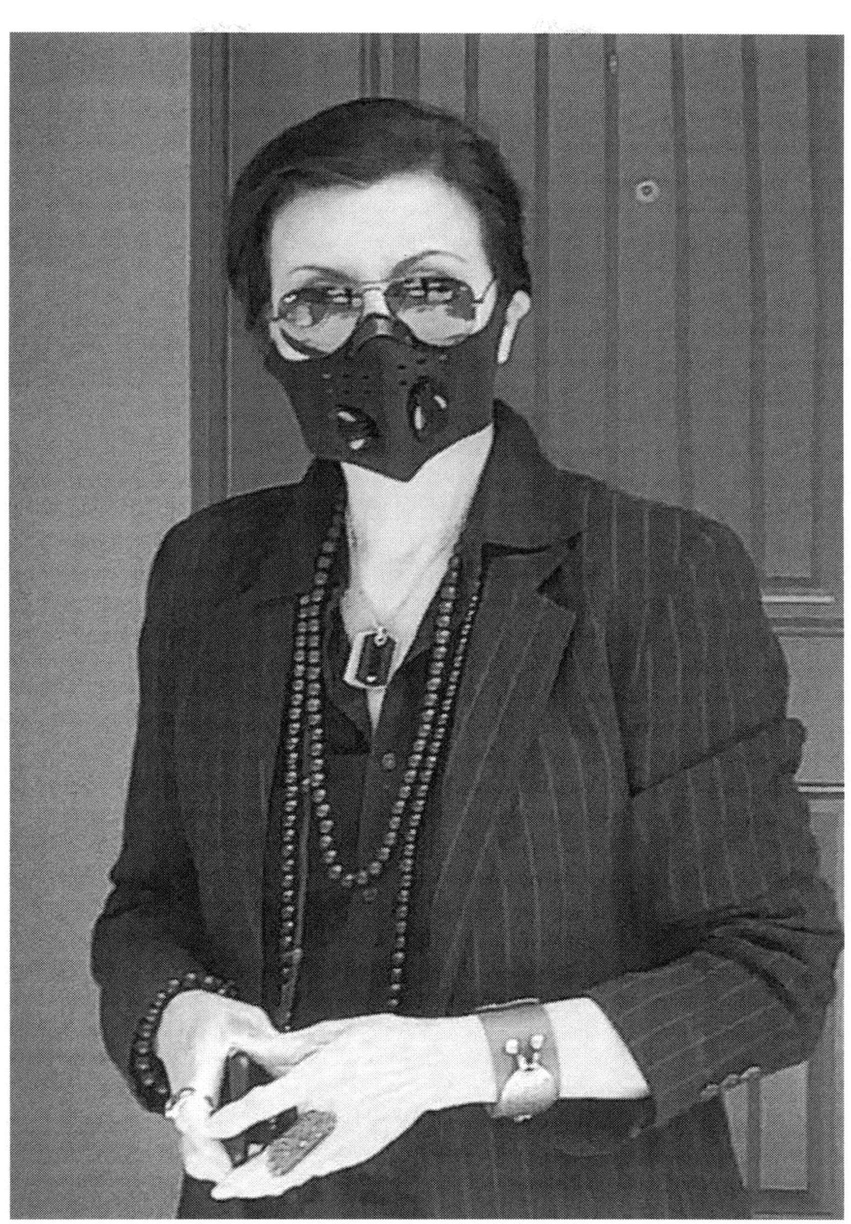

Picture taken during Covid-19 period

APOLOGY
&
ACKNOWLEDGEMENT

Nothing brings joy to an artist more than seing his or her work acknowledged and appreciated by the public. And all artists rightly can feel pride in his/her works. But my purpose here is to share with you some of the images that have given me encouragement in my pursuit of arts.

Over the years I have received many photographs, articles, and works of art from talented friends and artists. However, as time has eroded my memory, I cannot recall the names of all the artists who have shared examples of their work with me. Therefore I cannot obtain their permission to share such images for this book.

Please accept my sincerest apology and deepest gratitude.

Kiều Chinh

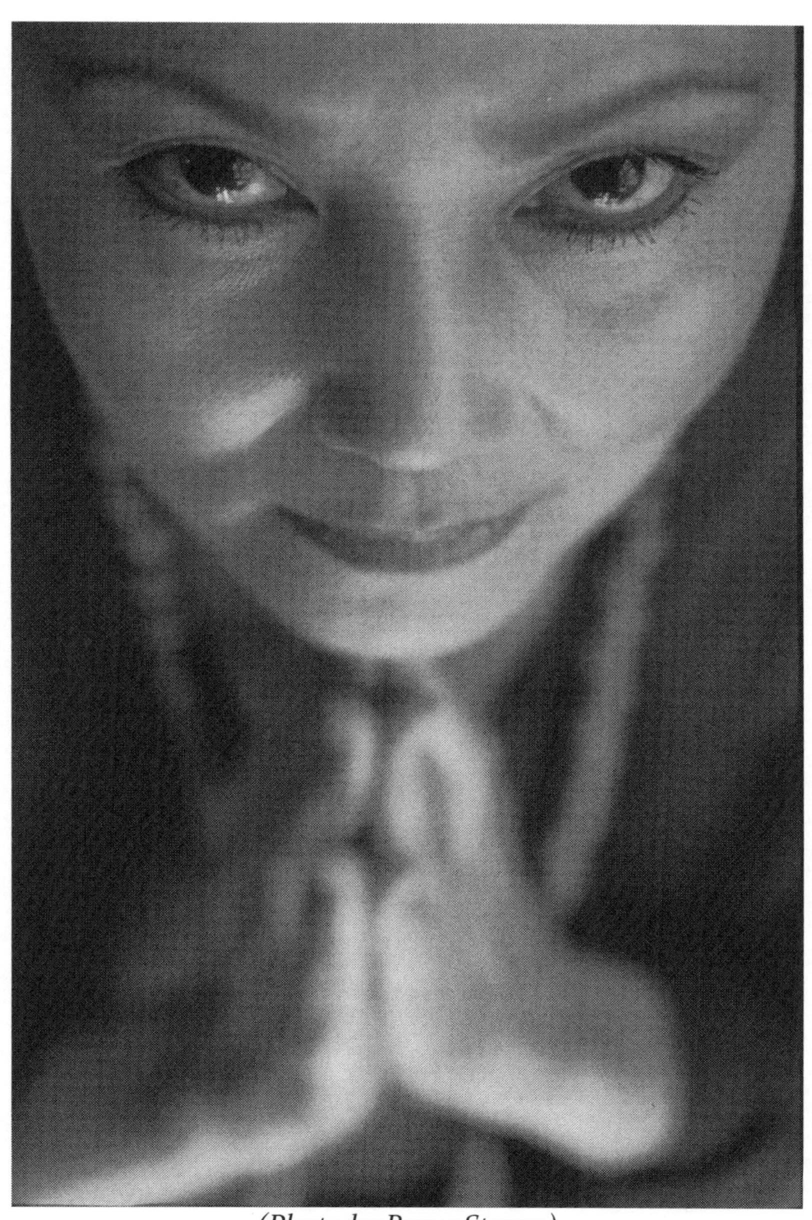

(Photo by Bruce Strong)

Made in the USA
Columbia, SC
20 April 2023

e11e4008-853f-42cd-82a7-5be97f412c86R01